D0231238

THE STRANGE LIFE
OF AUGUST STRINDBERG

AUGUST STRINDBERG

THE STRANGE LIFE OF AUGUST STRINDBERG

BY
ELIZABETH SPRIGGE

NEW YORK / RUSSELL & RUSSELL

FOR
VELONA PILCHER

CONTENTS

ILLUSTRATIONS

FOREWORD

BY FAR the greater part of Strindberg's voluminous work is autobiographical, whether it appears in the form of play, novel, essay, tale or poem. He revealed much of his life in a series of confessional novels, but even when he himself is not the principal subject of the work, his own experiences and obsessions permeate the pages. It is impossible therefore to study the writings of August Strindberg without seeing much of his life, but as he dramatised everything, and particularly himself, it has been difficult until now to gauge the accuracy of the picture. True, quite a number of his relatives and friends have written about Strindberg, but many of these take a specific period in his life and a special point of view. Now, a hundred years after his birth, it is possible to compare Strindberg's autobiographies with his letters, of which the Strindberg Society in Sweden has made a collection running into thousands. In 1946 Messrs. Bonnier published a fine selection of these letters under the title *Från Fjärdingen till Blå Tornet* (*From Fjärdingen to the Blue Tower*) edited and annotated by Dr. Torsten Eklund, the Secretary of the Strindberg Society. And in 1948, a few weeks before this biography went to press, the first volume of the Collected Letters was published, also by Bonnier, just in time for two very early letters to be included in this book.

My warmest thanks are due to Dr. Torsten Eklund, Dr. Gunnar Ollén and Messrs. Bonnier for permission to translate and use letters from both these volumes, and also to Professor Walter A. Berendsohn, who is engaged in collecting the Strindberg letters, and has given me both encouragement and help.

When one studies the letters and the biographies of contemporaries, one finds that Strindberg undoubtedly exaggerated some aspects of his life in his autobiographies, and it becomes clear that this was because certain common human woes, such as debt, hunger and hatred, grew into obsessions, and Strindberg used them as symbols of man's misery and emphasised them in the hope of forcing a cure. But there are also many dramatic passages in the autobiographical novels which read like invention and yet are borne out word for word in the letters.

The material for this biography has been drawn from these three main sources—Strindberg's work, a selection of his letters, and the Swedish biographies and studies listed at the end of the book. It has been a matter of exploration and deduction, but not one of invention. Strindberg chose the form of the novel for his autobiographies, and so, although this book is not fiction, I have told his life as a story. The passages quoted are translations mainly from his novels, but also from plays and letters, and sometimes from all three. One of Strindberg's chief perceptions was the law of recurrence, and in his work he echoes and reiterates from first to last. Except for the late, visionary plays, it would sometimes be difficult to guess in which period of his life a play was written.

My thanks go too to Dr. Greta Hedin whose support has been unfailing, who housed me in Göteborg during my researches—where at the 1947 production of *A Dream Play* I heard Strindberg's language in the original for the first time. Besides giving me invaluable advice and introductions, Dr. Hedin has sent me every Swedish book I needed.

My gratitude also to Mrs. Margaret Scholander, who gave me hospitality in Stockholm and helped me to get into touch with August Strindberg's relatives and friends. My thanks to his daughter Fru Karin Smirnoff for permission to use material and an illustration from her book about her mother, Siri von Essen, and to Strindberg's widow, Fru Harriet Bosse, for allowing me to quote from letters and her commentary.

Also to the two artistes, Alrik Kjellgren and Anna Flygare-Stenhammer, for sharing with me their vivid memories of Strindberg in his Intimate Theatre. And to Fru Birgitta von Hofsten with whom, one unforgettable Sunday, I traced Strindberg's Stockholm life from his birthplace to his grave.

My acknowledgements are also due to the authorities at the Nordiska Museum for allowing me to study Strindberg's manuscripts and to wander among his books, pictures and furniture, although his room at the Museum was dismantled for renovation. This circumstance, so disconcerting at first, brought me into closer touch with Strindberg's way of living, and gave me a clue to what in all humility I had to do—for the false top to his writing-table, complete with pens and the other paraphernalia of authorship for the use of souvenir-hunters, had been removed—and there was the real thing.

From the Nordiska Museum too comes kind permission to publish certain photographs and from Messrs. Bonnier to use others. I am indebted to Dr. Enid Starkie for allowing me to quote in the postscript of this book from her biography *Arthur Rimbaud* (Hamish Hamilton, 1947) and to Messrs. Jonathan Cape for permitting me to use material and include translations of letters from *Marriage with Genius* by Frida Strindberg (1937).

Finally I would like to thank Lady Low, Mrs. Anna Sturge, Miss Margaret Morris and the other friends in this country, both Swedish and English, who have helped me with translation and in many other ways, not least by simply letting me know of their own interest in August Strindberg.

ELIZABETH SPRIGGE

Shotters, April 1948

THE STRANGE LIFE
OF AUGUST STRINDBERG

CHAPTER ONE

1849–1867

Even in childhood I began to serve my sentence

TO DAMASCUS

IF JOHAN AUGUST STRINDBERG had been born when he was expected, his birthday would have fallen in March, in the days heralding the season he loved best, when the dark depths of ice cracked at last, the thick snow melted in sensuous streams, and Stockholm, his city, the Venice of the North, broke from her winter shrouds. Instead, he began his journey on January the 22nd, 1849, at the peak of northern winter, when the ice-cutter alone maintained a lifeline for the besieged city, when human beings were so muffled as to be scarcely recognisable and when, but for sleigh bells and church bells, all sounds were muted.

Riddarholm, Stockholm's ancient 'town between the bridges,' was Strindberg's birthplace, but while he was still an infant the family moved to an old house north of the water, overlooking a churchyard. Before long the little boy on the third floor came to see the Klara church as 'a mountain rising above the lime trees with a giant in a copper hat on top, who sounded the quarters in a high voice and the hours in a deep one,' and it seemed to him that the bell was always ringing— so much so on Sundays that people in the house could scarcely hear each other speak.

When August Strindberg looked back on his earliest years he always remembered the noise of bells and his sense of fear. He was a seven-months' child; he had been born too soon; he was over-sensitive and incomplete, and the world was hostile.

He was also born too late, for his mother already had a favourite son. Just before the birth of this fourth child, Johan August, Carl Oscar Strindberg married Ulrika Eleanora Nor-

1

ling, who had been his mistress for so many years, but she was sick and troubled and did not welcome this further care. She was grateful to Herr Strindberg for making an honest woman of her, for she was a tailor's daughter and had been in domestic service, whereas he was a shipping agent of good education, who claimed an aristocratic streak in his heredity, but this did not prevent him from bringing shame upon her. To add to the humiliation of the irregular union, he had gone bankrupt, and August was born when his father's fortune was at its lowest ebb. The family could not hold up its head among the neighbours; the child heard constant talk of debt and disgrace, and came to think of 'creditors' as a race of ogres who might at any time invade people's homes and take everything away. Poverty, however, did not stop the family from increasing until, although several infants died, there were eight children—three boys before August and three girls and one boy after him—all living at very close quarters with their parents, two servants and various other relatives.

This was Strindberg's introduction to human life which from the first fascinated and frightened him. He was unusually observant and he dramatised everything, always including himself. There was enough to eat, but not always enough of the kind of food he liked, so he saw himself as perpetually hungry; he cried easily, so he believed himself continually in tears, although in fact his smile too was quick and radiant. The parents were hard put to it to distribute affection and attention among so many children; justice sometimes miscarried, and August considered himself ill-treated and unloved —he thought he was always hiding from adult wrath; in fact he did everything possible to attract attention, for to be ignored was his worst punishment.

Watching the ghost sonata playing behind the façade of that gloomy house to the mournful accompaniment of church bells, the child worked out his own ideas of social life. On the ground floor he saw a General whose servant wore a skullcap and brandished enormous hedge-scissors; on the first floor was the Aunt, a widow in a lace cap who brought up her daughters in the pale reflection of bygone elegance; in other rooms were the Uncle, the Cousin and the Grandmother—relatives from both sides of the family, drawn together not by love but by economics, having as their common refrain 'what will people say?' and as their common dread 'the deputy landlord,' who pounced on them all for money.

But above that deputy, the boy soon discovered, was the landlord himself whom the deputy dreaded, and above the servant who frightened the children was the General at whose word the servant trembled. And when the General put on his uniform and cocked-hat, the whole household watched in awe, for this meant he was going to see the King who was higher than them all—yet still above the King, they said, was God.

Since a child was the lowest of all, August Strindberg felt the weight of authority pressing painfully on him, and he soon knew that, in spite of his weakness and timidity, he must rebel. Only so could he live—and he must live, for although he was bewildered by the world, 'he knew that he was good and could do things.'

The shipping agent, who loved nature, comforted himself for living in town by growing pelargoniums in the window-boxes. August shared his father's taste, and the pale petals with their velvet spots looked to him like his mother's white face and big dark eyes. He thought his mother very beautiful and kind; it was clear to him that she provided the food of which they all had such need, for after every meal their father thanked her. It was the mother who bound up wounds and dried tears, although she was also false and gave the children away to their father who punished them. When they were beaten it was their mother who comforted them—August Strindberg made the most of this comfort and loved his mother, but he could not forget her perfidy. He did not love his father, but at times he was sorry for him, for although he was the master, who must be obeyed, this stiff, correct and silent man seemed like an intruder in the home.

When his mother smiled at her eldest son and caressed him, August's heart twisted with jealousy. He imitated Axel's words and actions and thought out ways of doing better; he brought his mother his most cherished possessions, flattered her, did everything she asked and more, but still he could not win her heart. It often seemed to him that he could do nothing without doing wrong, go nowhere without being in the way, and that grown-up people's notion of being good was simply to sit still on a chair. He was full of activity, but what he most enjoyed was always stopped, and there was a never-ending chorus of 'did you do it?—what will Father say?—what will people say?—remember God can see you!' To be innocent was not enough, for, accused of lying, August sometimes confessed to sins he had not committed. He began to think that it was not safe to be himself, that if he wanted to avoid displeasure —and indeed he did—he must learn to be another. Yet already his ego was dear to him; even in his own weakness he discovered a kind of strength—he found that he saw more, heard more, felt more than those about him, and he dimly knew that he could love life if he were given a chance. Meanwhile he could only store up impressions of its strangeness and terror . . . a fire in the town and people burned to death, a wreck and someone drowned . . . stretchers carried through the streets and grave-diggers at work in the churchyard under the window, because cholera had come to the city, and he had to wear a copper disc on his chest and chew all day at a root.

Sometimes the family went to church to see a baby christened—he liked the white and gold church with its angels and candles and 'music as if from a hundred pianos'— but at other times everything was draped in black and they saw a baby buried. Then even the sweets served to the guests were wrapped in black paper—-August ate them greedily, but he could taste the blackness, and the older children pasted the black papers on the walls of their room so he was unable to forget the dead baby. Once he saw two hooded men with chains on their hands and feet, kneeling between guards, and was told that these were thieves doing penance. He could not get them out of his mind; he loved brightness, but his mind was filled with dark pictures, and in his ears the church bells chimed and tolled and tinkled—if for no other reason, then simply to mark the passing of time.

When he was seven years old, August Strindberg began to go to school and was unhappier still. At home there was an attempt at justice even if it miscarried, a blood-tie although no warmth of affection, a common background, the ease of familiarity, and the comfort of his mother's presence. At home

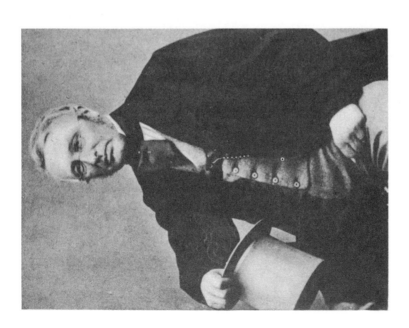

August fought to win attention, at school he tried to escape it, for attention meant pain—and worse, humiliation. His leather breeches and boots smelling of blubber offended his teachers and they took their revenge, while the better-dressed boys sneered at him and his family. It was no use being quicker than most at his lessons, for he only had to wait for the others and listen to their stupid mistakes—but while he feared the aristocratic bullies and despised their indolence, he was drawn to their bright faces and pleasant clothes and wished he were like them.

But although lessons seemed meaningless August Strindberg liked learning, and although he found the world unjust, he was eager to explore it. He examined the shape and texture of everything, and often saw second images in things. A face, a figure or a landscape would appear—in the grain of wood, perhaps, or in the pattern of plaster on a wall—and seem as real to him as the object itself. He began to observe that in all things were other things which many people did not notice, and his special vision became both an excitement and a loneliness.

After some years the family moved to the northern outskirts of the town. Finances had improved a little, but the shipping agent still felt the disgrace of the bankruptcy and shunned company, and besides this, the overcrowding in the flat had reached its limit, his wife was in wretched health, and he wanted his children brought up in touch with nature.

The first spring in his new home was a revelation to the eleven-year-old boy whose garden had been the churchyard where he might not step on the grass or touch the trees. Here was an orchard in bloom and a garden full of flowers and birds, while beyond stretched open country. This was something he could love which would not betray him, and he tried his utmost to make it his own. Although he was often tired after his long daily walks, for he still attended the Klara school close to his old home, he set himself to learn all that he could of nature. At the same time he had to compete with his brothers in their other occupations, for he burned to excel and was constantly afraid of being ignored or laughed at. Axel had a talent for drawing, so August must draw too; several of the children played musical instruments, and as he

5

had no special aptitude, he studied the theory of music and the lives of the composers, so that he might surpass the others in knowledge. He was genuinely fond of music too—in a family with less in common than many, this taste was shared by all, and the Sunday evening concerts when the family quartet and quintet played Beethoven, Haydn and Mozart were the pleasantest part of home life—but August's ambition was stronger even than his tastes. In the same spirit he shared in all activities—if he were alone he crept into the lake from the bank, if any watched he hurled himself from the roof of the bathing hut—his pride was greater than his fear, and all the time he had to prove himself through the opinion of others. He knew that he was considered queer; there was a fey look about his blue eyes and big white forehead, which with his frequent tears made servants gossip and call him a changeling, while at school some teachers thought him precocious, others a dunce. Sometimes when he wanted to speak the words would not come, at other times the futility of repeating over and over again what everyone knew held him obstinately silent. But although he feared punishment, August enjoyed being a martyr; anything was bearable when he could dramatise it, and sometimes he arranged to be passed over—in the division of a peach or some strawberries, for instance, or in the credit for some kindness to his mother—so that he could enjoy his own heroism and impress the other children with proofs of it.

His brothers and sisters also found August—this bridge between the boys and girls of the family—unaccountable. He was like the girls in many ways, including looks, yet pride kept him from their babyish games and timidity from rougher ones. Not only adults, but the older boys 'weighed him down,' so that most of the time he spent alone—yet if he chose to join in, as when the children acted plays in the attic, August was at once the leader, and the others felt his power and charm. His expression was often sulky, but his eyes, which he fixed intently on whatever he was contemplating, were very blue—and his smile compelled.

He examined human behaviour minutely, just as he did his nature specimens, eager to learn the facts and find out what lay behind them. Piece by piece life went under the microscope of his keen observation, magnified by an unusual awareness of hidden emotion. It was clear to him that without the father, the family would be destitute, yet he could feel no gratitude to him; he observed that every creature fed its young, and resented being asked to treat his parents' care as a special favour. Since he had not asked to be born, he could not see that he owed anyone gratitude, and his love for his mother was as tormenting as hatred. When he was away he was sick with longing and could feel the invisible cord binding him to her, yet when they were together their hearts were hidden from one another. She was dying because she had had too many children, and while his love for her was unresolved he could never be free.

Where, August Strindberg wondered, was this family love that people talked and wrote so much about—an eye for an eye and a tooth for a tooth was the law between the boys; they were all scarred with each other's blows. Yet his blood had some consciousness his mind had not, for if any of his brothers or sisters were hurt or sick he knew it at once, even if they were far away. He felt the pain in his own nerves and, although he usually avoided fighting, if one of his brothers were attacked he would fly to his defence, whatever the odds. He obeyed his impulses and analysed them afterwards.

Another discovery brought more questions. In the old house, under the shadow of bankruptcy, his family had seemed very humble, and in the capital he saw many rich people. Most of the boys at the Klara school were better-dressed than himself, but now the family moved again and August found himself playing with the children of peasants and attending a school where to be the son of a shipping agent was to be an aristocrat, where his leather breeches and greased boots were envied, and where his own hardships were slight compared with those of others. A glimpse of the summit of the social ladder gave him an idea of its span, for at the King's summer palace of Drottningholm he saw the pageantry of a royal household and was spoken to by the Crown Prince. He observed that the lackeys for all their finery treated his father with deference, and he was filled with pride until he found out that his mother, whom he had set among the stars, had been a maidservant. He did not know where to place himself; the superiority of his former schoolfellows had crushed him; now he met verminous children with sores on their faces and uncombed hair, and saw them punished for faults he knew they could not avoid.

Unable to discover why anyone should parse a Latin sentence, get by heart a row of dates or juggle with figures, August neglected his lessons, but where he found a link between the lesson and life he was industrious and very quick, and now he began to read for pleasure. Herr Strindberg, who was a man of few words but wide interests, had a fair library and encouraged the children to read nature books, travel, adventure stories and the Bible. Before long, in spite of his unreliability, August was looked upon as the scholar of the family, and when he was thirteen he was sent to the Stockholm Lyceum where the education was on advanced lines. Now he found that he had not only duties but rights, and that he was expected to exert his own will. He found this embarrassing, but presently made up his mind to give up Greek and learn modern languages, and he was confident that whatever he chose to study he could master, although still sometimes when he wanted to speak the words would not come.

For this education, better than any given to his brothers, August was for the first time grateful to his father, and he had the intense joy of seeing that his mother was proud of him. The elder boys were away studying commerce and languages, and the mother enjoyed the company of this strange fourth son whom she had never understood. August talked to her, read to her, explained Oscar's postcards from Paris as if he were a native of that city, and brought her the latest additions to his nature collections. She began to think that she might see a son of hers wearing the coveted white cap, sign that a boy had passed the student examination and was eligible for the university. August had heard exciting tales of student life and stared enviously at those wearing that emblem of adventure and liberty he dared not hope for, but now even this did not seem out of range. Yet he could not rest in his new happiness, but must research and analyse the whole time. His mother warned him against the sin of pride, but he wondered if it were not for their own honour rather than for his good that his parents wished him to be well

8

educated; he listened scornfully to his mother's conversations with neighbours and servants, and when she spoke to him of the humility of Christ and the vanity of worldly wisdom and warned him to remain 'simple,' he remembered that she had had no education, and detected in her the hatred of the ignorant for the cultured. How dared she call herself a Pietist —how think that she, who gossiped religion with a lot of old women, had a special knowledge of God? August Strindberg had no time to remain simple—he must push on and find things out for himself.

Nor did he dare to be too happy for fear it would not last; there was something ominous in the way that now, when she was well enough, his mother moved about the house, turning out drawers, sorting linen and the children's clothes. And then for days she would not leave her bed, and the faces in the house grew grave. These things he could not analyse— his imagination shied at the knowledge that his mother was dying.

One day she showed him golden rings and said they would be for her sons when she was dead. The one which would be his was of plaited gold with a heart entwined in it—he had never owned a personal ornament, and he kept imagining what it would look like on his hand at school. He was too shy and proud to approach the boys of better family, but he still admired their handsome faces and polished finger nails, and he felt that a ring of pure gold would prove, if only secretly, that he belonged to the élite. To have a white student's cap and a golden ring seemed the height of his ambition.

Then one night, two months after August Strindberg's thirteenth birthday, he heard the words he seemed to have been expecting all his life—'Mother is dead.' He had never really found her, now it was too late and he shrieked in despair.

As if dreaming he watched the strange play of death in the house—white sheets hung up in the windows as a sign of mourning, women stitching in the dim light to clothe them all in black, the household rules relaxed, people known and unknown coming to the house. His father's stern voice was hushed, and the boy had never seen such gentle faces or heard so many kind words. He wrote to Oscar, the only one of the children away when their mother died, reflecting the religious consolation in which the house was bathed:

Stockholm, 22 March [1862]

My Dear Brother Oscar

Now we haven't a mother any longer. She died the night between Wednesday and Thursday, we were all in with her but she wasn't conscious so she didn't know us. Sophie has laid her out and she is very changed. . . . We are very sad, but Pappa has calmed us by talking to us about it being God's will. . . .

Don't cry too much and despair, because God has willed this, but calm yourself and comfort yourself through God's word, as we have done . . .

Bids your devoted and grieving brother

AUGUST

Sometimes in his interest and sense of importance August almost forgot to grieve, and he watched the behaviour of his brothers and sisters suspiciously, sure that the babies could not really miss their mother, and that the others had not loved her as well as he, although his own conscience hurt him, for at the very moment of her death he had been thinking of the golden ring. When he found he was not grieving, he turned the knife in his heart until he was consumed with sorrow; when he had one of his attacks of melancholy he dignified it with the name of mourning and did not try to conquer or conceal it. Yet under all this subterfuge which did not deceive himself, the boy knew that his loss was real.

Soon the house was normal again, except that it swarmed with little black-clad figures, and the young housekeeper, 'Mamsell,' was now the mistress. August continued to write to his brother in France, telling him the news of people, plants, poultry and the weather—as if he, at thirteen, were responsible for the lot.

Brother Oscar!

Thanks for your letter. We are all well and the little girls are out the whole day we've had 22°+ in the shade the bushes are green. . . . I sowed radishes which will be ready on Sunday and salad . . . and our border is full of different kinds of flowers. My birds had two eggs each. . . .

. . . Axel and I have the two small rooms in the attic and they are very nice. Olle sleeps downstairs near Pappa the babies and Mamsell have the big parlour and Mamsell's very kind to the babies so you

10

needn't be afraid they're having a bad time. . . . We've left off our overcoats and are wearing only jackets. I am writing this by the open window in the attic gable and having great fun over a chaffinch who's building in the trees opposite. . . .

Write soon bids your friend and Brother

AUGUST

His mood, however, was not always so happy. He never failed to resent authority, and was soon at loggerheads with Mamsell, and in trouble with his father for interfering in her province. Then he saw himself as a bigger martyr than ever —a motherless boy, underfed and improperly clothed, who had to go without exercise rather than expose his outgrown shirt in the gymnasium, and whom the whole household conspired to humble because of his superior education—on the one hand treating him as a small child, on the other burdening him with menial tasks that were the servants' duty. Even at school his quick brain was not an asset; he had qualified already for the highest class, in which the boys worked for the student examination, but he was kept back because he was too young. Again and again he took a flying leap towards his unknown but compelling goal, only to be jerked back by the cruel bit of authority.

Before long the father informed the children that in order to give them a new mother he was going to marry Emilia Peterson, the housekeeper. The little girls were too young to understand and the older boys quickly adjusted to the situation, for although they had themselves been flirting with Mamsell, who was very attractive, they believed that everything their father did was right. But August was thrown into a frenzy: he had wrapped the memory of his mother in his fairest thoughts until she had become the symbol of all purity and radiance; as his body woke to adolescence he protected her from his own erotic thoughts, and he protected her from images of his father's lust. Now she was dragged from heaven to be desecrated—he could not understand how his father, an old man and a Pietist, could do this fearful thing, and Mamsell, too, prided herself on her faith. It was clear to August that their religion was only a cloak for their sin. He had just seen *Hamlet*, and now he saw himself as Hamlet. It was less than a year since his mother's death, and to be given a stepmother was an even worse fate than to have a stepfather. As he had clothed his mother in light, he now clothed his stepmother in blackness, endowing her with all the wickedness of fairy-tale stepmothers. He vowed to protect the younger children from her cruelty and to let his father see that to him at least this wicked woman was no mother.

He was fourteen now and obsessed with sexual images. Even when younger he had been disturbingly aware of a girl's presence; now his imagination was inflamed by the talk of schoolfellows, by his father's marriage and by stories of love. At the same time his hunger for knowledge took another turn; once he could name every plant in the environs of Stockholm, could distinguish every bird by feather, note and egg, and had collected specimens of all the minerals, his interest in these things flagged. Now he burned to know how everything worked; he broke up clocks and watches, musical instruments, toys—anything that fell into his hands—in a feverish effort to discover their secrets. Reproofs were of no avail; the driving force of adolescence was stronger than any check. They could keep him back at school; they could persecute him at home, but August Strindberg began to see that nothing could really hold him down. At a science lecture he was enraptured by the mysterious apparatus, and at once saw himself as a scientist, making bubbling magic in test-tubes. His father sympathised with this new enthusiasm and gave him books on chemistry and physics, and presently August decided to win fame by inventing a machine to illustrate perpetual motion. He ransacked the house for materials—whalebone from an umbrella, gut from a fiddle, parts of an old spinning-wheel, a coffee-grinder, a soda-water machine. There was no end to his ingenuity, and all other interests faded in the ecstasy of creation. Even his mother's grave was left unvisited. When the experiment failed, he flew into a rage and smashed his invention to pieces, but soon the creative urge returned and he began all over again. His own power enchanted him and he longed for the day when he would be grown-up and free.

He was better-educated than his elder brothers, but they were already working for their livings and so knew more of the world, and he wanted to know everything. When they

talked about sex, he was torn between shyness and the urge
to understand this thing which held the secret of the universe, but when presently he got hold of one of the books
they read, *Warning against the Enemy of Youth by a Friend of
Youth*, he received a cruel shock. This pamphlet, in conjunc-
tion with the address of a Minister at school, led August
Strindberg to believe that by giving himself sexual relief he
had condemned himself to death or lunacy at an early age.
It appeared that he had only ten years left, and even before
he was shut away for ever in tomb or lunatic asylum, his body
would decay, his spinal marrow and his brain would melt, his
hair and teeth drop out. Religion was proclaimed the only
salvation—but that would not save his body.

There was no one August dared turn to for advice, and he
stared in the mirror at his young features and the blond hair,
springing in vigour from his temples, watching in panic for
the first symptoms of decay. The gaiety of the world appalled
him, and he dropped all other interests in order to save his
soul. Now he determined to take the Saviour by storm, to fast
and suffer until faith descended in a lightning flash and he
knew that he was one of God's elect. And if by a miracle God
spared his life he vowed to become a priest—he had often
thought this an attractive career.

So August Strindberg resolved to be a Pietist, but no dim
follower in the wake of his stepmother. Whenever he talked
to her about history, philosophy or science, she sneered at him
for believing that there was any value in worldly knowledge.
Less humbly than his own mother, she too claimed a secret
understanding of God that set her, an ignorant woman, above
scholars, thinkers and writers, and she made her eldest stepson
believe that he shared her secret, so that they could talk of
God together, shutting August out in revenge for his better
education. Now he intended to beat them at their own game
and climb higher on the Jacob's ladder to heaven. He would
have preferred a new religion, but Pietism answered his
adolescent needs. It was a rebel faith, a puritanism which had
broken away from the complacent conventions of the orthodox
Lutheran Church, ignored the theologians and insisted on the
practice of Christian virtue, with feeling rather than intellect
as guide. The rebels had been dubbed Pietists in mockery,

13

half a century before; they had proudly made the name their own, and now from Court and cottage people flocked to join them. To be a Pietist you must be converted, you must repent, you must utterly renounce the world, the flesh and the devil— but the rewards were great. You walked with God; you gained an inner knowledge of hidden things; your place in heaven was assured—and your ego was safeguarded, for Pietism re-affirmed Luther's almost forgotten tenet of the individual conscience.

In the fight to save his soul August Strindberg encouraged his melancholy as a sign of holiness and sorrowed for the sins of the world. His mother had left a letter warning him against intellectual pride, but he saw no danger of falling into this sin—his mind was consecrated. Yet the flashing conviction that he was a child of God did not come, and he wondered if perhaps the Holy Spirit could not descend until he was con-firmed. Over this, although he believed that in his religious life none could thwart him, the elders had found a new way to set him back—his father had declared that he was not old enough to be confirmed, and his stepmother agreed, at the same time pointing out that, while unconfirmed, his religious views were negligible. Now, although at last he was in the top class at school, August was humiliated by having to join a group of ignorant young children to be prepared for con-firmation. He could find no point of contact with them, and the Pastor was stern and offered little grace or comfort. August Strindberg learned that he was guilty not only of his own sins but of the sins of his forefathers. He learned to pray 'Lord, create in me a new will.' He found himself trapped after all in the intricacies of dogma, and began to search for a way out.

His notion of women was the simplest—on one side were bad women from whom he must resolutely turn away his eyes, on the other beings like his mother who must be wor-shipped and protected. Living so much among boys—his sisters were still little—he had not been aware that there were girls who had much the same interests and problems as himself. Now he began to find a new pleasure in serious con-versation with the other sex, and one young woman especially became his confidante. She was a Pietist, but did not use religion as a substitute for culture—she was well educated

14

and a woman of the world, and she treated August Strindberg as an equal.

The yellow book became a nightmare memory and religion relaxed its stranglehold, but he burned with anger against these preachers who tortured the minds of defenceless children. He no longer fought his doubts: Confirmation had failed —at his first communion the Spirit had not descended, and he perceived that his wish to be a priest had arisen more from fear than from a desire to serve God, that his faith was based on fear, that in fear he had shut his eyes to truth. He proclaimed his doubts, and at the Pietist meetings they prayed aloud for the young waverer, but this only confirmed his scepticism.

Besides studying for his examination, Strindberg, now sixteen, was teaching younger children—a sore task for his impatient mind, but one which put into his pocket the first money he could call his own. Economic dependence had made a prisoner of him, and the fear of creditors, impressed on his infant mind by his father's bankruptcy, made his own small debts alarming—to owe anyone anything was to give him power over one's soul. His ability to earn lent him confidence and two friends took advantage of his open state; a schoolfellow introduced him to the pleasures of beefsteak, punch and the embraces of a pretty waitress, and a young engineer launched an attack on his cracking faith with the three 'instinctive intuitions' of the American preacher Theodore Parker. Beginning as an orthodox Unitarian, Parker had come to doubt the infallibility of the Bible and the exclusive claims of Christianity, and hot on the heels of his influence, Strindberg was caught up in the new theory of evolution. Cramped with school routine and Pietism, his mind responded eagerly to the exercise, and released from penance he grew more robust. Now he joined the Volunteers—Denmark was putting up a vain but gallant fight against the Prussians and the young men of Sweden were eager to be in arms—though it was not the soldiering that most appealed to Strindberg, but the chance to get out of the town. He had always lived in Stockholm, but he had not seen the setting of his city, and now 'he discovered where he was.' At his first view of the skerries he felt that he had returned to the land of his

15

fairest dreams or of a former existence. This was where he belonged: 'among grey rugged rocks and wooded islands thrown out into wide bays with the boundless sea beyond.' He was sure that whatever happened to him, wherever else in the world he went, he would always be faithful to this love.

He saw himself now as a child of nature with his origin in the earth at his feet. He contemplated the interdependence of creation, the mountains becoming earth, the seas becoming rain, and mountain and water together giving birth to forest. He considered how all creatures breathed the same air, how birds lived on insects, insects fertilised plants, mammals ate the plants and nourished man, and man looked upward to the stars. With this new view of the universe he recoiled from Pietism, listened to the bells with aversion and resolved to go to church no more.

His family and friends condemned his arrogance in taking such a stand, but in fact the youth felt far from confident. He had lived so long by the will of others that he seemed not to have a will of his own; he had been taught to pray—to look for strength outside himself, so when he looked within he found nothing. He was irresolute and weak, a mirror of changing impressions, full of discords and contradictions. It seemed to him that instead of letting him develop according to his own nature, the authorities had dug into his soul and uprooted good seeds with the weeds, and now they thought him proud because he could not bear any more pressure, because he flung off his fetters like a frantic animal. To his father's surprise he begged to be allowed to leave school and go to work, but when it was suggested that he should become a cadet, in spite of momentary temptation August Strindberg realised that the rôle of officer was not for him. He did not want to command; he only wanted to escape from having to obey; he thought it would suit him better to become a Professor, so that 'he could behave as he liked without losing respect.'

Everyone offered advice, but Strindberg had had enough of confessors and inquisitors, and turned his back on friends and relatives. Then he felt their claws stretching out after him; they called him ungrateful and he fled in terror. They had given him their friendship freely, now they were sending in the account, a bill which could never be paid—worse than any of the money debts that vexed him, a debt of gratitude which turned relatives and friends into monstrous creditors, like the men who in those early days had called to dun his father and could not be sent away, like the deputy landlord pouncing on the tenants for the rent. Only in this case it was worse, for it was his soul they were after.

Reading, learning, teaching, his mind was in a turmoil, and now that he had lost his faith there was no fixed point to think from. He tried to read poetry, but found it unreal, and plays irritated him because of the break the names made in the dialogue. The length of novels wearied him; he found biography more interesting, and best of all books about nature and science, but whatever he read he could not get away from the harrowing search for his own personality. Who then was he, since everyone had a different view? One thought him hard, another weak, one cold, another sentimental—proud, abject, manly, girlish, clever, ridiculous, and in addition to other people's diverse opinions, he had to reckon with his own experience of existing in other people. He would strike in rage, then weep because the pain he had inflicted was intolerable to himself; he would cower ashamed when another sang out of tune; when he meditated on the crucifixion he felt the agony and understood how the saints received the stigmata, yet he could not believe. Only when he drank was he at peace with himself, and he began to crave alcohol as earlier he had craved certain kinds of food. Now he learnt to dance, and his partners were the newest specimens to go under his microscope. The ones he admired most were fragile girls with eyes and lips dark against the pallor of their skins, but he did not aspire to such exoticism, and chose homelier girls to dance with. Then he would ache to have just such a being as his wife; his body could no longer endure without a woman, but even when he ignored his conscience, his taste shrank from loose living. From the time he was sixteen, he had been tempted to take some modest post which would allow him to marry, but in what line he could not decide. However, if he could get to the university, where one could be poor without humiliation and have brains without appearing proud, where one could drink and adventure without a sense of shame, he was sure his real life would begin.

17

In his last year at school Strindberg obtained a post for the long summer vacation tutoring a nobleman's sons out on his country estate. He believed that his tastes and talents would be appreciated by the aristocracy, and tried not to be over-awed by the patronising tone of his employers and the veiled insolence of the servants, implying that he was one of themselves. He wrote home that he was in paradise and did his best to believe it; the grace, the leisure and the luxury enchanted him, but he writhed in his dependent position, and his pupils bored him. He was tired of playing nursemaid, and to add to his discomfort he disliked and feared their dogs.

Strindberg's self-respect returned, however, when he was invited to preach a sermon and lent a gown and bands. He forgot that he intended never to go to church again, and only remembered that he had always wanted to be a preacher. His views gave him a little trouble, since he no longer believed in the deity of Christ, but the Pastor, who was used to students, assured his earnest young friend that if he believed in God that was good enough—even bishops had been known to omit the name of Jesus Christ from their sermons.

But August Strindberg could omit nothing—he was inspired. When the Baron asked for him, the servant took back the answer that the tutor was writing his sermon, and countless humiliations were wiped out. This was his chance to declare that although Christ was the chosen, beloved Son of God, whose teaching must be followed, every human being was also a son of God in his own right. He struck at the arrogance of the Pietists, believing that they alone held the keys of heaven—grace was for all, for rich and poor, for children, for lepers and harlots. . . . 'Come unto me all ye that are weary and heavy laden.' . . . 'To-day shalt thou be with me in Paradise.'

He laughed at himself as he put on the clerical gown, then had stage-fright, but in the end was carried away by his own eloquence. All his hatred of oppression, all his understanding of suffering welled up, and he was so much moved that he wept.

He saw at once that others were less moved than himself, but the mission spirit had woken in him and when he got back to school, as champion of the new faith he encouraged

18

the other boys to join him in cutting prayers. But so that the authorities might not take their revenge by failing him in the final examination, he worked day and night, learning once again lessons that he had forgotten—he was eighteen and he had been kept at school too long.

He thought the questions foolish and his own answers absurd, but none the less in September 1867 August Strindberg passed the student examination. Schooldays were over, the long painful years of childhood finished. Even his father's icy manner, even the indifference of his brothers and sisters could not depress him long; the white cap was on his head, the world stood open. 'He had the ticket of admission in his hand—there was nothing to do but enter.'

CHAPTER TWO

1867–1869

I did not want to be made a fool of by life
TO DAMASCUS

Uppsala, 21 Sept. 1867

Dear Pappa,

As I've now started on my new life I will give a short account of my state of affairs. To say what impression Uppsala life has made on me is difficult as I've only been here eight days, but what I and every youth most prize is the freedom and independence we shall never have again, freedom of study and action and intercourse, though not a freedom which means the letting loose of all desires and passions but a freedom bounded always by the laws of decency and morality— in short I am content and getting on well. The sacrifices I must make here will be amply repaid in the wisdom I shall gather from the lips of the learned masters. Regarding these sacrifices there is no danger, I'm not in want, but simply suit my needs to my means. Here briefly is my daily budget. . . .

It was a meagre budget, and in spite of his resolutions August Strindberg was disappointed. His hopes had been so high, his dreams so glorious; the white cap had been for years his emblem of liberty, the student songs he had learned had a medieval flavour of the wandering minstrel, the gipsy scholar and the knight of culture, and inevitably Strindberg had seen himself as a romantic figure at the university, picturesque in his poverty.

His reactions both to places and to people were swift. Uppsala was rich in tradition: the kings were crowned in the cathedral, the Archbishop had his seat there, great men had entered the world through these doors—August Strindberg looked at their statues and determined to do even better, but he did not like the place. The landscape was flat with no inspiring panorama of islands, the little town was unimpressive, the sight of so

20

STRINDBERG AS A STUDENT

many young men all bent on the same object as himself made him shy and hostile, the dusty atmosphere left by generations of learning oppressed him, and after a while he found his lack of funds a serious handicap. He had to share the meanest of rooms with another youth; the wealthy students could fill their bellies with meat and talk the night away over their bottles of punch, but he, who longed for gay society, rich food and alcohol, must share a loaf of bread and a jug of milk with his room mate. Soon he knew his companion's secrets, was familiar with his habits, could anticipate his every word; his friendship could not endure such trials, but when it broke and they ate their common meals in silence, Strindberg was lonelier than ever.

He had chosen to read Aesthetics and Modern Languages, which meant that he must learn the history of all the arts and master five foreign languages in three years. The grandeur of the plan excited him and he was eager to begin. He attended lectures on Shakespeare's *Henry VIII*, but calculated that at this pace it would take a lifetime to master any subject. As he could not afford private coaching, there was no alternative but to borrow what books he could and study in solitude. He made a friend of himself, criticising and encouraging his own ego as if it were a separate personality, an interesting and absorbing acquaintance. Thus cherished, his ego grew and he was so much taken up with it that he ceased to look outside at all. He read no papers, mixed in no conversation, knew nothing of what was going on in the world. It seemed that the world had no place for him, so he decided to ignore it. In any case the politicians, lawyers, financiers and pedagogues made life more and more complicated, whereas he, although craving gaiety, had a greater need still for peace and simplicity. Pent up in the small town, he felt like a wild plant whose roots vainly sought a little soil between the stones of the pavement, or like a captive beast pining for the forest. When he could bear it no longer he rushed out into the countryside and walked until he was exhausted. Nature alone exceeded his expectations and now, reading Rousseau, he dreamed of returning to her arms, especially as it seemed clear that he could never take a degree. His money laboriously earned by teaching would scarcely last a term; he had no frock-coat in which to solicit the aid of the professors, and in any case he found them uninspiring and soon ceased to go to their lectures. Fearing a rebuff, he shunned the company of boys he had known at school who were in better circumstances than himself; when he came in contact with the aristocracy, he felt his mother's blood—his slave-blood as he called it—boil up in him. He could not be at ease; so now, if he broke at all from his solitude, it was to seek out students whose plight was even worse than his own. Here he found two who owned nothing between them but a prayer book and played chess all day to pass the time; here were others freezing in garrets, waiting for the end of the term and the end of their ambitions and wondering what had induced them to come to Uppsala. Why had they—why had he imagined it would be otherwise?

The Pietists had told him that there was no virtue in book-learning, and in his bitterness Strindberg was inclined to agree. If the wisdom of the university was not for him, he would no longer consider it desirable, but his alternative was not religion but nature. In the desperate struggle for existence of all living things, he saw his own struggle not to be crushed. He was a source of unused power, but he was weak in his isolation. Family, church and state were cruelly strong; it seemed as if the individual must suffer for the sake of a rotten society—but at least he had escaped from the tyranny of religion. Hoaxed by their churches the pious fixed their ambitions on a hypothetical after-life, and let the wonders of this life pass them by, but Strindberg resolved to explore the mysteries of nature and in so doing learn to know himself. Sometimes he feared that after all his ego had nothing that was truly its own, that each one of his characteristics was derived from an ancestor—or again, that he had no characteristics at all 'except scepticism of everything that he was told and a shrinking from pressure.' Perhaps like a forced flower if left alone he would revert to type and be at rest. Yet, compared with his fellows, he found his senses strangely alert, and his eyes, on their long antennæ of imagination, glimpsed other worlds beyond normal range. This made him wonder if he were prone to hallucinations—he had been lent the works of Swedenborg, the mystic philosopher who had fallen a prey to megalomania, and he could see that it was dangerous to have the mind of a dreamer and live too much alone. The mind became choked with its own juices, and unless these were absorbed by physical activity they created phantasies which led to madness. He found the writings of Swedenborg completely mad and did not try to understand them; he could not discover any books that pleased him, and soon his disappointment with the university plunged him in listless gloom. He had always wanted to play a musical instrument, and so when the chance offered he learnt to play the cornet, and for the rest, as the winter mercilessly cut short the days, he whiled away the hours in games of backgammon.

Even in the heart of winter and the bitterness of failure, he rejoiced when term ended to see the woods and water in which his home was set, and found his nerves in tune again. Somehow he must still study for his degree—his father was determined that so much education should not now be wasted —but for the moment he had no choice but to teach. He had hoped for a country post, but fate decreed that the only answer to his application should be from the Klara school, the school beside the dismal churchyard, where he himself, eleven years before, had been mocked and bullied and beaten.

In the frosty dark of a winter morning Strindberg walked down the same street with the same bells in his ears and the same fear in his breast. His worst nightmare was to find himself back in this school—waking he would thank God for his deliverance—but this time he would not wake.

He and two women teachers were in charge of the lowest class, and between them must control, rather than teach, a hundred children. Some came from the dregs of the capital, families from which the upper classes turned their eyes away, but for whom none the less Strindberg knew that there was no help but charity. Pale, stunted children whose eyes and noses ran, whose fingers were frost-bitten, whose ugly features bore the stamp of suffering. It was hard to make himself look at them, but he overcame his shyness and repugnance by analysing their condition. Most of the children were hungry, and it seemed to him that they inherited their fathers' trade-diseases. Here he detected the lungs of the gas-worker, ruined through sulphurous fumes, here the bowed shoulders and flat feet of the blacksmith, here the contracted chest of the book-binder, the cough of the metalworker, the rash of the sweep, the myopia of the watchmaker. His own life seemed without purpose, but now, more in anger than in pity, he vowed that he would get justice for these people, from whom, he told himself, his own mother had sprung.

Nothing had changed in the school since he left—the same hymn, the Lord's Prayer, the same elaborate routine for going out to exercise or to the latrines. If one boy broke his rigid poise, if one pair of clogs made a clatter, the whole business was to do again. It was bad to be one of the herd; it was worse to be an overseer forcing this ridiculous regime on other young lives, demanding the impossible, the absolute. Strindberg's desk was on a platform—he saw it as a scaffold, stained red with blood.

If he were allowed to teach in his own way, following the sympathetic precepts of Rousseau and Pestalozzi, Strindberg believed he could interest the children and hold their atten-tion—he felt far closer to his pupils than to the other teachers, and he would have liked sometimes to joke with them. But gaiety had no place in the regime, nor would his pupils have understood it; he had to stick to the conventional method of teaching, to the meaningless questions and endless repetitions which had maddened his own young brain; he had to obey the ruling of the headmaster he detested and keep order by force, although he felt—and looked—too young for such a rôle. Angry and ashamed he caned these boys as he himself had been caned, and when this method failed too and he was at the end of his tether, he sent the culprits to the women teachers. For them Strindberg had an instinctive hatred—he saw them as narrow-minded, illogical and despotic. They would cane the children on their hands and repeat the strokes because, through the reflex action which they did not under-stand, the victims could not keep their fingers still under the punishment.

The nightmare had its compensations; although he was living at home and was not allowed to forget how he had fallen in becoming a mere elementary school teacher, by earn-ing his own living Strindberg had won real independence. At first his salary seemed riches—he contributed to the household expenses, he bought books to study for his degree, and he spent the evenings in cafés, indulging his appetite for alcohol. When he drank he grew eloquent, when he drank more the turmoil of his brain subsided and let him sleep. He saw himself as a Viking, half savage, half dreamer, born of a long race of Northerners who had taken their fill of mead and women. He had his mistresses now, but he did not love them—he fell in love with virginal girls whom he could not approach. Had he been able to approach them his vision would have been shattered; this way he could hold the object of his love sacred, he could long for her as he longed for his mother and dream of a marriage which would not violate her purity.

But drink and women were expensive, and now too he must have better clothes—he had been born with the tastes of a dandy. To make more money he gave private lessons, but as his circle grew, so did his expenses. There was nothing for it but to run into debt. It did not trouble him much; his mind was too full now for petty worries, for he had discovered that after all he could enjoy poetry. He laid aside his Italian grammar and plunged first into Schiller and then into Byron, and for the first time his unremitting search for himself was rewarded. He infused himself into *Die Räuber*, glorifying his own rebelliousness in Karl Moor's dramatic revolt against society and religion, and he identified himself still further with Byron's Manfred. The mystery surrounding this English lord, born on his own birthday sixty-one years earlier, and the suggestion of hidden sin seduced him, and in *Manfred* his own deepest thoughts came to life in the beauty of the poet's art. He had not thought before about the power of words, but now he determined to translate *Manfred* into Swedish for all to read. He tried, but although he was sure that he understood the very essence of the poem, he could not translate it. Usually if he gave his mind to anything, however difficult, he succeeded, but he could not write verse, whether blank or rhymed. Presently he gave up the attempt, but when a girl asked him to write a poem for her birthday, he was too proud to refuse. A friend came to the rescue, but as he had sent the same verses to another girl two years before, the fraud was detected. Shame overwhelmed Strindberg, and he ran, wildly, blindly, to hide himself in the woods. He had been reared in a sense of sin and he was living dissolutely, but never before had he felt so guilty. To cheat and lie and pass off another man's work as one's own was to be utterly degraded; he cursed his childhood, where first at home and then at school he had learned to lie, and longed like Manfred to flee from himself to the Higher Alps.

But spring came again, and as always many of his troubles melted with the melting snow. When he put away his winter overcoat which seemed heavy with snow and sweat and the dust of school, his whole nature revived. All over the city the double windows were taken down and light poured into the rooms; the ice cracked again and water streamed under the bridges. Strindberg's blood responded, his spirit leaped to freedom, and soon the school closed its doors on the blood-red desk and the sickening cane. Summer with its sunlit days and twilit nights stretched out before him—he must still teach, but away from the city, out of earshot of the bells that rang him back into childhood.

Now he studied the different types of people gathered in the summer colony, and it seemed to him that those who enjoyed themselves most were the townspeople who left all their cares behind in closed shops and empty flats, and gave themselves up to the sea and the sun. Nature in them turned outward to meet nature all about them, while the professors sat hunched over their books, irritated by every contact with reality, only able to enjoy life at second-hand. He no longer wanted to be a professor—there seemed no place in life for him at all.

A place was found by Dr. Axel Lamm, a Jewish physician, who knew the Strindberg family and had watched this quick-witted, difficult boy struggling into manhood. Lamm was sure that with his scientific bent and his interest in people, August Strindberg should become a doctor. Strindberg wanted any reprieve from the scaffold desk, but at first the difficulties seemed insurmountable. How could he embark penniless on an eight years' training? Dr. Lamm had the solution: his young friend should live in his house and tutor his sons. But then, Strindberg was not sure if he wanted to become a member of any profession—his main desire was to be free. In medicine, Dr. Lamm pointed out, he would escape from the class consciousness that tormented him; there would be neither pressure from superiors nor embarrassment from inferiors. Then Strindberg's conscience reproached him with deserting his post, but it was easy for Dr. Lamm to persuade him that he could do more for humanity through healing than by thrashing her children, and that there was no better road to knowledge and self-knowledge than the exacting course of medicine. Here was no creed, no dogma, no humbug, but the chance to penetrate life's mysteries and learn the truth.

So, in the autumn of 1868, when Strindberg was nineteen, he went to live with Dr. Lamm. The thought of a home with the homeless appealed to his imagination—*The Wandering Jew* was one of his favourite books and he was full of curiosity about the Lamm household. He observed that family ties were strong, yet there was no tyranny; the children neither feared their parents nor were expected to feel an impossible gratitude for each breath they drew. They had no fear of hell; they were not haunted by images of Christ's suffering on the Cross or imbued with a sense of guilt; they simply thrived in an atmosphere of kindliness and culture, and they had unconsciously imbibed so much knowledge that it was difficult for Strindberg to teach them. Here was no question, as in his first experience of tutoring, of being looked on as a servant—for that matter the servants themselves were treated as members of the family—but he felt himself pupil rather than teacher, even to those young boys. They had heard intelligent conversation all their lives; they had the run of their father's fine library; their minds and their bodies had been fed with richness—they had begun where he was getting to.

In Uppsala a year ago he had learnt to play backgammon to pass the time; now there was so much to do that he was thrown into confusion. He had looked forward to working in a fine laboratory, but he found it tedious to labour over experiments verified by others a thousand times. Only when he could try out something for himself were the retorts and the test-tubes and the flames of the bunsen burners once more imbued with magic as at that lecture long ago. To find unexpected traces of one substance in another thrilled him. He was breathless with anticipation, feeling that at any moment he might make a discovery which would solve the riddle of the universe. Then his whole being concentrated on his work and he felt close to truth. He distilled for himself some drops of prussic acid, and it gave him an extraordinary pleasure to know that under the glass stopper of the little phial he had imprisoned death. He could have gone on endlessly playing at magician, but to get a medical degree he must go to school again. Here he was, nearly twenty, faced with a whole string of new subjects to master, and worse ᴜɴan the new ones he must return to the Latin grammar—he was always being put back again to the beginning. Dr. Lamm's library offered him Goethe, Wieland, Lessing, Dickens, Chateaubriand and the romantic novels that were flowing from the pen of George Sand. Writers and artists gathered round the doctor's table and talked of Paris, of art, of the theatre. The Dramatic Theatre was close to the house, and there was a season of French comedies; night after night Strindberg slipped down to stand enchanted by the swift dialogue, the eloquent gestures, the graceful settings. Here was a people bred in sunshine, smiling at the world, whereas a Northerner, however much he loved his own country, seemed always to be craving for warmth, always struggling through heavy mists of melancholy.

With all these distractions it was hard to keep his mind on the rudiments of medicine or on his Latin grammar. 'His imagination had been set in motion and his memory would not work.' He loved to use his mind, but he hated to learn by heart, and already his brain was choked with undigested facts. Even politics interested him now, and he found himself reading the newspapers. These Jewish people lived like aristocrats; their house was full of fine pictures and *objets d'art*; they were cultured to the finger tips, but their outlook was democratic. They took democracy for granted and were not torn in conflict like himself. It was as if the Strindberg blood in which his father traced a noble streak had been unable to mix with the slave-blood of his mother, and the two strains still fought in himself. His tastes drew him away from the working classes, but conscience held him to them.

One evening when Dr. Lamm was entertaining, a tumult broke out in the street, and someone exclaimed 'It's only the mob!' Strindberg had been enjoying himself, but these

RIDDARHOLM "*Island of the Nobles*" STOCKHOLM

words crashed into his consciousness and shattered his pleasure like a stone hurled through glass. The mob! What was the mob but the people—his mother's people, his own people, the dark background which lent this scene its brilliance? The same shame which had overtaken him when he put his name to another man's verses mounted in him now, for having deserted his class and forced his way up to heights where he did not belong. In a moment he was down in the street where people were demonstrating because a statue of Charles the Twelfth, erected by public subscription, was to be unveiled in such a way that only the privileged with seats on stands would have a view. The crowd was threatening to tear down the stands, but whatever the cause it would have been the same to Strindberg. It was enough that people were being suppressed—he must fly to their aid.

During these months Strindberg began to understand how industrialisation was affecting markets and labour: country was at war with town; Sweden's union with Norway was uneasy; she was unpopular in Denmark because she had stayed out of the fight with Prussia—in fact like himself his country now had no vocation. He wished he could be a painter or an actor, living outside the rules in a world of his own. Yet when the statue of the warrior king was actually unveiled, August Strindberg was there again, marching with the student singers, among the elect until once more the people were at odds with the police, then in the crowd furiously fighting this symbol of oppression. This time in his frenzy he attacked a police officer who had hold of one of the demonstrators, and astonished at his effrontery the officer demanded his name. There was only one name for Strindberg's black boiling passion and it burst from his lips. 'Satan! And I shall take you if you do not let him go.' Yet, when a little later he stood in the window with Dr. Lamm and looked down on the stupid brutal faces of the crowd, Strindberg saw that conditions would be no better if these people were on top—both sides were tyrants and both slaves.

His social consciousness was increased by his first voyage outside Sweden. He joined a party of young people, with one of Dr. Lamm's sons in his charge, to visit the Thorwaldsen Museum in Copenhagen, and their travelling companions were hooligans, hostile to all culture, who sneered at the Jewish boy because his manners were different from their own. Strindberg saw more clearly still that if such men were to rule, ignorance would be joined to brutality. He could feel 'the nailed boots of the future rulers trampling on his heart,' yet he believed that if these people were oppressed he would risk his life for them. He belonged to both classes and hated both, and yearned to be admitted to that Bohemian world, outside the rules of society, of which he had an occasional glimpse. Instead he was forced to probe still further into human conditions, to see the difference between sickness in poverty and in wealth, to enter homes of terror and distress, to watch disease in all its stages, to hold a body in pain between his hands while the doctor operated. The practice of medicine was even more distasteful to him than the tedious study of text-books; his senses craved beauty and had to grow accustomed to vile sights and smells; he must dissect dead bodies and conduct nauseating searches of live ones. The only way he could bear it was to do these things mechanically and let his imagination soar—'to think of Faust while examining yet another specimen of urine.'

All the same Dr. Lamm was pleased with his pupil and Strindberg went up to Uppsala for his preliminary examination full of confidence. He did not pass, and the Professor of Chemistry advised him to return in a year's time better prepared. He left in a rage, convinced that the examiners had failed him because he was studying in Stockholm instead of in Uppsala and that they had a personal grudge against him. He had talked too grandly of his medical career, now he would have to bear not only his family's sneers for this new failure but the doctor's disappointment. He would have to go back to the beginning and for another year learn nothing new, simply go over the same dreary ground again.

In this mood Strindberg watched a troupe of actors strolling down the narrow Uppsala street, peering in the windows and mocking at the piles of old dusty books. At once he was infected by their mirth: how enchanting to laugh at all this provincial pedagogy, to make knowledge live upon the stage, to utter great truths and move the hearts of men and women! He decided then and there to be an actor. Even the old refrain

30

'what will people say?' was not strong enough now to weaken
his resolve. He forgot his disgrace, swept aside the doctor's
protests, ignored his family and, while still earning his keep
as tutor, gave his whole mind to the study of the theatre. He
translated Schiller's lecture on 'The Theatre as an Institution
for Moral Education,' and together he and Dr. Lamm wove
it into a newspaper article, criticising the government's lack
of cultural policy. The doctor was fond of writing articles
and Strindberg liked to help him. A copy of *The Lancet*
came from England, mooting the question whether women
were suited to a medical career. Strindberg instantly decided
that they were not, although he was by no means opposed to
education for women.

I strongly deplore women's state of subjection which does not
allow them any part in life's higher interests and the search for Truth,

he wrote to his friend Fredrika Roos at about this time, but
all the same his vision of the ideal woman was too delicate
and pure for the life of a medical student. In this Dr. Lamm
concurred and they wrote another joint article, but when it
appeared, the Editor had stressed their admiration for the
opposite sex but their objections to its descent from the pedestal
had been left out—women's emancipation was the order of
the day. In any case Strindberg had little time to think about
anything else, now that he was going to be an actor. He
struggled with his shyness and called on the Director of the
Dramatic Theatre; he felt embarrassed disclosing his heart
to a stranger, but when the Director advised him against this
hardest of all professions, Strindberg's mind was quite made
up. His vitality leapt to tackle anything new, and at the same
time his pride found protection in the Director's warning. If
it was so hard to be an actor, the shame would be less if he
were to fail again.

He did not, however, think that in this he could fail. He
loved the theatre and he had discovered Goethe's treatise on
the histrionic art. He followed the master's instruction fana-
tically, doing violence to his shyness and his fear of open
spaces by striding across the city squares at their busiest
moments, tiring himself out with gymnastics and fencing,
studying every movement of his body as he stood or sat,

entered a room or left it. He walked, as Goethe directed, with head erect and chest expanded, arms freely swinging and fingers lightly closed, and as often as possible he sought the countryside where he could declaim unheard. His voice died on the winds as he inveighed against heaven and earth. Himself a force of nature, he shook his fist and ranted against the church spires, the barracks and the palace that symbolised society. His ego swelled with satisfaction.

But even now he must go back to school, take a course at the Dramatic Academy, begin at the beginning and keep pace with the beginners. He could not endure this slow torture for long, preferring even the ignominy of working in the theatre as a greenhorn flung into a dance of which he did not know the steps—at everyone's beck and call, yet given no work. Children from elementary schools played parts they did not understand, and their very ignorance saved them. The whole work of the theatre appeared to him mechanical. Words were learnt by heart and feeling faked; the actors were indifferent; they never spoke of their art—the sacred art—but only of parts. There was no trace of a gay life behind the scenes; the actors sat in silence putting on their false beards waiting for their own entrances.

Strindberg hung about the wings through long rehearsals without a single line to say, not daring to read for fear of being passed over—and now there was much he longed to read. He resisted the creeping sense of disillusion; he had recognised the vital force of the theatre from the first moment he set foot in it, and Schiller and Goethe strengthened his feeling. He had been through much of Shakespeare in translation while still at school, but his response was weak—he had lost the meaning in the maze of words. Now he studied the historical plays again, and found *Julius Caesar* after his own heart. Lectures and text-books kept history in its grave; the theatre brought it to life and proved its message for all time. He turned to Öhlenschläger's *Hakon Jarl*. The Danish poet died a year after he himself was born, and in Sweden twenty years earlier had been crowned Scandinavian King of Song. These romantic tragedies moved and inspired Strindberg, so that depressed as he was by contemplating the seamy side of the theatre—the dust, the vanity and the jealousy—he could

still cling to his belief in dramatic power. He read *Brand* too
now, the savage satire that Henrik Ibsen, driven into exile
by poverty and misfortune, had written home from Italy.
Brand did not so much inspire as frighten Strindberg. For all
his break with Pietism he recognised something of himself in
the fanatical priest who sacrificed everything to his faith.
Strindberg wanted to be worldly, but he could not deny the
puritanical gloom that was conjured up by this powerful
creation. He wanted above all things to be free of restraint,
but he admired the Norwegian's denunciation of weakness,
and the courage with which he declared his views. Henrik
Ibsen, twenty-one years his senior, also knew the bitterness of
poverty, and had had years of drudgery as apprentice to an
apothecary before he won his way to freedom.

At last Strindberg was promised a part in *Maria Stuart* by
Björnsterne Björnson, the Norwegian writer who had succeeded Ibsen as Director of the Bergen Theatre. Strindberg
liked this play, and saw himself in two of the characters—
Knox, the moralist, hard as stone—not unlike Brand, and
Darnley whom he conceived as a kind of Hamlet. Here were
portraits of the two sides of his own nature, and he was sure
that he could play either rôle successfully, but all he was given
was the part of a nobleman with eleven words to speak—
eleven quite unimportant words. Bitterly he listened to the
ignorant chatter of the leading actors, watched them yawn
with boredom and heard them repeat like parrots words which
they neither thought nor felt. Was he never to spread his
wings? Presently he could bear his frustration no longer and
demanded his right to be tried for a leading part. The Director
coldly agreed to give him an audition: August Strindberg's
voice stammered out into the empty theatre—how could he
hope to move a handful of jealous actors?—those on the stage
with him did not even try to play their parts. He was sternly
advised to go back to the Dramatic Academy, and walked out
into the street weeping with rage and humiliation. He could
not even do this thing that he felt in the marrow of his bones.
He had no place in society and he had broken with his family.
Always he was told to go back, always the things that he most
loved were spoiled for him. Why had he been born into a
world in which he had no place? His upbringing had prepared

him for an imaginary after-life, but for the real issues not at all. He would go back no more—but was there anything ahead save death? He went home to his lonely attic, took an opium pill and lay on his bed half-hoping to die.

CHAPTER THREE

1869–1872

I am only asking for a loan with my future as security
Letter to Oskar Seippel, July 1871

H E A W O K E to seething memories; scenes from childhood and adolescence mingled in dreamlike fashion with scenes from Topelius's *Tales of a Barber-Surgeon*. The story he had just been reading told of a reconciliation between son and stepmother, and he wondered if after all his own stepmother might bring him and his father together. In any case, whatever the purpose, his mind was at work arranging memories, cutting out scenes, adding others, bringing in characters. . . . And then, as it were involuntarily, the action began; he saw the characters on a stage and heard them speak, and as the hours passed found that he had witnessed the whole performance of a play.

He wrote until exhausted, then collapsed on to the bed. Soon energy was restored, and at the end of four days he had written a two-act domestic comedy. He felt an extraordinary relief, 'as if a long pain were over, an abscess lanced at last.' Instead of dying he had been born again; out of chaos had come creation—he picked up his pen to write a letter and it wrote itself in verse. He, who a short time before had been driven to use another's talent, could not now help writing in rhymed and rhythmic lines. He was gloriously happy: as a child he had prayed in vain for a sign of grace, but now the Holy Ghost had descended; his brow had been touched by tongues of fire—he felt as if he had made love at last to the woman of his dreams.

But how could he tell if his work were good? He carefully set the scene—a candle, a clean napkin, a bottle of punch— and rushed out to collect his friends. Trembling he read aloud

35

to them—they acclaimed him without doubt a poet and a playwright and drank eagerly to his success. He had found his vocation, and when his friends had gone he fell on his knees and thanked God for this miracle.

He sent the play off under a *nom de plume* to the Dramatic Theatre and returned to the boards himself as a supernumerary. No criticism of his acting could hurt him now, when soon he might see his own creation living on the stage. Meanwhile he went on writing; the technique of drama delighted him—it was curious to remember how tedious he had once found the reading of plays, when now the interweaving of action and dialogue so stimulated his imagination. He began a full-length tragedy in verse—of Demosthenes leading the Athenians in revolt against King Philip of Macedonia, a play of patriotism, of the everlasting struggle between the classes, a poem in praise of liberty. At the same time he conceived another play to show that the strength of the great thinker *Jesus of Nazareth* lay in the fact that he was man not God.

A Name-day Gift was rejected, but the Director perceived talent in it, and when he discovered the author's identity urged him to renounce acting and concentrate on the greater task of writing, to which end he should go back to Uppsala and take his degree. Again they were pressing him back while he was straining forward—this time with his goal in view. But *Hermione*, the Greek tragedy, was also returned by the Royal Theatre, and everywhere he met with the same advice. He could not even escape his fate on the score of poverty, for now that he was twenty-one he inherited a small legacy from his mother. He went home to claim it, not as a prodigal son or a failure, but as a promising author, not asking a favour but demanding his rights.

So now he was back again in the pedagogic den. Whatever direction he took his steps led round in a circle, and these repetitions gave him an uneasy feeling of being up against a personal enemy. However, this time he was neither penniless nor a greenhorn; his new talent gave him self-confidence and his experience of medicine and the theatre proved him a man of the world. He had proper clothes and made the most of his height and his hair. When he was a Pietist his locks had drooped like his spirits, now they sprang upward from his forehead in a blond mane and his blue eyes sparkled.

The scope of the course he must cover confused him; but there was no need now to play backgammon in order to pass the time. He still had the meanest of rooms and slept on a plank bed under a leaking roof; he could only afford the simplest food and missed the luxuries of the doctor's house, but he was no longer lonely. Uppsala's young poets sought him out: they bound themselves together into Runa, a guild of song, to study the Scandinavian and Icelandic sagas and break the conventions of the day by returning to the origins of culture. Now he shared the secrets of his soul: over the drink—they claimed mead as their heritage just as surely as Nordic literature—they discussed and analysed, were grave, gay, lewd and sentimental. When they had drunk a lot they asked one another if they believed—by which they meant if the one believed that the other had been 'called' as poet. Strindberg learnt to play the guitar, and as the breath of spring returned, the songs of Runa woke the sleeping streets.

He burned the draft of *Jesus of Nazareth*. True, he had now read Darwin, and although he still believed in a divine power, he must in reason proclaim himself anti-Christian, but all the same he felt that the complete refutation of Christianity was too big a subject for a play. He destroyed several other sketches too, but he still hoped for a dramatic success which would let him out of taking a degree, and he was advised that a one-act play in verse was the most likely form of drama to be accepted by a theatre. For this he chose Thorwaldsen as a subject neither too grandiose nor too banal, and one that was of topical interest since this year, 1870, was his centenary. The character of the famous Danish sculptor invited drama—Strindberg saw something of Ibsen's Brand in him and much of himself. Like the members of Runa, Thorwaldsen's call was not to religion but to art, and his father had urged him to forsake Rome and art for the Danish shipyard, just as his own father had extracted a promise that he would not waste time writing but read for his degree. Thorwaldsen in his studio in Rome with his hammer raised to smash up his great figure of Jason was an attractive scene to work from.

In Rome took fourteen days to write. On the day it was finished a letter came from Stockholm bringing far less money than Strindberg expected; he owed every cent of it and had no idea how he was to buy his next day's dinner, but that problem had to wait until he had tried out the new play on his friends.

On April 1st, 1870, he wrote his cousin Oscar Strindberg, a young business man in Stockholm who was something of a poet himself, an enormous letter describing his financial plight and his dramatic success:

> . . . I went home—finished my work—and went up with it to friend Arvid—and there was friend Axel—I read my play aloud—the last line died away—not a word!—then Arvid got up—whispered something in Axel's ear—and they invited me out for a walk. I agreed—and we came 'by chance' to an inn—they asked me to have a drink—I went in. We sat down in one of the small rooms—everyone was silent—then the girl came in with a *bottle of champagne*—I trembled with joy—had no words for my astonishment and delight—because I understood what they meant—then the cork hit the ceiling—then tongues were loosed—it was a glorious moment—and now the critics can slate me all they like—I've spoken to the hearts of two young men who have understood me. Soon the glasses were empty—then I was seized with that divine recklessness which is the essence of youth and makes all its troubles so light—I took back a bottle of punch—the last coin went—long live recklessness! no dinner to-morrow—what matter when to-day I live like a God! . . .

The next day Strindberg tended a student who was sick and destitute, and bought food for them both on credit. He pondered on all this brotherly love; he was touched by his friends' unenvious admiration of his work and wrote his cousin that after all 'there is something in this Uppsala life I like,' but at the same time he was aware that these friendships were only a makeshift. Without the love of a woman he could only be half a man, and whenever he caught sight of a father, mother and children sitting together round a table, he felt miserably lonely.

In Rome was accepted for production at the Royal Theatre the following autumn. His friends' faith in him was justified; his failure as an actor and all his other failures were wiped out. He tried to study, but it was impossible; besides, it was the month of May, a month to sing and drink, to write poetry, play the guitar and fall in love. Soon term was over and the Runa brethren continued their revels among the fishermen on Kymmendö, an island in the Baltic skerries. Strindberg was the soul of the party, although sometimes when the bacchanal went on too long he suddenly sickened and broke away to seek himself in solitude.

When at last, in September 1870, the curtain rose on his own scene—Thorwaldsen's studio in Rome with a touch of a Stockholm studio and a breath of La Vie de Bohême—Strindberg was faint with excitement, but he saw at once that the play was nothing but a painted mockery. He heard the audience laugh, but could not think why; what he had taken as witticisms fell on his ear as childish nonsense, what he had imagined high emotion was foolish sentiment, what he had believed poetry was mere doggerel, and his use of foreign words, which had seemed so effective, was pretentious and silly. He could find no virtue in the play at all. His legs trembled, electric shocks ran through him and he began to cry; a friend took his hand to calm him, but in shame he ran from the theatre as once before he had run from his own hypocrisy. He was tempted to plunge into the swirling waters of the Stream and wash away his guilt, but at the end of the performance his friends found him in a humble café, drinking himself into oblivion.

The critics were lenient with the anonymous author of *In Rome*, but when Strindberg got back to Uppsala he found much censure. The student newspaper denounced his effrontery in disguising his own insignificant personality with the famous figure of Thorwaldsen. Strindberg was deeply hurt and his old shyness of strangers returned.

Now his full-length prose play *The Freethinker* was published. His mind full of Karl Moor, Faust and Brand, he had created his own Karl who, through the influence of Theodore Parker, sacrificed all he most loved to truth. Strindberg had poured his soul into this play and rejoiced that it should be his first published work. It fell at once into the hands of a cynical reviewer who held it up to ridicule. Strindberg was furious: he could dissect himself with utter ruthlessness, but this derision shattered his humility. Critics be damned! He was a writer and he would write the truth. He plunged into a new play reiterating the religious rebellion of *The Freethinker*, but this time on a grander scale with the Danish Romantic Öhlenschläger as his master, and the Icelandic sagas, which he read in the original, lending him atmosphere.

Herr Strindberg now arranged for his son to live in the house of a parson's widow, in the hope of keeping him from dissipation and holding him down to his studies, but the plan was vain. The young man's body and mind were in a fever—he was in love for the eighth time—with a girl who was betrothed to another—he had made friends with an older man whose penetrating criticisms of human behaviour opened his eyes further, and he had discovered Kierkegaard. In 'Either-Or' he found his own perpetual conflict mirrored, and began to analyse it again in the light of this new, stern knowledge.

How he scrambled through the Latin papers he could not tell, but the blessed word 'passed' freed him from that toil for ever, and now he turned to the thesis he must shortly present. He had chosen Öhlenschläger's *Hakon Jarl* as his subject, using the play as the basis of a discourse on the conflict of Realism and Idealism in man and in art, and extolling Kierkegaard's hatred of compromise—although personally he found it impossible to choose between ethics and aesthetics. If he could not have Both-And instead of Either-Or, Strindberg saw himself condemned to veer eternally from one pole to the other.

The thesis was returned with the comment that it appeared suitable for an illustrated weekly, and once again Strindberg was thrown into a rage. He had bared his soul with all its contradictions and weaknesses; he had wasted his loftiest thoughts and finest imagery only to be insulted. He detested Uppsala; in a fit of pessimism partly induced by the suicide of another student—a haunting seductive image—he had burned his Viking play, and now he was exhausted.

When he reached home at the end of term, he felt as if he had returned to harbour from a storm at sea, and found comfort in his own old truckle-bed and the company of his sisters. Now that they were growing up they brought comfort to the house—the feminine touches he identified with his dream of home. Even his father had mellowed with the years; he sat over his ledgers all day, but at night old man and young shared their interest in the great things of the world. In this soothing atmosphere a new play sprang from the ashes of the one Strindberg had burnt, still on the Viking theme but now condensed into one act with Björnson's successful drama *Between the Battles* as its model. These were halcyon days, but they could not last. As soon as his father tried to exercise parental authority Strindberg fled to the fishermen, and as he was now quite without means of support, much of the summer was spent trying to find money to take him back to the hated university in the autumn.

Kymendö 17/VII 71

Oskar Seippel!

It's not on the grounds of an old chance acquaintanceship that I ask help—for that is—without disguise or flattery which I remember offends your frank nature—my purpose—no, I approach as a stranger—although availing myself of an old privilege to use an intimate form of address—and beg you at least to read my letter to the end so you won't take me for a cadger having to meet debts at all carelessly incurred. . . .

He then gave Oskar Seippel, a childhood's acquaintance now in business, an accurate account of his career to date, explained that it appeared necessary for a young man to have a degree if he were to get anywhere, and went on:

. . . My 'Jason' statue is half made—must I destroy this work of my youth's strength—of my laborious days and sleepless nights? . . . Help me! it is hard to beg when one's so young—but I'm not begging really—I'm only asking for a loan—with my future as security.

And to John Fredrik Rossander, another business man, he wrote:

. . . Sir, help me! I am only twenty-two and am begging you for a loan—no, I am begging for work—for without a loan I cannot work—and I'm pining every day and every moment to get away from the peace and joy of country life back to the old hellish horror of Upsala—only in order to work—Give me hope and courage again —because I yearn to be in a position to try out the strength I've mustered during the summer rest—and I need not assure you that J shall always gladden you with the sight of what's said to be an unusual phenomenon—a grateful person.

For all these efforts Strindberg returned to Uppsala almost penniless, but *The Outlaw* had gone to the Dramatic Theatre, and he was full of health and vigour. He strode about with his books and necessities in a knapsack, sleeping half-dressed on any couch that offered and eating whatever his friends could give him. He felt so well that for a while he laughed at his predicament, but at the first hint of being unwelcome he hired the meanest room he had yet inhabited—an attic which his friends assured him smelt of suicide.

The Outlaw was put on, but it was not a success, and to his annoyance the critics suggested that it derived from Henrik Ibsen. True, like himself, the Norwegian had been influenced by Öhlenschläger, but the rugged quality of The Outlaw sprang straight from the Icelandic sagas and the emotion was Strindberg's own. He saw himself clearly in five of the characters, pleaded the cause of each and understood them all. He thought Ibsen was taking too strong a hold in Sweden— Brand was powerful, but he found Peer Gynt 'obscure rather than deep,' even though it was a good antidote to Norway's nationalism. He felt that in Sweden young and old had fallen into an apathy, a belief that now they could doze till Domesday. Considering the course of history, he sometimes wondered if Norway might not yet swoop down upon her sleeping sister.

In any case Strindberg did not want to be under Norwegian or any other influence, although he often doubted if anything were original. All Swedish culture appeared to derive from other culture, and he was tormented by the notion that he himself was only a chance product of other people's lives. Nothing satisfied him now; he angered his masters with criticisms of Dante, Shakespeare and the Swedish classics, but in secret he lamented his strange inability to admire anything whole-heartedly. He had nothing to believe in and nothing to worship, and to add to this emotional blank winter struck hard on his poverty. All the same his humour was irrepressible and he wrote his cousin Oscar lively accounts of his hardships.

A stove-pipe ran through his attic and once a week, on washing-day, it was warm; then he stood against it with his books propped up in front of him, but for the rest he must chiefly stay in bed and read, as darkness fell, by the light of a candle stuck in a bottle. But he could still watch the arrival of new tenants and hope to find a beautiful girl as his neighbour; he could still analyse his own sensations and everybody's behaviour—he had learnt to distinguish true friends from false and he lavished gratitude on those who showed him kindness. Sometimes his plight struck him as ludicrous, sometimes he wondered how long he could resist the temptation of suicide. He could not conjure up a vision for a new play, and one day, watching a painter create the radiant colour of summer in darkest winter, he felt that no man could have a richer gift than this. He borrowed materials and locked himself into his attic to learn the magic art; his efforts were good for a beginner, but his friends looked askance at this new development. He noticed that nowadays people often looked queerly at him, and wondered if he were going mad, and even when he was most sure of his sanity, he was sometimes seized with panic at the notion that others thought him mad and were planning to have him shut up.

Into the midst of this uncertainty, among the bills and complaints that made his mail a menace, came a letter from the Royal Palace commanding his presence. He thought it was a hoax—why should the King want to see a down-and-out student, an unsuccessful playwright, the son of a maidservant? But as everyone assured him that the letter was genuine, presently, sick with nervousness, he crossed the threshold of the vast Stockholm palace round which the water and the traffic swirled. His first glance at Karl XV reassured him. This King was no tyrant; he was a tall handsome man who looked ill, smoked a long pipe and had a kindly manner, and he explained to Strindberg that he had seen and admired *The Outlaw*, and that as he wrote a little himself he liked to meet other writers.

Strindberg returned to Uppsala with a cheque in his pocket and the promise of a quarterly stipend from the Privy Purse until his studies were. finished. In one day he had risen from destitution to honour, and he could assure himself that this good fortune was not due to patronage but to the sincere regard of one man of letters for another. Now he need owe neither money nor gratitude—food, fires and brandy would stir his frozen blood, and he would work with all his strength.

His back grew straighter and his chest expanded, yet somehow this new dignity estranged Strindberg from his friends, and sometimes the consciousness of other men toiling like slaves, while he was privileged, oppressed him with a sense of guilt—he had been reading *Les Misérables* and its message bit deep. He plodded on with the curriculum for the degree, but he could please neither himself nor his tutors, and although he scraped through the papers in philology, astronomy and constitutional history, he did not do well, partly because in the *viva voce* his aphasia returned. He was sure now that he would never be able to speak a foreign language fluently and would at times have difficulty with his own. Some said that the cause of this trouble lay in the two scars above his left eyebrow, one the result of a fight and the other of a fall, and he took this to mean that they suspected cerebral damage—in other words that they thought him insane. Presently he wrote to a mental home, where he had heard that patients were allowed freedom and could work on the land, described his dreams and hallucinations, his fears and aphasia, and asked to be admitted for a cure. The alienist replied that hypersensitive people often passed through such crises and that these experiences were by no means symptoms of mental derangement—and Strindberg was slightly reassured.

But now he wanted to write again, and instead must read all the philosophers. Each system fell short and increased his impatience; Darwin's stark views seemed closer to the truth than these spiritual meanderings, and he aspired to find it out for himself, but constantly lost the thread of his own thought in the mass of other people's words. He saw that after all the royal stipend was a cage; he lay on his sofa surrounded with text-books, made notes for a new play and longed to be free.

As if in answer to this thoughts, after only two quarterly payments the King's bounty ceased without any explanation. Strindberg was indignant, believing it preferable to die of cold and hunger than to be made a fool of, and he also suspected foul play. However, now he was free; he was twenty-three and would be a student no longer; he had taken all Uppsala had to offer, and would shake its dust from his feet for ever. What did a degree matter? His mind was filled to bursting; 'his personality had sucked a drop here and a drop

44

there, and all that it had assimilated was now his own.' Away from the narrow streets and narrow minds of the university his soul would expand—his friends had named him Eagle and now like an eagle he would spread his wings.

CHAPTER FOUR

1872-1875

I only have to look and listen round about me to discover that I can't live here
Letter to Eugène Fahlstedt, Stockholm, September 1872

BACK IN Stockholm Strindberg at once found employment on the radical evening paper *Stockholms Aftonpost*; he made friends in the artists' colony and continued his painting, and at the same time was introduced to a line of thought for which he had been unconsciously seeking. At Uppsala he had not heard of Buckle's *History of Civilisation*, although it had been in print for several years, and he felt that he would have been saved much misery if he had read earlier the Englishman's contention that doubt did not indicate a mind's weakness, but rather its health and will to progress. Buckle came closer to formulating a doctrine of Both-And than any philosopher Strindberg had read—the historian affirmed that the highest aim of man was truth, but declared that truth was relative to situation. This shed an entirely new light for Strindberg on history, himself and his work, and he determined to earn his living as a journalist while he wrote an historical drama, which this time he would by no means condense into one act.

His central figure, Master Olof, was drawn from Olaus Petri, the fanatic blacksmith's son who had led the Reformation in Sweden. In Strindberg's first researches he saw him as a saint and hero, but now he understood how this young reformer had in the end surrendered to compromise. Following Buckle, the theme of *Master Olof* was the relativity of truth.

Strindberg's whole attention was not, however, turned inward to this work, for he found the capital stimulating after the sleepy university town, and he liked to contemplate the

46

activity of the docks—loading and unloading of boats, opening of locks and lifting of bridges—and to listen to the familiar sounds of his childhood—creaking of cranes, clanging of chains, hooting of steamers, screaming of gulls, the clatter of clogs and wheels on the cobbles, and above all other noises the ringing of church bells waking sad yet nostalgic memories. Time was passing quickly but he still felt himself 'a child believing in truth and fairy-tales alike.'

He had more disturbing things too to watch than the traffic in the harbour. As a reporter he went everywhere—to Parliament, Church Councils, Law Courts, Police Courts, shareholders' meetings, philanthropic gatherings, festivals and funerals, and he had a sense of looking right through the façade and seeing corruption. At Uppsala he had perceived that the short cut to laurels was paved with bribes and flattery, and in one of his first newspaper articles he called for the university to be moved to the fresher air of the capital, where the student would have a chance of developing as a normal citizen, but as he saw more of the city's life, he was less sure of its benefits. It seemed to him that trapped in a web of their own making—a suffocating tangle of obsolete laws, stupid conventions and economic pressure—people took every opportunity to do each other down. The leaders of religion made it fashionable for the rich to sin and seek salvation, and irrevocable for the poor to be oppressed; the political parties threw principles to the winds and intrigued with one another for power; lawyers and civil servants were pompous in form and cynical over misery; the aim of the financiers was to make their own money and lose other people's; the theatre was a hive of jealousy; art critics and dealers destroyed the artist; publishers bought artists' souls along with their manuscripts; the army only existed in case the peasants rose, and journalism was about the dirtiest job of the lot. The journalist must always pander to what the editor believed to be the opinion of the majority, and at the same time must play safe—not extol the working man nor criticise a clergyman or an influential person.

Strindberg thought of his childhood as very gloomy, yet in those days, when his mother had failed him first through illness and then through death, he had believed that outside his

cage life was fair, and even at Uppsala he had been sure that
the people he glimpsed in their homes were all happy and
loving. Now this illusion broke too, for even the closest
families appeared to be held together by fear, deceit and greed
—by every human emotion, but most seldom love. He was
convinced that all bondage was evil and had taken it for
granted that women ought to have the same human rights as
men, that a woman should choose for herself if she would
be wife or mistress and if she would take the highest creative
function of motherhood. He had asserted that her voice should
be heard in the government of home and nation, that her
property should be her own to dispose of—in fact that as a
human being she should be completely free. Now he saw
modern woman interpreting this freedom as the right to
squander half her husband's money, while with his share he
must pay the bills, and to spend the day—since she was not a
slave bought for labour—lying in bed, attending meetings to
further the rights of woman and amusing herself with her
friends, while her husband, worn out with work, returned to
a neglected home. Strindberg remembered how his own father
had been made to feel an intruder and saw how children were
used as unconscious accomplices in the game. Altogether it
seemed to him that society had got itself into an appalling
mess.

He had good friends with whom to share his disillusion.
The Runa brethren had broken up, but now he was initiated
into the more sophisticated brotherhood of the Red Room.
These artists and rebels met in a red-furnished room at Bern's
Restaurant to drink and parley; their dress was inspired by
Montmartre—a frock coat was as conspicuous here as was the
lack of one in Uppsala—and the chief bond was originality.
The Runa brethren had gone back to the Icelandic sagas; the
members of the Red Room allowed no antecedents—'new'
was commendation, 'old' implied worthless, and the only
point of the past was that it was finished. They were sceptics
and egotists united by a sincere hatred of hypocrisy.

The violence of the Red Room's views inflamed Strindberg,
and he went further than them all in his contempt for the
established order; yet a part of him shrank from the clamour.
What a morass it was whichever side you took! How he wished

life could be effaced and begin again in purity. He loved the early morning before man had tainted its freshness, springtime when every leaf was perfect, infancy when all was innocence. He wanted to bathe the world in light, until not one dark place remained to harbour evil. He felt himself 'a bird forced to live in a mine, beating his wings against the shaft in search of air and light.'

In the early summer *Stockholms Aftonpost* sold up— nothing radical, Strindberg reflected, could last long. However, this meant that he was free once more to write, and in spite of the Red Room's avowal that the past was dead, his historical drama *Master Olof* had grown steadily in his mind. So when June came he left the distracting city and settled down as usual on Kymmendö to work it out. He resolved to break the tradition of historical plays with their opera-like construction—his work was a symphony in which all voices were interwoven, and they spoke with the language of everyday life. There was no verse, no declamation and above all no consistency. As in life itself large events and small made up the action, tragedy and comedy were indivisible, and so were the different sides of each character. The nature of Master Olof himself, as he developed from the seed of Olaus Petri, was complex and vacillating. Strindberg had no use for 'the strong character,' fixed by each word and gesture hero or villain. Olof was an idealist, an egotist, an adventurer—ruthless and yielding, melancholy and gay, sceptical and loving. He was not a type, but a human being with a soul, and so too were the opportunist king Gustavus Vasa and Gerd the revolutionary. All were in movement, all in conflict, and the behaviour of each character was, as Buckle had shown him, true to his circumstances and his time. As Strindberg wrote, the thread of his own life wove into Olof's, for he too had rebelled against religious cant—and it was not Catholicism but spiritual stagnation that his Olof fought—and he too had been a king's protégé. There was a Brand in him and in Olof, but his Brand was less consistent than Ibsen's and so must be more true. In the joy of feeling that he had touched truth at last, Strindberg could not keep up with the torrent of his thoughts.

This was a happy summer; several of his friends joined him

on the island and his stepmother and two eldest sisters paid him a visit. Strindberg enjoyed playing host to them and watching his friend Hugo von Philp falling in love with his sister Anna. In the sense of relief that always came with writing, he was in harmony again with life. The radiance of creation was still about him when he went back to Stockholm to read *Master Olof* to his friends.

He saw at once that the play was doomed. No one clapped him on the back and called him a genius, no one invited him to celebrate with a bottle of champagne. Indeed, long before he reached the end, two of his friends were asleep. True, they had been working hard all day, but if a play could not keep a tired man awake, it was worthless, and if the others, whose tastes were modern, found the treatment too unconventional, what chance had it of being accepted by a theatre? The inspiration that had kept Strindberg in flight gushed out of him; he fell to earth and was trapped again.

There was nothing to do but send the play off to the Royal Theatre and 'anæsthetise himself' by painting pictures while he awaited the official verdict. It came one evening by the mouth of his former editor, and although Strindberg had guessed which way it would go, when he heard that his work had been rejected he was ill.

The Director urged him to rewrite the play in verse and remould the characters, but he did not see how he could. It might be possible to modify the form, but if he were to paint Gustavus Vasa as more of a hero, or Olof as less of a renegade, he would be a renegade himself. Meanwhile no theatre would perform the play, no publisher would print it; he had no inducement to write another, and neither job nor money.

It was clear to him now that all his prayers for grace had been prayers for genius. He had never ceased to pray; Darwin had finally shaken him from the Pietism that had clouded his childhood, but not from his belief in divine power. The gift of words had descended, but now he was forsaken and hollow, and believed that if there were any progress in the world it must be man's doing—'no God could have so slight an influence.' So man was free, since there was none to bind him, yet freedom was worthless; only the obtuse and the tyrannical were successful, and Strindberg had no intention of playing the fool for their amusement. As he dragged himself through the days the sameness of everything oppressed him— he was always seeing the same faces, hearing the same remarks, anticipating the same actions.

He read Kierkegaard again and found him terrifying, yet the Danish philosopher whirled him along in a kind of dance of death which was a distorted pleasure. His own thoughts struggled like fish in a net until they strangled themselves, and he noticed once again that people were staring at him. He wished he could fall into 'a kind of quiet madness which might make him wise again.' Otherwise, presumably, as the alternative was to starve to death, in the end he would shoot himself.

At his lowest ebb Strindberg was offered night work correcting the proofs of a morning paper. It was a cruel solace, for now he could not even forget his troubles for a few hours of the night, and for his pains he scarcely earned enough to keep him alive. He could not pay his debts; he dared not fall in love. But still his friends of the Red Room were patient with him; his brother Axel, employed in an insurance company, but a fine pianist and a conductor in his spare time, had joined the circle, and between them the members lent August Strindberg money, bought him drinks, and still inflamed his mind with their ideas. 'Everything must be new!' he would cry, and summon all his eloquence to destroy the old and pour scorn on the repressed and timorous.

Plunging deeper into melancholy he found he could breathe more freely. He had read his Schopenhauer at Uppsala, now the fashionable German writer, Karl von Hartmann, rationalised his pessimism. In his recently published *Philosophy of the Unconscious* this clever young man, only seven years older than Strindberg, expounded the view that the Unconscious was composed of Will and Reason, but that in action Will became divorced from Reason. Thus Willing led to a despair for which the only cure was Reason's tenet that the whole of existence was inevitably painful. When human beings were enlightened enough to understand that individual happiness was impossible either here or hereafter, there would be, von Hartmann declared, a collective effort towards non-existence, and the world would cease to be.

51

With morose pleasure Strindberg took von Hartmann's views as a confirmation of his own suspicion that everything was nothing; he now felt that it was an awareness of having been born into nothingness which had made him cry so much as a child, but the adult way was to accept pain as inevitable and alleviate it as best one could. The bourgeois was an optimist because he was not conscious—his good fortune perhaps, but not his merit. Conscious life was suffering, but Strindberg saw how once man had taken the measure of his littleness as an atom of the cosmic dust, he was free to make what he could of life. With this conscious pessimism as a prop his self-confidence returned. He still could not write, except an occasional article or a half-hearted alteration to *Master Olof*, but inevitable suffering was a satisfactory tenet to work from.

As his vitality returned, so did his love of the theatre, and presently he went off to Göteborg to try his luck on the boards once more. He could not see how he, to whom a dramatist's characters were more real than life, could fail to act them. Yet he did fail again and returned to winter and grinding poverty. Now if he saw a spark of hope he stamped it out; he was resolved to make the worst possible of a bad world. He stared at the dung-heap and was obstinately blind to every flower that bloomed on it.

King Karl XV had died without renewing his favour, but again came unexpected relief. Strindberg was offered the editorship of a new periodical, designed to further the interests of the insurance companies. He refused at first on grounds of ignorance, but as he had given up hope of writing, and no other work was in view, he finally accepted, and the absurdity of being selected for such a post amused him. He was always stimulated by the new, and now he must rub up his mathematics and study the law of premiums and compensation. He dived into statistics and worked his way steadily down to bedrock in order to understand the system thoroughly, which involved exploring not only the figures but the human lives behind them. As a result, the first numbers of his paper were surprisingly interesting, even to the lay reader, but the insurance companies, who supported the publication, were uneasy. Presently a new

52

marine insurance company was started. Strindberg investigated and found a subject worthy of his venom, a fine illustration of the fact that for some people the greatest discovery of the century was that they could live on other people's money more cheaply than by their own labours. The new company was advertised as a democratic, profit-sharing concern; Strindberg examined the figures and discovered a skilful trick played within the letter of the law. The smallest shareholders who paid in cash, because cash was all they had, stood to lose everything. The other assets were no more than big names on worthless pieces of paper.

As editor he criticised such methods of insurance, and at once a number of companies withdrew their support of the paper. Experienced financiers explained that he was mistaken, magnates fought him, but Strindberg would not yield. He saw his duty now as guardian of the public interest, and he was determined to keep the periodical going. With his friends as guarantors he borrowed money from the Riksbank, and each new loan brought with it a new illusion of solvency.

With the eleventh number the crash came, and Strindberg crashed with it. He could not pay his debts, and his friends could not make good their guarantees. He had defrauded the people who entrusted their savings to the national bank—he was guilty. The sickening sense of guilt that had been instilled into him in childhood, and which he had tried in vain to shed with his Pietism, tormented his conscience. He fled to the sea and the arms of a woman, but presently he fell into a fever in which he saw the creditors lying in wait for him and heard their voices demanding that he be given up to them—since he had used their money, they had shares in his body and his soul. He wished he had been put in prison—that might have brought him peace.

When the mists cleared, Strindberg found that for the first time in his life he had been seriously ill. He was still shaken with ague, and all his senses were painfully sharpened. The burden of awareness was intolerable, and he gazed at the waves, longing for them to enfold him like a mother's arms and blot out the cruel world. Death, the sea, his mother and his mistress were mingled in his distraught mind, and he saw another reason for his dark sense of guilt. He was perverted—

53

'his desire for his mother was an incest of the soul.' The terror of this thought increased his passion and when, shortly after, the girl left him for another man, Strindberg broke down completely. A mere physical tie could be broken without violence, but he felt he had given his soul into this woman's keeping.

He rushed out into the forest, yelling defiance at the hostile powers, lashing the branches of trees, whipping the striplings to ribbons at his feet. He climbed to the top of a hill and, as there was still a pine tree above him, he climbed to the top of this too and challenged the forces of the universe. Strindberg recognised this as one of his attacks, and he knew that anyone witnessing the scene would think him mad, but he reassured himself with the thought that he was only translating his inner struggle with hostile powers into action—he was 'acting a poem of desperation.' In fact he felt it would be a relief to be mad, everlasting darkness would be more merciful than this light which only showed him the nothingness of life, impotence would be less terrible than this power which consumed itself in sheer frustration. Once Strindberg had despaired because he had no vocation; now he was a poet without a song, a lover without love.

As he could not make up his mind to die, Strindberg was now forced to the most distasteful course in life—to live with his family in disgrace until he could find some way to escape again. These were hard, cold, bitter days—for him there was no fatted calf, and Master Olof seemed as dead as his heart.

But always when his need was desperate, some friend had a little money to spare, and if nothing else held comfort there was still the sea. Before long he was out at Sandhamn on the coast, learning the weather wisdom of pilots and coastguards, and when presently a telegraph clerk was needed, he took the post. He found the office routine tiresome, but it amused him to tap out the weather reports over the wires, and the regular life restored his health. He began to paint again and the urge to write returned, so he sent a description of a wreck to *Dagens Nyheter*, one of Stockholm's leading daily papers. As this was printed he sent more, until one morning came the offer of a well-paid post on the staff of the paper—the originality and vividness of August Strindberg's style had won the interest of the editor.

54

So the wheel turned and Strindberg was a journalist again, but this time not a common reporter nor concerned with finance. From the observatory of the editorial office he could survey the world and watch history in the making, and he found this kind of journalism was far more in touch with life than the academic professions. At Uppsala his mind had been stuffed with indiscriminate information and ready-made conclusions; he had been expected 'to digest rotten thoughts that others had chewed for a lifetime and then vomited.' Now he was wholly concerned with the living and the new.

All the same a journalist was still expected to pay respect to what was commonly respected, and Strindberg still could not control his pen. It took the power unto itself; vivid, biting words streamed from his hand and left him with a blessed sense of pressure removed. This was the most agreeable post he had held and he wanted to keep it, but his pen insisted that newspapers should tell the truth. It pointed out that politics had become nothing but a compromise between public and private interests, it warned of the misery caused to ignorant people by Christian propaganda, it exposed the swindles practised under cover of the country's admirable pro-Jewish sympathies, and encouraged art to break the conventions. As he loved the theatre best, he chastised it most severely. He could find neither plays nor players to please him, and the complacency of writers, managers and audiences enraged him. To be accepted as an intellectual all one had to do was talk about Shakespeare. This smugness explained why there were no Swedish plays of distinction—Norway had her Björnson and her Ibsen, Denmark her Öhlenschläger, and the rest of Europe abounded in playwrights. Sweden alone slept, content to play foreign plays badly, although her history was dramatic, her language beautiful and her theatres second to none. Strindberg tried to shake her from her catalepsy by drawing attention to the lack of drama in her present life. She dozed while other nations fought for freedom and struggled to progress; she had no passion and therefore her theatre was dead.

As he wrote, he felt the editor's enthusiasm waning, but complaints could not alter his flow. All he could do, when these became too frequent, was to offer his resignation, but when it was accepted he could not bear to let this door too shut against him. To have no outlet even for his descrpitive writing would mean not only penury, but mental stagnation, for the theatre of his mind was closed. The playwright had died with Master Olof; the journalist must try to keep alive.

He wrote to the editor begging to be allowed to go on writing for *Dagens Nyheter*, even though he was no longer on the editorial staff, and ended the letter:

One mustn't be stiff-necked when one wears paper collars or talk big when one's hungry.
I have been very hungry.

This humility, which did not come easily, bore fruit, and newspaper articles and a few translations continued to earn Strindberg a precarious livelihood and procure him the absinthe which alone now gave him an illusion of happiness.

He knew he was on the downward path; he could see the wheel slowly turning, bringing the sickening recurrence of his fate—hunger, debt, humiliation, to which was now added ill-health, a frequent ague that had troubled him ever since his illness the year before.

He was twenty-five and had tried so many professions that he was intellectually bankrupt. The Red Room had dispersed and he was glad of it, for in this state company was at best only an irritation and sometimes he was seized by a real attack of agoraphobia.

Again an event changed the pattern. In spurts of energy Strindberg had applied for many posts, both high and humble, and his most ambitious bid succeeded. In the autumn of 1874, in spite of not having a degree, Strindberg was the winning candidate for the post of an assistant librarian at the Royal Library of Stockholm. Overnight he became a Royal Secretary, an Extraordinary Amanuensis. He was recognised and respected—'acquaintances saluted him in the street as if he had returned from a long journey,' and social circles to which he had never aspired opened.

His salary was not large and he eked it out by giving lessons in a girls' school—work was easy to get now that he was a Civil Servant. His pupils found him strict, but although he was impatient with their mistakes they perceived his kindness, and he turned history and nature-study into treats. He also still added to his funds by writing articles, and he not only translated von Hartmann into Swedish, but also some of the American humorists. Their view of life pleased him; its *reductio ad absurdum* seemed the logical outcome of pure pessimism, and finding that Mark Twain already had a translator, Strindberg tackled Bret Harte.

The Royal Library filled a spacious wing of the vast palace, and besides innumerable prints and manuscripts housed two hundred thousand volumes in its graceful rococo rooms. Strindberg, who at school and college had struggled angrily with mutilated copies and out-of-date editions, now had the knowledge of the ages in his keeping. Here the centuries, each in a unique and splendid binding, shared time and space, here theologians and magicians, philosophers and historians, poets and scientists, lived side by side at peace.

But in spite of this good fortune Strindberg was depressed. On April 10th, 1875, he wrote to one of his old college friends:

. . . The breaking of Spring is a terrible time for sensitive natures —I have suffered horribly. To work all day in order to eat, and then eat so as to be able to work all the next day is a vicious circle. It is *l'homme machine*. And it's for this that one fights one's way through an appalling youth, for this that one puts off dying. Work turns man into a brute. . . .

How few of the Runa brethren, he pointed out in this letter, had come to any good—one had actually died, but most were spiritually dead:

And then they say one shouldn't drink Absinthe! Oh hell! . . . Farewell to you! You've never yet stuck your fingers in the dirt, so you've been lucky enough to keep yourself clean and still have the cleanest nature I know. Poverty makes people very evil, or if not evil, mean and petty—one doesn't see much of the world from a dung heap—Devil knows it's not only specially weak natures whose souls get hurt battling with filth.
Master Olof has gone to hell too!

Seven men, all of them in good health and four with private incomes, stood between Strindberg and promotion, and even if in time he were to become a head librarian, he could not see how this would help him to be a writer. Indeed sometimes the vast accumulation of knowledge which lined the walls of the library pressed on his brain. There were secrets here which his soul needed, but how without direction could he find them? In childhood he had been curbed, now he wanted guidance and was too free. He liked the Chief Librarian well enough, and enjoyed shocking his conservative colleagues with his radical views, but all the same he felt a fish out of water in this refined atmosphere of learning. Then someone suggested that the newcomer might like to classify the Chinese manuscripts, of which no one so far had been able to make a catalogue. To the surprise of all Strindberg calmly accepted the challenge, and at once turned his energies to the study of the Chinese language, which pleased both his eye and his mind. Now he could forget the present and lose himself in ancient Oriental wisdom.

But one thing would not let itself be forgotten, and that was his heart. On the one hand he must have someone to adore, on the other he wanted to revenge himself for the misery women caused him. He had had several more love affairs since the 'she-devil' on the island betrayed him, and his cynicism had earned him the reputation both of a Don Juan and a woman-hater. He knew both labels were unjusti-fied. In spite of women's treachery he worshipped them, and although he was a member of a secret society for the promo-tion of free love, still more secretly he disapproved of promis-cuity, and believed that he would remain only half a person until he found his one true love and complement. His God was distant and obscure; his friends no longer counted—all that he had to worship was nature and woman, woman who was nature and the mother of all life. He must worship, and part of the ritual was to spit upon each idol as she fell and then set up another.

In May the honeysuckle and the lilac bloomed by the library windows; in the harbour beyond flagged boats rode at anchor, and further out the green bay and wooded slopes shimmered under the light blue dome of the northern sky. Strindberg could not but be ready for adventure at such a time.

It appeared in the guise of Ina Forstén, the Finnish fiancée of an old friend who asked Strindberg to protect her while she was in Stockholm, as her young man, an opera singer, was in Finland. Strindberg did not want the charge, and

explained that he was the devil incarnate and quite unsuitable. Ina Forstén hinted that she knew better—he was
not wicked but only unhappy, and she could help him to
escape from his morbid ideas. He assured her that her own
ideas were pure rubbish—'she was dishing up the old stuff
again and offering him as fresh fruit preserved stuff, badly
canned.' All the same he could not deny that Ina Forstén
was intelligent, and argument with a young woman was a
sensuous pleasure.

Presently he took her to visit her fiancé's mother, and to
make the situation more dramatic pretended that he too was
betrothed. Ina asked him many questions, to which he
invented appropriate replies, and gave him a great deal of
advice. They went for walks together and to concerts and
theatres; the habit of her company grew on him and he began
to dread the day of her departure.

Algot Lange wrote from Finland, begging his fiancée not to
see so much of August Strindberg, whose reputation was
deplorable. Ina Forstén showed Strindberg the letter, declaring
that she could not understand jealousy. He retorted that this
was because she could not understand love, for love was the
highest consciousness of possession, and jealousy was the fear
of losing what one possessed. He confessed that he was not
engaged and that he loved her—she must choose between
Lange and himself. This she would not do, and he saw that
she was a flirt, a *mangeuse d'hommes*. Nevertheless he continued as her cavalier until his old friend offered to shoot him,
whereupon Ina decided that it was time for her to return to
Finland.

Ina Forstén had taken the manuscript of *Master Olof* to
show some influential friends, and just before she left she
told Strindberg that these friends were as much impressed by
the play as she was herself, and that they wanted to meet the
author. So between them *Master Olof* and the Finnish girl led
Strindberg to his fate.

CHAPTER FIVE

1875–1876

It was in Drottninggatan
in a brilliant June-day blaze
on a crowded pavement—
the meeting of our ways.

Then past shop-window glass
you vanished in the tide,
the rustling of a gown
and sound of small heels died.

Over hats and parasols
your blue veil flowed.
Then sank in the human wave
that slowly on you closed.

But I, I hunted for it
as a banner from the sky,
when I go out to face the storm
I always hoist it high.

So STRINDBERG wrote after his first brief meeting with
Siri von Essen in the fashionable shopping quarter of Stockholm in June 1875. His vision of corn-gold curls under a
picture hat hazy with blue veiling made him conquer his
shyness and accept her invitation to call, much as he hated
ringing at strange doorbells and meeting strange people.

Here fate played him another trick, for Siri von Essen and
her husband Baron Wrangel were living in the very house in
Norrtullsgatan to which the Strindbergs had moved when
they first left the Klara churchyard, and to which they had
returned again later for some years. As Strindberg entered
the courtyard under the tall ash trees he knew so well, the
ghost of his childhood walked in front, and a host of memories
came to meet him. He feared to wake them further, and half-

expected his father to open the door and scold him for being late or for leaving some task undone. Even the unfamiliar servant could not change the familiarity of the atmosphere, and through the strange furniture Strindberg saw the well-known objects of his home, and his mother, worn out by child-bearing. In her place now was this young Baroness, this girl with the face of a child and the grace of a woman, who looked too young to have borne the baby at her side, too innocent to know the lustful embraces of a man. So might his own mother have looked, so might she have smiled if life had been kinder to her.

Strindberg was warmly received, for both the Wrangels were keen theatre-goers, and before her marriage Siri von Essen had even had some training for the stage both in France and in Finland. They had seen Strindberg's first plays and read *Master Olof* with the greatest enthusiasm, and to add to the felicity of the meeting they knew his sister Anna and her husband Hugo von Philp and were also devoted to Ina Forstén. The Baroness, who was also Finnish, was shortly going on a visit to her parents' home, and it was soon clear to Strindberg that she hoped to be charged with a romantic mission and had no regard for Ina Forstén's engagement to another.

Strindberg could not bring himself to think of Carl Gustaf Wrangel as the husband of this lovely Siri—a diminutive of the name Sigrid which exactly suited her sylvan charm—but as an individual he liked the Baron. He was a few years older than himself, had the easy aristocratic manners which Strindberg admired and envied, and his rather too full face was made interesting by a pair of mournful blue eyes and a melancholy smile. Strindberg was sure that although now Wrangel must be in an ecstasy of happiness, he knew something of sorrow, and he was further disposed in his favour because, although he was a Captain of the Guards, he was also a keen amateur of the arts. Indeed he, like Strindberg, had been granted a stipend by the late King—to enable him to study painting at Düsseldorf. The two young men made friends at once in a common lament that Sweden no longer had a King who understood the importance of culture.

Strindberg found the atmosphere of the house happy and

61

peaceful; although the Wrangels' furniture was costlier than the pieces of his memory, the present style was less formal, and modern easy chairs lent the drawing-room, which had been the austere dining-room of his day, an air of intimacy and repose. That such contentment could exist in a house that had held such pain amazed him, and his old longing for a happy family life revived. When he bade his new friends good-bye, they begged him to come back in a few days' time and dine with them informally. He left in a daze; here the tragedy of his mother's death had fallen on him, here the miseries of adolescence, the fear of living decay and damnation. He felt that the sadness of his childhood would be redeemed in the happiness of this young couple, and that he could believe again in the goodness of human nature.

So up he went, more and more often, to the house whose garden had first shown him the secrets of nature, and whose drawing-room was to teach him the secrets of happiness. Sometimes it surprised him a little that the pair should want his constant company; they did not seek privacy—they were more like good friends than lovers, but it was so pleasant to be welcome, so comforting to be treated as a member of the family, that Strindberg repressed all thoughts that might damage his pleasure. He was proud that the neglected child of that old house should come back to it as the intimate friend of this aristocratic couple; he never tired of looking at them— the tall soldier in his blue uniform, picked out with yellow and silver, and the girl—her angelic face in a gold halo of hair, her Byzantine slenderness lending modern clothes a classic beauty. Her wrists and ankles were exquisitely slender, her feet the smallest he had seen, and to complete this picture of feminine perfection was her small replica, the three-year-old Sigrid. Strindberg still believed himself in love with Ina Forstén, but in Siri von Essen he saw the soul of his mother, the very soul of woman for which all his life he had been seeking. Even as a boy, while he danced with the homely maidens, his desire had been towards those other shapes in whom a spirit shone. She was here; now he could worship, and the hollow in his breast was filled.

He did not lust for her. He worshipped her absolutely—as the virgin mother. He could not imagine her in sexual relation with any man, but her husband was part of the exquisite pattern of this home which must never be changed. He was sure that he would adore Siri von Essen in this way for ever, and that this did not conflict with his feeling for Ina Forstén.

The Baron insisted that both he and Strindberg must accompany his wife on the first stage of her journey to Finland, so one evening they steamed out among the islands —Strindberg's adored skerries—and in the unending twilight of the northern summer sat talking of their three lives which fate had twined together, and swearing eternal friendship. When dawn came Strindberg was shivering with ague and fatigue, but the captive poet in him broke free, his tongue was loosed and he lost all sense of his body. His adoration of light, his passion for beauty, his longing for truth broke out in a torrent of words, and he felt his soul drawn out of him by those two pairs of intent and fascinated eyes.

At last the men had to leave their lady, but still they clung to each other. The house was desolate; the sight of the child depressed them still more. Strindberg tried to laugh at such sentimentality on the part of a Guards Officer and a Royal Secretary, but without Siri von Essen each of them seemed to have lost his individuality. At the library he searched for her type among the masterpieces of the past, and in the Manuscript Room Queen Christina's letters, yellow with age, became for him 'the whispered words of Baroness Siri.' He wrote verses in French to enclose in the Baron's letters to her, and she replied to her two correspondents together.

After a while, however, Wrangel's demand for Strindberg's constant company ceased, and when they met Strindberg found his friend altered. He had lost both his dignity and his melancholy, and when he had had a few drinks he told pornographic stories and made lewd jokes, which Strindberg always found intolerable. Presently he lost all reticence, talked to Strindberg of his mistress, explaining that his wife knew about the affair, that the girl was her own cousin, Sofia In de Betou, and that Siri did not care, as she was completely frigid.

Strindberg was embarrassed by this forced knowledge, but it did not damage his image of perfection. What Wrangel called frigidity, Strindberg saw as Siri von Essen's exquisitely chaste and virginal nature. Her husband's concupiscence must be satisfied elsewhere, which was regrettable, but unimportant, and he would not let the unfortunate disclosure spoil the friendship that meant so much to him. He saw himself and Wrangel as branches grafted on to the stem of Siri's beauty, and as soon as she returned from Finland the trio once more became inseparable.

All the same when Ina Forstén finally threw him over for Algot Lange, Strindberg believed his heart was broken. He could not sleep, took sedatives and wished them a thousand times stronger, and his only comfort was to talk to the Wrangels of his despair. He could at least explain to Siri von Essen that Ina Forstén was a mere husband-hunter who knew nothing of love, and when inevitably Siri asked him what then love was, he could let the poet free again to describe this passion stronger than all others, 'this irresistible force of nature, this storm, this cataract.'

Siri understood, for she too was an artist. Strindberg had felt it as soon as he looked at her, and now he learnt the truth of his intuition. During all those grinding years of childhood, while he had been struggling to keep his soul alive, this delicately nurtured Finnish girl had been trying too to break through the narrow perceptions of parents and governesses and escape into beauty. She had a love of the theatre which matched his own, and she had studied many plays, especially French ones, in which language she excelled. Indeed, she would have liked more than anything in life to go on the stage, but she had been married very young, and the Baron's position made it impossible for his wife to be an actress. She would not do anything to hurt him, but Strindberg learned that in private she rehearsed her favourite parts as if she were going to play them, and that she believed she had talent. He found that in spite of her apparent good fortune, she was restless and unhappy in her conventional social and domestic life.

Strindberg felt the greatest sympathy for Siri von Essen. He knew so well the bitterness of frustration, of feeling oneself a wasted power and an unheard voice, and besides this he was sure that her husband's infidelity must be a secret grief to her. He suggested that she should become an authoress, since her excellent letters proved that she had the ability to develop this way of expressing her imagination, and Siri tried her hand at some articles, but without enthusiasm. She was convinced that she was an actress, and confessed to Strindberg that a literary career would only interest her if she could make a great deal of money. He saw that his paragon had the fashionable notion of earning her own living.

He was anxious to help her in any way he could, yet for himself, Siri was neither actress nor writer. She had nothing to do with careers or domesticity but was simply the Madonna of his dreams. True, he had set the picture of Ina Forstén in a lamplit circle of flowers, had seen her dark eyes stare pensively at him 'like the eyes of his mother, like the dark velvet spots in the pale petals of the pelargoniums,' and had worshipped. But now this idol was overthrown and the altar of his heart was bare. He was tortured by the thought that no woman would ever really love him, and as God appeared to have forsaken him, he sought solace in the devil. He had certain friends who practised orgies in a hidden laboratory; here the altar bore a skull, a bottle of cyanide and a punch-stained Bible with surgical instruments for book-markers, here liquor flowed from retorts, and the evening usually ended in a visit to a brothel. In this way Strindberg tried to rid himself of the obsession of sex.

He still managed to pursue his exacting work as sinologist of the Royal Library, but he was becoming all the time more confused and hysterical. The Wrangels still insisted on his company—nor could he stay away, and in between his visits he wrote them long letters—in Swedish, German, French and mixtures of all three languages. He turned his very soul inside out, condemning life, denouncing himself for blackening their fair lives with his misery, and imploring them —his only comfort—not to give him up. Often, now, Sofia In de Betou was one of the company, and this added to Strindberg's confusion. Siri showed no jealousy of her rival; indeed she seemed actually fond of her young cousin who was, Strindberg could see, better suited to Carl Wrangel's tastes than was his wife. Siri von Essen outstripped her husband in vision and intelligence; Strindberg thought people talked a great deal of dangerous nonsense about women's emancipation, but it was clear to him that Siri had not been born to be this man's housekeeper or bedfellow. Wrangel admired her and she was mildly fond of him, but Strindberg saw that they had nothing in common, whereas when she talked with himself their souls took fire from each other. It seemed to him that she bore her trials like an angel—he knew now that she also had financial difficulties to contend with. The Wrangels too were persecuted by creditors, which explained why they were living in such an unfashionable district, and Siri was a prisoner, a captive butterfly. Her lack of interest in her home surprised Strindberg, but he admired her unusual lack of complacency—he saw much of himself in her, and longed to set her free.

So it continued until in the autumn Strindberg could no longer deny to himself that he was physically attracted by Siri von Essen. Now when they walked together, he was aware of a magnetic current flowing from her body into his, and felt that their very beings were fused. 'Her small feet, keeping pace with his own, were so much a part of him that he seemed to be walking on four legs and he was conscious of the unborn lives within her yearning for the quickening act of love.'

But the idea of an intrigue with another man's wife was abhorrent to him, and although he ached for love, he did not at all want to be the hero of a passionate romance. Above everything in the world still he wanted to be a great writer. He decided to escape to Paris—the centre of civilisation which since boyhood had called to him—there he would vanish from the Wrangels' lives for ever.

He obtained leave of absence to study in Paris, and staged a farewell feast in his attic for the friends who had given him the happiest months of his life, setting the scene carefully as if for a play—the shabby furniture disguised, the candlelight falling on the red Bengal roses, the tinted wine glasses and odd pieces of porcelain he had picked up cheap at sales. It was the first time Siri had been in a bachelor's apartment, and not only did she find it beautiful but full of pleasant mystery. They drank wine, ate oysters and relived the pleasant days they had spent together, and in token of everlasting friendship Baron Wrangel presented Strindberg with an opal ring. Ina Forstén's approaching marriage was the ostensible cause of Strindberg's sudden desire to travel, and indeed the thought of this was painful to him, but he was in such misery and confusion now that no emotion was clear any longer.

He had chosen to go to France by boat because he believed that the jolting of the train was harmful to the spine, and also because he would have less chance to change his mind—but the way to the open sea was long, and the thought of his exile grew hourly more intolerable. Suddenly he found himself gazing as in a dream at a scene he knew by heart; the boat was passing the group of islands in which lay Kymmendö. A host of memories invaded his mind and he felt himself losing control. A pilot boat was on its way out from the islands; he sprang on to the bridge and demanded to be set ashore, informing the captain that otherwise he would have a raving lunatic on his hands for the rest of the voyage.

On shore Strindberg felt impelled to follow the same dreadful course as when, two years before, after he had been so ill, his mistress gave him up. He plunged into the heart of the forest, dashed himself against the trees, cried aloud—and ran, searching for he knew not what, fleeing from he knew not what. When darkness fell, he groped his way back through the woods in an ecstasy of fear, his senses so sharpened by terror that he could tell each kind of tree by the note of its dying leaves.

He went to an hotel and wired to Carl Wrangel that sudden illness had forced him to abandon his journey, and soon he felt so ill that he thought he might die. He longed for the tender care of a woman, but he sent for the local priest —once again, as he wrote Wrangel in long incoherent pages, he had been driven back to God.

Dalarö Thursday (7) *October* (1875)

Faithful Friend!

On a sickbed in haste—fever coming!

The Lord hath smitten me—'Saul, Saul, wherefore persecutest thou me,' said His servant who has just left me—I made no journey —Now since I've found Him my Saviour I understand everything! And suffer everything gladly. He has visited me three times before. . . . Hear my secret—

East from Dalarö is an island—I've talked of many trips—on the island is a hill—on the summit of the hill stands a pine the top of which I've lopped—on the highest branch hangs a sling with stones in it and a pole like a lance—When one sits in the tree-top one has the fir forest below—the sea beyond—There I preached and inveighed—when I was suffering from my illness.

I went through the most frightful agitation of mind that last time —my whole soul had grown into hers—every small thing in my room stood there for her sake in its special place, to make it pleasant for her—her soul which dwelt there— . . . everything was wrenched away. . . . Do you not think that a soul—such a delicate organism as a soul—can go to pieces—I had my third attack on the steamer: after seven hours we drew near Dalarö. I attracted attention—people watched my movements till I realised my condition and asked the Captain to put me on shore—after that I was driven by spirits out among the trees. . . .

God means something by all this. I disobeyed His call to enter His service. . . . The worst of it is, but it's inevitable—if I recover—we must separate—I must be alone with my God—You have been my idols—such one must not have—She will not save me . . . with you I talk of her—I mustn't any more—I've done with all that—my fairest dreams——

And so for pages he wrote on.

The Wrangels visited him and were friendly and reassuring, and after some weeks Strindberg returned to Stockholm. Everyone believed that he had had a nervous breakdown as a quite natural result of overwork, but Strindberg felt that fate had fooled him again.

The winter passed like an uneasy dream; his work was the only clear part of his life—the Chinese catalogue was finished and won esteem, and he was following it up by research into references to Sweden in Chinese literature, and vice versa. At the same time he wrote many articles for periodicals, and began once more to revise *Master Olof*, transcribing it on the best hand-made paper, and painting a title-page in the style of medieval illumination. He felt that if he could forget women altogether he might now become a contented citizen, but this was the last thing he could do—he flirted with both Siri and Sofia, and the Baron's regard for him was cooling. As if forced to act in a second-rate domestic comedy, night after night found Strindberg in the Wrangels' house or the house of their friends, one of a horribly intimate quartet, endlessly repeating scenes of flirtation, suspicion, jealousy and reconciliation. The whole affair disgusted him, but he could not keep away, and truth was hidden by veils of sentimentality just as the earth was hidden by depths of muffling snow.

But soon came the Ides of March, and Strindberg had always felt that March was a fateful month for Northerners. Under the ice the forces of nature rallied—when it cracked and the air was filled with the sensuous fragrance of melting snow, passion was loosed and the destiny of lovers fulfilled. So now the players in this tragi-comedy could no longer hide the secrets of their hearts. Strindberg saw the friendship between himself and Wrangel as a fake—they had the inherent antagonism of the aristocrat and the proletarian and were only held together by the spell of a woman. Wrangel no longer loved Siri—he had eyes only for his mistress—but for the sake of his reputation he was unwilling to leave his wife. Siri did not love her husband—Strindberg, the poet, was the lover for whom she had been waiting all her life, yet although she talked of freedom and a Bohemian life, she was afraid to forfeit the security of convention. Strindberg himself was timid, hypersensitive, excitable and vacillating; he could see his own faults and those of the others as clearly as if they were characters he had created, but beyond all analysis now was the fact that he adored Siri von Essen, and saw himself as the swineherd who would win the white skin and tiny feet of the princess.

Yet for a little while, although they knew the truth, the three protagonists tried to trick one another, hoping in this way to slip back a year to the first carefree days of their friendship. But they could not go back, nor remain as they were— they must go forward to their fate.

As soon as Strindberg had admitted to himself that he was in love with Siri von Essen and none other, he was tormented with jealousy. Even to see her dancing with another man was painful, and as she was a natural flirt he suffered acutely. But he also had at last the overpowering joy, which he had feared was not within his destiny, of knowing himself loved. And now he could pour out his adoration, although he spared her nothing of the truth as he saw it.

[12 *March* 1876]

Forgive me!!!!!!
Sunday morning.
I will, I will be mad!

Now I've talked about it all. Who to? To the spring, to the oaks, to the willows, to the anemones, and the bells sang and the lark said: 'Carry on!' What have I talked about?—I love you!!! And I walk in the streets as proud as a king and look compassionately at the crowd—why don't you fall on your dirty faces before me? Don't you know that she loves me? Who? The princess, my princess, the loveliest woman in Sweden, she who has the bluest eyes, the smallest feet, the goldenest hair, the fairest forehead, the most exquisite hands. . . . You are not worthy to hear this!!! She with the noblest heart, the proudest spirit, the finest feelings, the fairest thoughts! Mine, my beloved—and she loves wretched me.—If she doesn't soon throw me over I shall go mad with pride.

Thank you for yesterday. Wasn't I dignified? I'm making progress. I was meant to be born a woman. Beloved, forgive me, O, how I hate, detest, despise my friend Carl! How deeply he has offended me! How dare he stop adoring my love!—He can't see her for a harlot! O my God! She who loves me is so superior to him. He, with with the aid of the law and religion and the consent of her parents, stole her beauty and youth and favours, and then threw her away like a withered flower, he denies me the right to gather up what he has thrown away. God in heaven, I shall go mad! . . .

You're opening your *home* to infamies. You let lhim rouse his ardour at her side to quench it later in your arms, thinking about her. You demean yourself to share with her. I shall go mad! And your husband permits himself to insult you by such a request—under the same roof as your innocent little child. My God, it's too much! . . . How can you stay in that room—doesn't it revolt you?—you're walking in filth—you, the queen with the sunlit forehead, whom I love so deeply, for whom I have suffered torments—you are becoming evil—your wings are losing their power—you will sink if you don't raise yourself!!!! Honour! What is honour? A word? No, it is something—I know now—it is something men invent in order to rid themselves of female encumbrances they are sick of. No, honour is something—but God preserve us, isn't love something too, isn't it more, isn't love more than honour, more than everything?—yes! my heart's dearest. Oh when shall I be able to tell you this? When shall I be able to cast off the iron mask—for an hour only and show you and tell you with my trembling lips and burning eyes that I love you. I must do so or I shall die—I must fall on my knees, put

70

my head in your lap and kiss your hands a thousand million times, I must tell you that I love you so that you believe it and are happy— you don't believe me—oh, I love your very soul—have I not done this? A year! Then do not be afraid of me, my dearest. But I love your beauty too, I must hold your hand, I must look into your eyes, I must kiss your forehead or else truly I shall die. You think this means my love is sensual?—O no—haven't our souls loved each other all this time without once tiring or giving up? Then why are you afraid? Our poor senses and our bodies are surely meant to express our emotions—how could I love you if I were unable to see your beautiful true eyes and hear your kind and gentle voice? O, sometimes I should like to be a thundercloud and embrace and absorb you—I should like to be the sun and draw you up as dew.— We must meet for a ringing second which is not bought too dearly with years of silence. You can rely on my strength—I do not speak now of honour, although it is for me a matter of honour to protect you, to love you, to support you, if—insignificant as I am—I can do this without your losing all respect for yourself. O, how I love you! And he dares to think the other more beautiful—let him go in peace with her.—O, I love you so that the whole of my being is shaken to its foundations. I shall commit crime for your sake. I shall do this now at once. Like this. Listen!!!

Do you think you can win back your husband's so-called love?— No—he no longer believes that you are beautiful—you who are so lovely—how I thank that monster for letting me have you to myself, how I love that trollop who holds him fast while I kiss you!— You have his friendship, I have that too and as my friend he is the finest, the best, the noblest I have ever known and I love him. But as your husband, as my love's cruel tyrant I hate him. Now I'm going crazy!

Are you going to continue to throw open your home to such base-ness—aren't you ashamed—why should you be more ashamed if you who love me ask to come to the bed in which I lie and kiss my eyes to purest dreams? Your room was a temple to me, a shrine whose mysteries were yours alone. It is defiled—don't you hate that room? Oh, when I saw inside it yesterday evening I began to tremble.—If you let this go on you are no better than she and I cannot respect you. . . .

You let yourself remain in the keeping of idiots—you *who have genius*—you have it, you see that's why they persuade you you're foolish and weak—because they are afraid of you . . arise, young lioness, shake your yellow gold mane and send out shafts of fire from your glorious eyes so that the fools tremble, cut loose from this loathsome menagerie—out into the forest, into fresh free nature where a heart, a head and an embrace await you and a love that can never die like the former one. Do you know why that died? You continued to grow, to develop. He stood still—now you are ahead of him and he's left behind for ever. Our love cannot die because we

71

both grow, we both have wings, we can never tire of one another because we are new each day—we have our goal outside love—therefore you see there's no danger—for if love should slacken *we* have the fire of genius to heat it. . . . In the Lord's name—I'm talking in sacred seriousness now—is your husband's future more important than my future?—what have you to thank him for besides the friendship he has shown you?—is your craving for life never to be satisfied—are you not to fulfill your destiny—are you to wither in the bad air of a bedroom?—you were not born to bear the children or be the maidservant or bedfellow of a male friend—raise yourself from your degradation or I shall not believe in you. Why should we, king and queen in the eternal imperceptible world of the spirit, concern ourselves with their petty little claims? In the devil's name how I despise you sometimes—beloved, pardon, pardon, pardon, a thousand thousand times. . . . Will the world crumble because the Swedish Guards get a blemish through one of their officers treating his wife infamously?—Are you to sit at table with an officer's trollop? Are you to be your husband's coupler?—God in heaven, can you forgive these words for my great love's sake—yes, you must forgive everything!—

. . . You shall work, *I can* get you and us work—you will be famous—and if they—that's to say society—censures you, it won't be our civilised society—and in any case you *have me.*—Woe to any who harms a hair of your head or your reputation! . . . Are your feelings so small—is your love not big enough to give you courage? You want to meet me in the daytime—oh, no place becomes you better than the splendid salons of the temple of Art—don't they tell you, all those works of art, how much one must suffer and dare if one wants to be more than the crowd—? Oh, I have sat in the palace window and watched you coming round the corner of Fredsgatan—I could see your lovely sun-streaming forehead a thousand miles away; do you know that then the square and the air were shining and I thought the sun had come out—but the day was overcast—and I waved my handkerchief. You didn't see it—oh, how sad I was—how sad I've been! Don't forget that now I am nothing when I am not with you—why do you admire your husband—admire me, love me—if it becomes intolerable fly to me—my room shall be your home and I'll live somewhere else—you shall look at my books which I despise but which determined my future . . . you shall water my flowers—oh, how beautiful and happy they will be when you look at them with your friendly eyes, your beautiful, dangerous, glorious eyes! I shall kill myself if I can't be beside you in peace and tell you that I love you—my salvation. You said you put your peace, your life, your happiness in my hands. Do this and you will be doing God's will!!! You need not be frightened of me. . . .

. . . Remember I shall force you to come to me, to fly to me—I shan't visit you for some days—if you can't live without me, then come—no pride! between us. . . .

72

Why am I cold and sarcastic with you? I love you and sometimes want to leap into your embrace but am held back by fear of being driven out of Paradise. That's why. Oh see for once my tenderness! . . .

Beloved creature, you don't believe that you have genius—you think genius is just sharp wits—by no means—I have not the sharpest wits—but fire; my fire is the greatest in Sweden, and *if you wish* I will set fire to the whole wretched set-up!—You have fire, it is this dusky flame which troubles you, it has smouldered for so many years and so many damn fools have tried to quench it. Come! Fulfil your high destiny. You shall be an actress—I shall make you a theatre of your own—I shall play opposite you—and write—and love you— you have a great sin on your conscience, you have wanted the gift of genius without risking martyrdom—oh this is a lovely martyrdom! Fulfil your destiny, become the greatest actress or authoress in the country!—

Now I'll stop—don't kill me—read all my letter—don't despise me—I have really suffered intolerably. . . . Forgive me—believe in me steadfastly—however I behave believe in me. . . . Oh, oh, save me and I will save you!—forgive me all this—I love you, love you, love you!!!

If you're afraid to become my wife, you're afraid of the prose.— Oh, don't you know that I have a magic wand that strikes water from the rock?—that I can get poetry out of filth if I must? Oh, I shall grind a coffee mill so that it sounds like music—I shall go to the market and buy potatoes but I shall always put a flower on top—I shall lay the table as if van Huysum had painted a still life, and how I shall work—then I shall have peace from my accursed restlessness —read my letter all through—do you not hear how it vibrates with love for you, my queen.—

. . . Don't you find life without work or purpose wretched—you who can give this country its greatest author—and I shall be that— you don't know who or what I am—I am unique—I have not met my superior yet—yes, in you, Maria—you with the most beautiful name I know, alas, I am ashamed when I think of what I have said. . . .

If you have not the courage to live without me—if you have not the courage to live with me, then die with me and let our love continue on the other side of death, pure and holy and free from these wretched bodies that drag everything down. Die with me—oh in your company I will gladly give myself up to the eternal unknown spaces, where our souls may embrace one another and need not be ashamed or ask permission of any but God.

Now forgive me all this, you must, you must—because I love you!!

Siri begged him to help her, to go to Carl himself and tell him that he loved her: 'O, sacrifice your pride for once to your love! You'd let me die. . . . Haven't you the courage to say "I love your wife—our love is pure?"'

He hadn't; the thought of such a conversation was paralysing—he felt that he and Carl would be talking on quite different levels. In the end he wrote him a formal letter, and followed this up with an enormous 'Epistle' in six chapters to the two of them together. Wrangel, however, took the matter lightly—he could not see why they should not all four go on indefinitely as they were now.

But Siri von Essen loved Strindberg and the difficulties and perils of illicit love strengthened her feeling. She was not so much tied by convention as he thought. She had always wanted to live dangerously, and now she wrote long letters to her mother explaining that she had not been made for peace and a bed of roses. She admitted that she was a bad wife, a bad mother and a hopeless housekeeper. She had been born less a woman than an artist, and to fulfil herself she needed dangers and difficulties and a high purpose. August Strindberg brought her all these things, and to deny him would be to deny life itself.

The fact that the Wrangels were friends of Strindberg's sister Anna and her doctor husband Hugo von Philp, whom he had introduced to her in their student days in Kymmendö, made it easier for Strindberg to see Siri alone without breaking the social conventions, but his conscience at once reproached him:

Dearest Sister,
　　Don't call on the Baroness to-day.
　　I shan't forgive myself for a long time that your home became an assignation—that was never intended—and you must understand that it was not your unfortunate brother's mistress you opened your home to—it was an unfortunate woman who has been spiritually tortured by her husband and desires to flee from her home—your bedroom is not desecrated because I kissed her forehead there—I don't suppose I'll ever meet her again.
　　Forgive me for dragging my sorrow into your home—it will be harder for Hugo to forgive this.
Your brother
AUGUST

It was not long, however, before the lovers braved the conventions, and Siri von Essen came to his attic. In her happi-

74

ness, the first real happiness of her life too, he found Siri von Essen even lovelier than before, and believed that at last he had found the woman who would make him whole.

The difficulties of the situation were, however, greater than he had expected. He wanted to use all his spare time on his play—Siri was to go on the stage although he was not convinced of her talent, but he knew that she could have for her lover the foremost playwright of Sweden. *Master Olof* might have faults—what play had not, what living creation was perfect?—but he was convinced of its worth and determined to .work at it and for it until it found a theatre. Lying fallow it had sapped his creative energy and made it impossible to conceive a new play, but in his new knowledge and experience of love, he was sure he could improve certain scenes. Now that he understood the subtle interplay of a man's and a woman's temperaments, the changing stress as power shifted from one to the other of them, the interdependence and independence of each, he was impatient to breathe new life into his creation. Instead, he found himself involved in a horrifying pell-mell of family affairs. Scandal, recrimination, financial claims and legal arguments made chaos of reason and good feeling. Siri's mother, Elisabeth von Essen, wrote from Finland, imploring Strindberg to refrain from luring her daughter to disaster, and countless other relatives of all concerned joined in the fray. The Wrangels' house, where happiness had blossomed on a stem of sorrow, became the abode of fiends.

Strindberg could not understand why he was so much involved. Carl and Siri had agreed to divorce on grounds of her determination to go on the stage, and it was arranged for her to visit an uncle in Copenhagen until the legal formalities, mercifully brief in Sweden, were concluded. The little girl was to go on living with her father, but Siri was to see her as often as she wished. This part of the business troubled Strindberg a little, for he was sure that a child should not be separated from its mother, and although Siri wept at parting from Sigrid, he did not feel that her maternal love was profound. She had not wanted another child by her husband and now she feared that she might have one by her lover. If this occurred, Strindberg intended of course to marry her, for otherwise society would make life intolerable for them all, but he did not really want to marry. He could not see that he and Siri needed a legal bond to seal their union; he detested promiscuity, but he still believed in free love and took it for granted that she did too. His only grief was that they could not have a child, for this to him was human fulfilment, and he was sure that if Siri bore a child in love, her maternal instinct would wake—it was impossible for him to imagine a woman without it. However, as things were, when Siri came back from Copenhagen she could live in the freedom she so much desired and envied in himself. But her relatives did not share this unusual point of view, and sometimes during the interminable discussions Strindberg felt as if he had taken on the whole burden of Siri von Essen's family. He loved her, he believed he would love her always, but the shadow of responsibility was already stealing over the sunlight of his happiness.

CHAPTER SIX

1876–1882

The good time, the springtime of my life had arrived
A FOOL'S DEFENCE

FOR ALL their sakes they tried to avoid more scandal. They spread abroad Baroness Wrangel's determination to go on the stage, and Carl's commanding officer helped the argument by informing him that if his wife became an actress he would be obliged to quit the Guards. But by now all Stockholm knew of the affair between the Baroness and the Royal Secretary, and the gossip-writers made the most of their prize. No one was likely to believe that Baroness Wrangel had deserted her husband out of pure love of acting.

Strindberg went on doggedly with his work and recommended Siri to do the same. He would still have preferred her to aim at authorship, but as she was set on a dramatic career he urged her to study diligently and take every opportunity of visiting the Copenhagen theatres. Her letters depressed him a little; they were so full of other people, of the success she was having in what he surmised to be second-rate artistic circles.

When Siri returned, her mother came to Stockholm to chaperon her, but one by one their friends dropped them. They could only think that they had behaved too well. Society winked at adultery, but disapproved of divorce. Even the theatre manager they approached with a view to Siri's début declared that he would have nothing to do with a runaway wife. These were difficult months. After all Siri found that she missed her little girl, and life under the watchful eyes of her mother and her Aunt Augusta was more like a return to the hated restraints of childhood than newly won freedom. Her dowry had gone to her husband, and her mother had to let rooms to aid their slender resources. Siri had never been hard-up before and she was frightened. She was more frightened still that she would have an illegitimate child, and her fear saddened Strindberg. Secretly he believed that unless she could bear the fruit of their love, their union was immoral, yet to comfort her he must assure her that she need have no fear, that he would 'cheat nature,' and if in spite of his care nature won, he would take all the responsibility.

Presently Siri found a well-known actor and actress prepared to coach and sponsor her, and with renewed spirits went off to stay with them in the country, while Strindberg buried himself in work. Now when the lovers met, it was no longer under the curious eyes of the gossip-writers, but beneath the benign countenance of nature, and happiness seemed to be turning their way again when a heavy blow fell. In January 1877, just as Siri was to make her début, news came that the little Sigrid was seriously ill. Siri flew to her bedside, but the child was dying of an inflammation of the brain, and only survived a few days. Carl was broken-hearted and Siri's tears flowed unceasingly. She hardly needed her mother-in-law's assurance that the tragedy was a judgment on her wickedness, nor did Strindberg need Siri's reproaches to reawaken his sense of guilt. He had always been uneasy about the part he had played in Siri leaving her child.

Presently Carl sent for him. In his grief he wanted his old friend beside him, as well as Siri with whom an affectionate relationship had never been broken. Presently they were all three drinking, dining and playing cards together in a melancholy imitation of the old carefree days.

As soon as was considered proper Siri, under her maiden name of von Essen, made her first appearance on the stage— as Camille in a play by Leroy. She was at once a great success. The scandal was good publicity and Stockholm flocked to see her. Her performance showed promise and her looks were exquisite; she was besieged with photographers, flatterers and flowers. Her dressing-room swarmed with admirers, and Carl followed her about like a faithful dog. She was in transports of delight, but Strindberg grew gloomy; he had lost his gentle, childlike love and found in her place a painted actress, who seemed to him mannered, conceited, hard. On the stage she

78

looked angelic, in public she was radiant, but she did not care how slovenly was her person or her room when she received her lover. Without cleanliness and order, Strindberg's spirit sickened; even at his poorest he had been fastidious, but Siri now seemed to revel in squalor, and the same deterioration showed in her speech which grew vulgar and full of stage slang. She laughed at Strindberg's prejudices and reminded him how eager he had always been to break conventions. Why had he become such a prig? Sometimes he laughed himself at his inconsistency, but all the same he grieved. He had struggled up the ladder to culture and better living, in the holiness of his love he had purged himself of grossness, and now she, who had been born at the top, seemed bent on pulling them both down into the gutter.

Her second part, Jane Eyre, was not quite such a success as the first, but it secured her a year's contract at a higher salary than his own, and she was naturally elated. She did not often let Strindberg help her now with her work—his experience as playwright and dramatic critic seemed to count as nothing with her; she preferred Carl's less severe assistance when she was studying her parts. She appeared more interested in her dresses than her art, and sometimes Strindberg felt that he was already cast aside like a gown she had tired of. Then again she would turn to him with tenderness, and in the double rôle of child and husband he would find peace in her arms. They were both artists, both egotists, both idealists, and at moments each had the power to give the other a glimpse of the heaven on earth to which they both aspired.

Nevertheless they were far from achieving the perfect spiritual union for which Strindberg had hoped, and without which physical intimacy seemed to him brutish and ugly. He tried to keep alive his feeling of reverence for Siri von Essen, but in reaction to the staidness of her former life she was all frivolity and wildness now, and this did not make reverence easy. His emotional difficulties made the disappointment over his play the more bitter; it was five years since he had begun to write *Master Olof*, and now he had rewritten it completely in verse. Just as he himself had become outwardly more conventional since his appointment as Royal Secretary, so his play had conceded to tradition by becoming

79

more heroic and abandoning its prose form, although Strindberg hoped his verse was striking enough to be recognised as original. He did not restrict himself to traditional poetic language, but used the whole Swedish vocabulary.

From his window as he wrote he had watched the New Theatre built, and his hopes had mounted with every brick. Now the theatre was finished, but a Norwegian play was billed. *Master Olof* had been rejected again. Five whole years of creation were wasted—all his other work was only an opiate and a stopgap. However, at least his position at the library brought him into contact with cultured and influential people, and he was no longer quite unknown. He resolved to swallow his distaste for seeking favours and do everything he could to get his play accepted, if not in Stockholm then in Göteborg, and meanwhile he set to work on a volume of short stories about his own experiences at Uppsala. He thought it was time people knew what this much-vaunted university life was really like.

Just a year after he had tried to run away from his tangled emotions, a friend invited Strindberg on a trip to Paris. Siri did not try to stop him, and they talked less of what they would do when he came back than of the old days when they had been happy. Both of them understood that the time had come for them to part, perhaps for a short while, perhaps for longer, and they sadly agreed to leave it to fate to decide when they next should meet.

The journey refreshed him; the divorce proceedings had been so sordid, and everything that had happened since so polluted with scandal, that he really felt as if he were 'flying from a heap of offal.' The excitement of new places stimulated his old adventurousness—and at last he was in Paris.

He liked the feeling of this more southern land, where the sun was not so impatient to be gone; much as he loved his own country, it seemed to him that Northern man was for ever struggling to get back to the warm origins of humanity. Roaming the streets and sitting at cafés with his friend, he enjoyed the impact of new impressions and the freedom from recognition, and he energetically visited libraries, museums and theatres. He had looked forward specially to Raphael's pictures in the Louvre, but now that he saw them he had the impression that, in his greater finish, this painter had lost the inspiration of his master Perugino. On the whole Strindberg found the highest art not so high as his anticipation, but this was something of a relief, for he had expected a revelation too great to be borne. On the other hand he found the theatre purely disappointing; it seemed to him an outrage that such bagatelles, such artificiality should reign on the foremost stage of the world.

Gradually the charm of novelty faded. As autumn drew on, the streets grew wet and dirty, Strindberg's mind was sated and he found the pressure of the great city heavy. He began to have a sense of anxiety which he could not explain, but which brought back his fear of strangers. He gave up going to cafés and sat in his hotel room, reading the newspapers and brooding. He had written to Siri, but she had not answered, and now in his loneliness he forgot the stranger actress and only remembered the mother-mistress of his heart.

When at length her letter came, it informed him that she was pregnant and implored him to come back and marry her. He took the first train, too happy to fear bonds and responsibilities, or to remember the jolting of his spine. He thought his own country had never looked so lovely as in its October gold—and he had never been so much in love.

Siri reproached him with her condition, but Strindberg was patient. The knowledge that she was bearing his child filled him with tenderness and wonder, but he understood that it was difficult for her. She would soon have to find an excuse for retiring from the stage, and she had another trouble too. Her mother had fallen ill and it was believed that she had not long to live. Siri had broken away from her, and now she feared that her own behaviour and the death of her child had contributed to her mother's illness. She wanted to be reconciled with her, but although Elisabeth von Essen had grown used to her daughter being an actress, she still did not tolerate her association with August Strindberg. Siri dared not tell her that she was carrying his child; indeed, it would be born so much too soon after their wedding for propriety that they decided to conceal its birth until a later date. It was not surprising that Siri von Essen's spirits were low.

Strindberg's own affairs were going better than usual. The

volume of stories had been accepted at once, his salary at the library was raised, and he was invited to review books for Finland's leading magazine and art for the Swedish Academy's journal. While the banns were read and preparations made for the wedding, he plunged into work, relying on marriage to wipe out the shame and ugliness which, in spite of his belief in free love, had attached to the irregular union. He was glad now to shoulder the responsibilities of a household if in this way their true love could be saved.

Not long before the wedding Elisabeth von Essen died. Siri's heart was heavy; in the first year of freedom she had lost her child and her mother, and her hope of fame was not fulfilled. She had parts, but not leading ones—most often she was cast as a society lady, rôles which required looks rather than ability. Sometimes she doubted if after all she had much talent, but she never doubted her will to be an actress, and it was hard, before she was really established in the theatre, to have to leave it, bear a child and become once more a housewife. Strindberg wanted marriage now, but Siri von Essen feared that for his wife this would spell slavery.

He tried to reassure her, for he was as anxious as Siri that their individual lives should be enriched and their liberties unharmed. When the child was born, she would act again, and meanwhile he encouraged her to write articles and translate plays from the French. Certainly he was overjoyed that they were to be married, but this did not lessen his contempt for most of the marriages he observed. Siri and he were artists, and theirs was to be the union of free souls. This year even winter could not freeze his happiness.

August Strindberg and Siri von Essen were married on the last day of 1877, three weeks before his twenty-eighth birthday, and Carl Wrangel, Sofia In de Betou, Algot Lange and his wife Ina Forstén and many relatives and friends attended the wedding. Strindberg left his attic and took his books and his pelargoniums to the little flat in the centre of Stockholm's newer residential district which Siri had fitted out with furniture and pictures from her old home in Finland. The craftsmanship and texture of his wife's heirlooms added to his joy— ever since childhood he had wanted to live among graceful harmonious objects.

STRINDBERG AND SIRI VON ESSEN AT THE TIME OF THEIR MARRIAGE

Siri too was happier now that they were man and wife. Outside the winter raged, but inside they made their own summer, closing the shutters, bolting the door, lighting the candles and pouring out the wine. He played the guitar, they sang and read, he wrote her poems, and the days drifted by in gentleness. His wife's dresses and jewels enchanted him; even her untidiness he saw now as a sign of intimacy, and he could keep his own room as austerely as he wished, since they had agreed to do away with the old-fashioned practice of sharing a bedroom. 'I am writing on rose-tinted paper,' Strindberg wrote to a friend, 'partly because I have no other, partly because I'm newly married. . . . What indescribable happiness it is to be married!''

After a few weeks Siri was prematurely confined; the baby girl was at once taken away by a wet-nurse, but she was too weak to survive. Yet another death—this time of the child of their love—marked their union. Yet, in spite of her distress, Siri felt some relief that now there was no hindrance to her career and her social position, and with his reason Strindberg agreed; but his heart yearned for the child, and his conscience smote him for agreeing. He thought it a crime not to welcome any new soul to this earth—he himself had been unwelcome and for this he had never forgiven his parents. He felt as if he and Siri had killed their child by wishing it out of the way.

The stories—called *From Fjärdingen and Svartbäcken* after two districts of Uppsala—came out, and although the reviews maintained that Strindberg's descriptions of university life were exaggerated and biased, most of the critics praised his lusty style. August Strindberg was spoken of as the pioneer of Swedish realism, and he saw that even if he could not win fame as a playwright, he was at least becoming known as an original writer. When shortly afterwards *Master Olof*, in its latest verse form, was at last published, the critics ignored it, and Strindberg himself felt that it had lost much of its worth in over-revision. He resolved that his new work, a full-length novel called *The Red Room* after the coterie of his journalistic days, should give no one a chance of ignoring it. In this book he developed still further the style which had proved so successful in his short stories, and followed up his denunciation of university life with an exposure of the hypocrisy and cant with which he saw the whole of society to be riddled. He had been reading Dickens and admired the Englishman's compassion for the simple and the poor, his dislike of officialdom and his call for reform—but to break through Swedish complacency Strindberg believed he must be more ruthless. He had studied the technique of *Madame Bovary* and steeped himself in Rousseau. He sharpened his words to a fine cutting edge to rip up dishonest company promoters, hypocritical churchmen, self-indulgent philanthropists and grovelling journalists. He had appointed himself the conscience of his country.

Meanwhile the new coterie that formed round the young couple was a very different affair from that of the Red Room. Siri's good looks and high spirits made her popular, and a marionette theatre and moonlight drives in the park gave Strindberg, too, the light-hearted pleasure he had missed in youth. With sufficient money for good food and wine and a servant to run the house, his vitality was no longer wasted. Afetr his day's work at the Library he could still write for hours, and he conceived a store of themes for further stories. Now that he had found this autobiographical vein, he did not see any reason to leave it until he had transferred all his experiences to paper. In his pen he had absolute conviction, which gave him relief from the uncertainty he felt in himself. He was not sure that his wife found him a good lover, and although she told him that she had never been happy with Carl Wrangel, the image of that giant still disturbed him. Nor was he sure that he wanted to be a good lover in the accepted sense, for sexuality shocked him, and while he did not doubt Siri's fidelity, the way in which she dissipated her affection offended his taste. She coquetted with men and embraced her women friends with sensuous pleasure; she even flirted with her young maid, and she laughed at her husband's objections, confessing freely that she loved people, specially when they were young and pretty. It was all in character, all part of the temperament that made her an actress, but Strindberg remembered cynically Carl's early assertion that his wife had no temperament. She could not refrain from making love even to her dog. Strindberg had always, as Siri

84

well knew, detested dogs, but now, after the death of the baby, he had neither the heart nor the courage to forbid her to bring her spaniel to her new home. To her it appeared an angel, to him a goggle-eyed monster that barked and slobbered, made messes and was given all the titbits. Even now, when he had plenty of good food, Strindberg's obsession about hunger remained. He craved nourishment and love, and it offended him that Siri should squander these treasures on an unclean animal—and one which into the bargain was bound to remind her of her old life. At first Strindberg tried to ignore these flaws in their happiness, then found that in avoiding trouble he was missing intimacy. It was better to have constant quarrels and reconciliations, which were all part of Siri's stormy, provocative nature, than to drift apart. He usually gave way to her in the end, partly because her will was strong, partly because he who had suffered so much from domination had no wish to dominate another. All the same he brooded over their discords, while she quickly forgot them, although she found his uncompromising, fastidious ways a nuisance.

Presently the economics of the household caused further friction. In the second year of their marriage *A Doll's House* came to Stockholm, and woman's emancipation became more than ever the progressive slogan. Strindberg found Ibsen's play absurd and Nora a provoking nitwit, but he believed implicitly in independence, and Siri had charge of her own income and he of his. But this arrangement, conceived to improve the mechanics of marriage, only led to constant arguments as to which was responsible for this or that expenditure, and as neither of the pair was really practical their accounts became a hopeless muddle. To add to their private problems, Sweden was going through a financial crisis, and presently Strindberg's bank failed and left him in debt. However, if he did not know how to use money he had learnt how to make it. Articles on a wide range of subjects found their way into the periodicals, and now *The Red Room* came out.

The reviewers fought over it. Strindberg's style broke the academic rules and his realism offended good taste. Many of the novel's characters were based on well-known persons, and the original showed through the disguise. His criticism of the existing order was merciless, his descriptions of poverty got under the skin—it was a brilliant, offensive and beautiful piece of work. Every revolutionary rallied to the author, and the conventional and reactionary were out for his blood. August Strindberg was proclaimed the Swedish Zola, although he had not read the Frenchman's books; he was admired, detested, feared and well on the road to fame.

The Red Room at once sold two editions and brought Strindberg the money he needed. Letters poured in from home and abroad, and Edvard Brandes, the radical writer brother of Georg Brandes, leading critic of Northern Europe, wrote assuring Strindberg that he was destined to become the reformer of Swedish literature. In reply Strindberg poured out his heart to the distinguished young Dane.

Dalarö, 29 *July* 1880

Honoured Herr Doctor,
Your kind letter has given me much encouragement and joy, both because you are an eminent man and a progressive man, and because I am considerably isolated, pretty well alone in the fight I pride myself on having made my own. Your recognition and still more your sympathy have given me courage, because here in our country one lives a dead man's life, tearing everyone else to pieces out of pure jealousy (a fault of all small nations) so that no party can ever be formed; yes, this was shown when, after *The Red Room* came out and the author was made the object of a meanly dirty attack, not a single voice was raised in protest.

You can judge therefore how proud and strong I felt at the reception you gave me, not as author or genius (because I have little of that . . .) . . . but as a fighter. Though what use I would be to any party I can't conceive; not much I believe, because I'm still engaged in piecing together bits of my broken pitcher, not fully clear to myself, seeming only a conglomeration of rejected opinions. . . . I have scarcely anything left but my big beautiful hatred for all oppression and all gilded rottenness. Added to which I am swift in attack, but then comes my humanity and I suffer for having scourged my fellow beings, even when they deserved it. Therefore I cannot be a trustworthy friend nor an enduring enemy. . . .

A few words about my political opinions in case you should want to recruit me!—I am socialist, nihilist, republican—everything possible that is opposed to the reactionaries. This from sentiment, for I am Jean Jacques' *intime* when it comes to a return to nature; I should like to join him and turn everything upside down to see what lies at the bottom; I think we are so much entangled, so terribly much regulated that things can't be put right, but must be burnt up, blasted, and then begun again afresh.

As to the questions of the day, well—they are such small questions, the daily affairs here at home, that I really don't know them. They are mostly concerned with grants and loans.

But Norway! That could set us a fine example if it would break its humiliating bond with Sweden. A young sound country bound with one that's played out, decayed. It doesn't make sense. But Norway should do this now before it is overrun with civil servants—that is reaction, that is damnation! I am myself a 'Royal Secretary' so I can judge in this matter. . . .

. . . You Danes are still suffering from these wretched 'Aesthetics.' You worship form, Beauty, but that is only the exterior, and you— you have at least had your Kierkegaard. O that man! . . .

If Strindberg felt himself isolated, in his corner at the Royal Library he was none the less a hero, for simultaneously with the equivocal success of *The Red Room*, his treatise on *Sweden's Relations to China and the Tartar Lands* won recognition at the French Institute, and he was awarded a medal by the Imperial Russian Geographical Society.

Fate seemed at last to have relented, for now, two years after their marriage, Siri was expecting another child, and this time she was glad. The thought of her pregnancy was poignant to Strindberg and he was deeply aware of his paternity. The sense of guilt that marred their physical love vanished and peace returned. Yet he feared this birth—as if he himself were to be born again. He had been born to fear —how was he now to receive this child, this soul, this stranger? He knew his own weakness—how was he to rear another life?

All the same he awaited the child as a welcome guest, and these months were the happiest he and Siri had shared. The pains of childbirth seemed to rack his own body, yet he could not believe that a mother's agony was not fully compensated in joy. When he held their infant daughter in his arms, Strindberg knew ecstasy, even though the melancholy thought came that only thus, through another body, could a soul win immortality. He was a child again in his child, but Strindberg felt himself already 'a plant going to seed.' His youth was over—there was a successor in his house.

He gave his readers no respite. When they ignored *Master Olof* he presented them with *The Red Room*, and now that they were convinced that he was an atheist and an anarchist, he brought out *The Secret of the Guild*, a play he had conceived five years before on the theme of the building of a medieval church in Uppsala. When the great bell was rung, the tower collapsed, for the master-builder did not really know the secret to which in his arrogance he pretended. Father and friend forsook him in his wretchedness, but his wife was loyal—and the secret was faith. Neither moralist nor churchman could take exception to this play and it immediately went into production. The reactionaries praised Strindberg's return to the fold and the revolutionaries deplored his defection.

And still he worked—cataloguing a new collection of Japanese manuscripts, keeping up a flow of prose and verse for periodicals, bringing out another volume of short stories, this time about seafaring folk whom he could wholeheartedly admire, and collaborating—because to his annoyance it was physically impossible to do the whole thing himself—in a comprehensive volume on Old Stockholm. It 'anæsthetised' him to write about the past; he imagined that he was telling stories of the old times to his children—his own childhood seemed already to belong to antiquity. Even more directly than in *Master Olof*, Strindberg's present aim was a new and truer way of writing history, and he was sure this could only be done through the study of human personality. When he observed how a man's opinions, actions—even his handwriting—changed in relation to those about him, he could not envisage objective history. To Buckle's theory of the relativity of truth Strindberg added his own view that nothing was entirely objective.

In addition to this strenuous work, he was the moving spirit of the Strindberg 'Club' which was now a favourite rendezvous of Stockholm's *avant-garde*. The club had a secret password and its activities were entertaining—Siri von Essen acted, Strindberg wrote, translated, directed and indulged his taste for fun.

His star had indeed risen. In spite of the failure of the bank he had paid his debts, in spite of his enemies he had won recognition, and soon his wife bore him a second daughter. They took a summer cottage on Kymmendö, which in spite of some unhappy memories he still adored, and with his own hands Strindberg built a log cabin to write in down by the water's edge—he was working on a play for Siri's return to the stage. It needed only the Dramatic Theatre's decision to put on *Master Olof* in its original prose version for Strindberg to feel that all his labours were at last requited.

He had lived with *Master Olof* for nearly nine years, and in spite of all that had happened and all his other work, saw more of himself in this early play than in anything he had written since. An attack of rheumatism and uncontrollable nerves kept him away from the first performance—in the Christmas week of 1881—but when he heard that it was well received, his youth, his inspiration—the buried poet—sprang up from their grave. Once again, as in those first days of marriage four years before, summer bloomed in darkest winter; he swept all the books from his writing table, and in fourteen days composed a romantic fairy play. He still criticised society, but now he could be gentle; he could smile—life was good-evil, and he saw that the distress of human beings came more from lack of understanding than from vice. In *Lucky Peter's Journey* the hero's bitterest experiences were only milestones on the road to his heart's desire.

Subject to a few alterations the new play was at once accepted, and Strindberg went on with *Herr Bengt's Wife* for Siri von Essen's second début, and at the same time made researches for a popular history of Swedish culture. To his dismay he found himself extremely tired; his head often ached, his food disagreed with him, he still had rheumatism and his nerves were out of tune.

As Margit, the nun whom Herr Bengt rescued from the cloister, Siri looked her best, and the audience received her with enthusiasm. Yet her acting of the part fell short of Strindberg's vision, and his conception of it was not in accord with her tastes. The setting was medieval, but the matter visibly autobiographical. Ibsen had proclaimed his view of marriage in *A Doll's House*, a play that Strindberg found 'sick like its author,' but which none the less set every housewife dreaming of a career and filled chivalrous young men with remorse. True, it had been laughed off the stage in Berlin, but such a penetrating critic as Georg Brandes had—in Strindberg's opinion—been taken in by it. In *Herr Bengt's Wife* Strindberg gave his own more complex, more poetic—and he believed truer—version of the eternal drama, in which after many hazards love finally conquered, and the sanctity of marriage and parenthood was saved. This was August Strindberg's reply to Henrik Ibsen, but it was also the cry of his heart.

Siri would have preferred a less personal, gayer rôle, but her success brought further engagements, while Strindberg grappled in gathering gloom with the history of Swedish civilisation. History appeared to him more and more futile—an unending walk in a circle; civilisations rose and fell, social systems came and went, religions changed, and man remained ignorant and unhappy. However, he at least derived satisfaction from his new way of presenting the subject. Other historians viewed events through the medium of privileged persons—and the events were largely military campaigns. Strindberg revealed the texture of national life—the varied pattern made by the lives of the common people. He was not concerned with the castles of kings and nobles, but following Rousseau's decree that for true culture one must return to nature, he went for his material to nature's children—the artisan, the fisherman and the beggar.

When *The Swedish People* was criticised for the way it swept aside time-honoured personages and precepts, Strindberg felt more isolated than ever. No one supported his views, and without any party or school of thought behind him, his very existence sometimes seemed precarious. He did not see how anyone could exist if he were not a link in the chain of his own time, yet his special vision forced him to break away. His depression soon changed to anger—if people shut their eyes to every truth that surprised or displeased them, what hope was there of breaking the circle in which they walked blindfold? He could not forgive life for falling short of his expectations: marriage, art, religion, history, all failed to fulfil their promise. He saw that his mission was to destroy—destroy in the hope that when all false images were razed to the ground truth would rise. He was back in the savage humour of *The Red Room*, but for his new assault he eschewed the form of the novel. Successful as that book had been, it could be dismissed as fiction. His new work disdained any disguise. He marshalled his scepticism, his scorn, his effrontery and his wit, and in *The New Kingdom* leapt brazenly to the annihilation of all that the Swedish Constitution stood for, all that the bourgeois held most dear. He refused even to take the prevalent sentimental attitude towards prostitution—why should he be sorry for those who were clearly not sorry for themselves? And while respectable citizens lamented that Sweden's young genius had gone to the devil once more and was now past praying for, the New Theatre produced *Lucky Peter's Journey*. The same citizens wept at the play's goodness and beauty and could not make the author out.

The following summer Siri went off to play *Jane Eyre* in Finland while Strindberg stayed behind and wrote her advice. He looked after the household, first in Stockholm and then on Kymmendö, meticulously supervising the servants, the provisions, the accounts and the health of the children. When Siri was due back, Strindberg suggested that he should continue with the housekeeping, so that she might be spared such cares—she had never got over her dislike of domestic affairs—and there should be less cause of friction. Quarrels made him ill and he had enormously much to do. In spite of his high working speed, journalism and correspondence now took many hours, and at the same time he was composing a book of stories in a setting of Swedish history, while the poetic urge had returned with such force that it could not be denied. His writing-table and scripts were scrupulously neat, but his mind refused to be kept in order. He began to prepare a volume of poems in prose and verse—here again he must destroy, must break down the dignified academic forms that fettered thought, explode the tradition of lyrical language and set poetry free. Even beauty, he decided, must give way to truth.

Sometimes nowadays Strindberg saw a strange expression in Siri's eyes. He began to think that the incompatibility of their temperaments was making her actually dislike him, then suspicion dawned that she believed he was going out of his mind. She had friends now who were closer companions to her than himself, which could not surprise him considering his preoccupation with work, yet he was hurt and jealous, particularly as when he was free she seemed to have no time to spare for him. Even if she could no longer hope to become a great actress, the life of theatre entirely absorbed her and she lived in an emotional whirl. Her flirtations tortured Strindberg, and when presently, on the grounds of economy, she invited a woman friend to share the flat, he suspected that they were carrying on a love affair. The walls seemed saturated with whispering voices, the women's faces bore secret smiles, when he spoke they looked not at him but at each other, and exhausted as he was, he felt that no one cared for his comfort. The food grew daily less to his taste, the children were kept out of the way with a nurse, the bills were enormous and there was little to show for the expenditure except Siri's clothes and cigarettes. In his overwrought state, her constant demands for money seemed to Strindberg to bring a taint of prostitution into their marriage, and the ideal union he had hoped for floated steadily out of reach. Yet in his heart it still lived, and in the seclusion of his study he gave it birth, writing again and again of man's desperate need for his mother and his wife.

CHAPTER SEVEN

1883–1884

I have played my cards and lost. Shuffle the pack and deal again
Letter to Jonas Lie, Ouchy, December 1884

BY THE time the stories and poems were ready for the publisher, Strindberg was on the edge of a nervous breakdown, and his doctor urged him to travel. Siri too had been unwell—her chest was not strong and it was thought that she might benefit from a change of climate, and although she regretted leaving her work and her friends, Strindberg hoped that the break would improve their relationship. For himself it was a good moment to uproot: his father had died this year which marked another milestone on his own journey; he was thirty-four—youth was definitely over and he had been a Civil Servant long enough.

They decided to go to Grez, a village near Fontainebleau which had become something of an artists' colony and had in its circle a number of Swedes, including the well-known painter Carl Larsson who was a staunch admirer of Strindberg's work and had prepared his way by describing him in France as 'our Émile Zola.' In the autumn of 1883, therefore, the Strindbergs set off with the two little girls and Ebba the nurse, making their way by one-night stands to Grez in Nemours. The journey was arduous and expensive—Strindberg gave money freely to anyone in need, even when he was short himself—but to squander it on expensive hotels irked him. However, Siri would not tolerate cheap lodgings, and he soothed his annoyance by writing boyish descriptions of Germany's water-closets to his friends, and telling them that he thought the racket made by Karin and Greta must have cured some Germans of their sentimentality about other people's children.

They found the artists' colony amusing, and Siri von Essen wrote a description of it for a Swedish magazine, but Strindberg was in no mood to settle down and soon decided that they must go on to Paris. Each move was an ordeal for Siri, for whenever routine was upset Strindberg was more than usually irritable, and as Ebba knew no French, the arrangements devolved upon herself. Nor did Paris please Strindberg when they got there; he had the impression that people scented themselves instead of washing, and that if they were not stealing they were begging—nobody so much as opened a door without expecting a *pourboire*. He entirely agreed with Rousseau that the metropolis was not the heart of a nation, but an ulcer corrupting its blood. Strindberg's welcome among Paris writers, however, was gratifying. His own country treated him with suspicion, but here at the hub of European culture he was accepted as the leader of modern Swedish literature. The two Norwegian authors, Björnsterne Björnson and Jonas Lie, who with Henrik Ibsen formed Norway's great trio, immediately took the young Swede under their protection. Inspired like most Scandinavian writers of the day by Öhlenschläger, Björnson aimed at 'creating a new saga in the light of the peasant.' His trilogy *Sigurd the Bastard* had won him international fame, and from the time Strindberg began to write he had admired and feared Björnson—he could not but fear such a giant of a man who wrote as he wished and yet made a success of writing. Besides, the portraits of Björnson showed a robust and vigorous man—and in the presence of marked virility Strindberg was never at ease. Once Björnson had come to Stockholm and Strindberg had kept out of his path, but he had felt 'a tumult as if a storm had gone over the city, as if a magician had passed by.' He recognised in this Norwegian a being stronger than himself who might have power over his fate.

By the time they met in Paris, Björnson, in the prime of life, had become more of a political agitator than a poet. He travelled about Europe preaching radicalism, and his play *The King* had been denounced as treason. Strindberg and he had much in common, and Björnson welcomed the gifted young Swede with such fatherly solicitude that Strindberg forgot his alarm. Before long Björnson and Jonas Lie, the Norwegian

94

novelist, who had also been a student at Christiania with Henrik Ibsen at the time of Strindberg's birth, became his closest friends. Björnson assumed the part of protector, whereas Lie's approach was subtle and oblique. Unlike his friends, Lie had not discovered his literary gift until he was nearly forty and had been in turn lawyer and journalist, but now he was recognised as Norway's leading novelist and enjoyed a stipend from the Government. He lived mostly abroad and was a good deal of a recluse, but he and Strindberg found themselves magnetically attracted. Their imaginations struck sparks; they hypnotised one another and gave birth to thoughts that both had fathered. At first this relationship fascinated Strindberg, but as the weeks passed he felt as if he had been seduced into a kind of debauchery of the soul. His thoughts were driven from their proper course, and material he needed for his work was dissipated. The pressure on him of the two famous Norwegians grew heavy; they wanted to alleviate his poverty and ill health, interfere in his marriage and plan his career. He shrank from their patronage, and discussion of his marriage was especially painful. Far from improving their relations, this journey seemed to be driving him and Siri further apart. She did not like Paris; they had had to move twice already, and she found it hard to keep their rooms warm and to provide the kind of Swedish food they all preferred. She had little time or strength left for the theatre and had only managed to see Sarah Bernhardt a few times. Over these difficulties Strindberg's new friends were unsympathetic; they had questioned visitors from Sweden about Siri von Essen's acting and formed the view that she had no talent. They thought it foolish of her therefore to pine for the stage—the career of August Strindberg's wife should be enough. Björnson particularly expressed this view, and it was hard for Strindberg to argue with him, for while the older man criticised Siri von Essen, who detested him (she too found Jonas Lie fascinating), nevertheless Björnson was a lover of women, whereas Strindberg's views on this subject grew ever more complicated. He had begun work on a volume of stories about marriage which exploded chivalry and romance as senseless fantasies, and showed the real relationship between the sexes as a fight based on the instinct of reproduction and the economics of living. Yet he admired Siri's spirit, and understood very well that it was not in her nature to relinquish the theatre whatever the relative merits of her art and his. No sight was so moving to him as that of a woman sitting peacefully at home with her children and her sewing, but he had fallen in love with a woman who had openly declared that she was unfit for domesticity, and he had let her believe that in him she would find release from captivity and boredom. He had promised her a theatre; now she had borne him two children and a third was on the way. But she said herself that at last her maternal instinct had awoken, and in spite of their difficulties they had times of happiness. He confessed to her that he was writing a diatribe against married life, and begged her, if she read the stories, to remember that the marriages he described were purely hypothetical, and that the sole aim of his attack was to spur men and women on towards a better relationship, instead of allowing themselves to be fooled by a romantic illusion which could only end in despair. He assured Siri and himself that nothing could be further from his intention than to wound her or to injure their marriage.

Siri was glad when Björnson and Lie failed to persuade Strindberg to settle down in Paris. For a while he had been tempted—the cosmopolitan capital was inspiring after the insularity of Stockholm—but constant company, however congenial, exhausted him, and after three months of it he was aching for independence, solitude and nature. The Strindbergs made for themselves the most Swedish Christmas possible, and then, in January 1884, when Paris was at her darkest and dirtiest, they moved on to Switzerland. Strindberg, writing joint letters to Björnson and Lie, described the joyful arrival in the sunlit land—how Siri was so much moved by the first sight of the Alps that she burst into tears, while he himself 'darted round the railway carriage like a squirrel, trying to see out of both windows at once.' Soon he was writing ecstatically both to Stockholm and to Paris, describing the splendours of the landscape from the veranda of their sunlit rooms overlooking the lake at Ouchy near Lausanne, and the comfort of good food, wine, tobacco and wood fires all at a low price. The spirit of Rousseau seemed to breathe over the whole land, and Strindberg sometimes felt that the good Swiss air was making him sentimental; he was tempted to throw down his weapons and give up hurting his fellow creatures, then once more he recognised his mission to destroy everything that was false.

His poems came out in Sweden and roused more indignation. The ruthless young critic of society could not even keep to novels, plays and essays, but had crashed into the sacred world of poetry with his ugly realism, his invective, his polemics and abuse. That he could write conventional lyrics was proved by some of the early work he had included in the volume, but since he had taken on the function of destroyer, he had abandoned the beaten track of prosody. He adapted form to his violent need for expression—he wrote in verse that changed to prose and back again, played havoc with rhyme and metre, made wanton use of classical names and technical terms—even the word syphilis appeared in one poem—and he began the book with a blazing defence of his methods.

The critics blazed back, although here and there a reader was caught by the author's extraordinary vigour of thought and expression, or by touches of beauty and tenderness as startling as his violence.

While his readers disputed, the poet walked in the mountains, studied the work of John Stuart Mill, took lessons to improve his French, German, English and Italian, and made up his mind to think as a world-citizen rather than as a Swede. He was convinced now that socialism, internationalism, and particularly the organised Peace Movement, which he met in Switzerland for the first time, were the only cures for the evils of civilisation. He considered devoting some summers of his life to 'discovering Europe, just as Stanley discovered Africa.' He would discover the peasant and write about him—not about local custom, costume and folk dancing, but about the thought and action of the peasant in his relation to culture and progress. He would rouse the peasant to an understanding of his own importance.

For the first step in this campaign, as spring broke, Strindberg went down into Northern Italy, but here he met with disillusion. 'At first the orange trees duped me, but later! . . . The Mediterranean . . . *humbug, Sir*!' He could not see the beauty of the country for its badness. This was the playground of the rich, and the peasants were apathetic and corrupt. He returned with relief to Ouchy—'The Alps are still there.'

Here on April 1st, 1884, Siri gave birth to a son, whom they called Hans to match the second girl Greta, and during the summer the family moved to Chexbres further up in the mountains, away from the heat and the tourists. Strindberg now made his first contribution to the French Press—an appreciation of Björnsterne Björnson, and he wrote a pacifist story for his new volume *Utopias of Reality*. This book showed something of the fair future to which he was dedicated, while the collection of tales called *Married* attacked old rottenness. Life in Swiss *pensions* provided excellent copy in the way of parasitical wives, and in the war of the sexes Strindberg could not be pacifist. Since coming to Switzerland his own marriage seemed more secure; if Siri von Essen felt frustrated by her exile from the theatre she did not show it, and Strindberg tried to hide the moods of suspicion and jealousy in which even his wife's tenderness—the very mainspring of his happiness—appeared as a subtle sadism. If he were not walking or working—and walking with Strindberg was always a preparation for writing—he was with his family. He could not bear Siri long out of sight, and he spent hours playing with the little girls, perceiving in the elder, Karin, an intelligence he was eager to foster, although he did not share Siri's hope that both daughters would go on the stage. He declared it would be better for them to train as midwives. The other guests at the *penşion* saw Strindberg as a devoted husband and father, and a modest, courteous and hardworking man. Yet underneath this composure he was at fever pitch; his health had not much improved and he was once more taking bromides in order to sleep. He had to write continuously now in order to support his family, but in any case he could not have stopped. 'His brain worked without respite, grinding like a mill, and he had no relief until he got his thoughts down on to paper, and then the same agony started again.' He wrote and wrote his small neat script, while sweat poured off his forehead, and he did not even pause to read through what he had written.

Nevertheless he and Siri had come through this testing time, and now on her thirty-fourth birthday she raised her glass and thanked her husband for seven happy years.

In September they moved to Geneva, and in the same month Albert Bonnier, Stockholm's leading publisher, who had been enterprising enough to print Strindberg's poems, brought out *Married*. The public fell to; no subject could have been more topical or controversial, and almost everyone, from the staunchest reactionary to the boldest progressive, found something in the book to shock him, for not only did it condemn modern woman, repudiate birth control and ignore divorce, but it strongly attacked the upper classes and the Church. Woven into exaggerated descriptions of marriages which Strindberg had observed, was much autobiographical material, drawn not only from his own marriage but from his childhood. He described the fear that had haunted him after reading the pernicious yellow book—that by masturbating he had unwittingly doomed himself to lunacy—and castigated Pietism for enjoining celibacy, and thereby perverting youth's natural virility. He represented Confirmation and Communion as humbug devised by the Church to keep the lower classes in their place; he even went so far as to detail the commercial value of the wafers and the wine, which 'the priest foists on the congregation as the flesh and blood of the Agitator executed more than eighteen hundred years ago.'

Most of the stories, however, were caricatures of married life with touches of humour to relieve the so-called realism, and touches of tenderness which gave a clue to the author's underlying sentimentality and his plea for the perfect marriage which had not yet been achieved. In the preface, which aimed at destroying the Nora-cult with which, in Strindberg's view, Ibsen had infected Scandinavia, the author put forward his own view of women's rights. Co-education he deemed essential and boys and girls should have the same facilities in a new and progressive educational system; women must be eligible for all occupations and keep their maiden names when they were married. Sex preference—but also all false romanticism and mystification—must be swept away; then only could Strindberg see hope of a better relationship between the sexes.

He expected censure; the prudish were bound to find the stories indecent, and in a letter to Albert Bonnier he had already suggested that they might try to have the book suppressed. But when, within a fortnight of publication, he received a telegram informing him that the book was impounded and author and publisher both charged with blasphemy, Strindberg was taken completely by surprise and very much frightened. It was not after all his treatment of sex but his treatment of religion that had caused this disaster. Now the enemies of whose machinations he was always aware had found a legal way to attack him. He wrote to the court refuting the charge and prayed that the matter would blow over.

His protest was ignored and he was overwhelmed with letters urging him to return to Stockholm and face the proceedings. His friends declared that Strindberg must not consider this a purely personal issue, for it raised the whole question of freedom of speech and religion, and all lovers of liberty, whether they approved Strindberg's views or not, would uphold his right to express them and Albert Bonnier's right to publish the book. The penalty for blasphemy, according to Swedish law, could be two years' hard labour, and Strindberg was warned that if he let Bonnier face the charge alone, he would be convicted of abject cowardice. Björnson, in particular, was imperative in his counsel, and Strindberg replied with a furious letter telling the Norwegian to leave his books and his affairs alone. At the same time he wrote again to the court, admitting his responsibility as the author of *Married*, and was at once requested to appear in person.

Siri, who was not well herself and feared that he would break down under the ordeal of a trial, begged Strindberg to remain in Switzerland, advice hotly supported by some Russian Nihilists with whom he had made friends—no one in Russia, they said, would be so crazy as to give himself up to his enemies of his own free will. Pressure to go, however, both from outside and from his own conscience, was stronger than his fear, and when presently young Bonnier, Albert's son, himself a member of the firm, came to Switzerland to discuss the whole matter with the author, Strindberg had no choice. Leaving Siri in bed in Geneva with some undiagnosed malady, and one of the children ailing too, he set off with Bonnier on the long journey north, so depressed that he was sometimes unable to contain his tears. He assured his companion that if anything were to happen to Siri, he would shoot himself. The future had never looked more black; he had often feared that he might end up in a lunatic asylum, but to have given his enemies this right to put him in prison was a still more ironic fate.

His imagination played such tricks that by the time the train drew in to the islands of Stockholm, he half expected to be manacled and thrown into gaol. Instead he was met by a cheering crowd and there were calls for a speech as he stepped on to the platform—now that Strindberg was a martyr in the cause of freedom the progressives were prepared to overlook his reactionary attack on woman, which even his preface did not absolve. Difficult as he always found it to speak in public, Strindberg tried to tell the crowd of the necessity for realism, but it was too enthusiastic to listen—he was swept to the hotel to find his room heaped with flowers, letters, telegrams and petitions. The papers were full of him, and there was a gala performance of *Lucky Peter's Journey* in his honour. Even Björnsterne Björnson, in spite of Strindberg's insulting letter, had an article in a Stockholm paper declaring that the *Married* proceedings were a scandalous attempt to suppress intellectual freedom by brute force. Strindberg sent Björnson 'a sentimental telegram,' but the Norwegian followed up his general support with personal criticism and once again the Swede was furious. Björnson was by nature romantic and aggressive, and Strindberg shrank from both these qualities in others.

In spite of his shyness he was persuaded to appear at the New Theatre that night, the eve of the trial. In the foyer two young women pushed through the throng to speak to him; for a moment he did not recognise them, then as he embraced them tears came into his eyes. 'Life is pretty strange,' he said, 'when I can scarcely recognise my own sisters.'

As *Lucky Peter's Journey* continued, the audience grew ever more enthusiastic, until in the scene satirising the lack of religious liberty, it rose to its feet, waving, clapping and stamping, while the performance appeared to go on in dumb show. At the end Strindberg was called again and again before the curtain, yet as he stood there, bowing, his mind was filled with foreboding. There was little difference between the cheering of an excited crowd and its booing; neither demonstration was based on understanding, and he had no wish for this kind of fame. Besides, with the trial to face and the threat of imprisonment hanging over his head, this acclamation smacked of an orgy before a sacrifice. His supporters were loud, but the conservative Press made the most of *The Red Room*, *The New Kingdom* and the poems, in their condemnation of August Strindberg as a blasphemer and an altogether vicious influence on his country. To-night he was given a laurel wreath, but to-morrow he would be in the dock and he could not hope for mercy.

With his hair falling in disorder over his damp forehead, his eyes blazing and his body trembling, as he felt his enemies closing in on him, whose only weapon was his pen, Strindberg defended himself without legal aid; but many distinguished men, in spite of their avowed dislike of Strindberg's work, entered the witness box to uphold the liberties of author and publisher. Strindberg's defence was that he meant in deadly earnest every word that he had written. He was concerned with telling the truth, and in giving the facts of the commercial value of the wafers and the wine used in the Communion Service and in calling Jesus Christ an Agitator, he had not intended either to mock or to blaspheme. On the contrary, he had exposed tricks which to him, a deist, seemed profane, and incompatible with true religious feeling—and he took back nothing of what he had written.

The trial dragged on for weeks, and Strindberg's friends were afraid his health would crack. However, he was guarded by a detective and took the view that 'people were more afraid of me than I of them,' and he had besides certain private springs of strength. He dramatised the whole affair and saw himself as Brand, defending his individual creed—an antidote to finding himself a public 'show' with his picture on packets of cigarettes. Then also, here in Stockholm, although he called it 'the land of the mastodons,' the vision of Siri von Essen appeared to him as in the first days of love. In these streets where his youth lingered, he caught glimpses of her child-like face and yellow curls in a mist of blue veils—and once more he wrote his wife love letters and thanked her for standing by him in the dark days.

On the 17th of November came the verdict—Not Guilty. The police, whom he had expected to escort him to prison, had to help August Strindberg to escape from the court, and the streets round his hotel were packed with cheering crowds—many of them workers who had heard that this author was their champion. That night there was a banquet at which he begged his supporters to remember that it was not his acquittal they were celebrating, but the victory over the enemies of free speech—and truly, as once again he left Sweden to rejoin his family in Geneva, Strindberg felt humiliated rather than triumphant. He was played out, and as he had no martyr's crown, he knew that his enemies would gain power. If he had been condemned for his views, his health might have suffered, but he would have gloried in his innocence, whereas his present punishment brought no spiritual reward, and his freedom did not give him the wherewithal to live.

In long letters to Jonas Lie, deploring 'B.B.'s' behaviour, Strindberg explained that he 'hadn't cared a damn' about the case, and had 'only come home to set Albert Bonnier free,' that as a result of his attack on the upper classes he was threatened with destitution, and having no piece of earth to nourish him and his children, was dependent on his 'natural enemy' the capitalist. Yet 'Albert Bonnier is so persecuted that he dares not publish my work.'

Strindberg had had bad dreams at the end of the summer, which he now saw as premonitions of disaster: 'I believe in dreams, for my brain works sharpest when I'm asleep.' But now the fight was over:

... Now I take my leave of the Swede and the world and go out again into the desert to think and read about the great questions of the future. . . .

His one comfort was Siri's loyalty, but if she gainsaid him by a single word or gave him one ambiguous glance, he believed that she had gone over to the enemy.

CHAPTER EIGHT

1885–1887

All this I have borne without a murmur, because I believed myself the father of that child.

THE FATHER

TRUE ENOUGH, as soon as Strindberg had left the country with a cleared name, his antagonists' rage boiled over and his supporters had little left to say. The papers were full of insults and abuse; an Archbishop denounced Strindberg and his followers to the Swedish Academy, and educationalists clamoured for the suppression of his books as injurious to the morals of the young. Now he saw himself truly persecuted, but his growing fear was not only of the enemy outside, but within. He began to watch himself horribly changing. Although he had long since ceased to believe in the deity of Christ, he had stood up in court and declared in full faith that he believed in God. In his rôle of Reformer, he had even fasted and drunk water, purging himself before his God in the cause of purity and truth. Now this faith in a beneficent deity crumbled, and he saw the world directed by quite other powers.

The rays of his searching mind were focused on evil and his belief in its power grew. Other people's hatred poisoned his very blood-stream—how then could he think it altogether by chance that two of his opponents, on whom he had concentrated vicious thoughts of revenge, quite unexpectedly died? Perhaps it was not for nothing that during the trial one man had called him Lucifer. He had a power within him for good, but it was useless; his fellow creatures would have none of it, instead they invited him to use his power for evil.

No one would publish his description of the trial, and now the need to make money was imperative. The doctors thought

104

that Siri's lungs were affected, and the children too were far from well. 'At night he heard the threat of hunger and want rising like a flood to engulf them,' and the precariousness of the children's future filled him with alarm. He decided that he must once again become a journalist—but most Swedish papers were closed to him. French periodicals welcomed his contributions, but pay was small, and to make a living in this way he must be near Paris, so in the summer of 1885 he moved the family back to the artists' colony at Grez where their travels had begun. Now Strindberg was once more in the full fire of his friends; Björnsterne Björnson refused to be shaken off, and since the trial Jonas Lie and Edvard Brandes had been corresponding about their anxiety for Strindberg's health and future. They all fell on him, exhorting him, for his own sake and that of art, to give up any idea of being a journalist or a reformer and make proper use of his great literary and dramatic gifts. These writers believed implicitly in Strindberg's genius, but had come to the conclusion that he was quite without power of selection. It was essential therefore that some wise and trusted friend should go through his scripts before they were offered for publication. On this point Siri von Essen was in agreement with them, and it occurred to Björnson that she was just the friend Strindberg needed to perform this office. As soon as he suggested it, Strindberg was filled with suspicion; not so long ago Björnson had criticised Siri von Essen for wanting to pursue her own career instead of fostering her husband's—now he wanted to put her husband under her supervision and censorship. Björnson had supported the right to free speech, but was unable to forgive the criticism of women. The longer Strindberg contemplated the *Married* proceedings, the more convinced he was that, although he had been charged with blasphemy, his real offence was the portrayal of women stripped of romantic camouflage, and that women were behind every attack on him. He had been informed that the Queen of Sweden herself had read *Married* and asked that the book should be impounded, and now Björnson, the champion of women, was trying to place him under a woman's—under his own wife's—domination, while at the same time other people, and notably Sweden's foremost emancipated women, were writing to poison her against him. While he was composing *Married*, Strindberg had still believed in woman and in marriage and had pleaded for love; now he conceived a second volume without this faith. He had assured Siri that the book was fiction, but he painted the new stories from life and not least from his life with her. The devil took possession of his pen, and this time his victims were not only emancipated women, but also the perverted and unsexed. He threw down the whole female sex and trampled on it in fear and fury, just as at those long-ago orgies he had thrown his sacred image of womanhood to be desecrated along with the stained Bible and the polluted sacraments.

His hatred appalled him. He wrote to his friend von Heidenstam, a Swedish writer who had remained faithful through his fall, begging him to understand his misogyny 'which is only the reverse side of my fearful attraction towards the other sex.' Strindberg was trying all the time to understand it himself, to explain it and justify it to himself and to others, and he blackened Siri von Essen to relieve his own sense of guilt. He could honestly assure her of his fidelity, for he was by nature monogamous, but he knew that he had betrayed her none the less. She had believed that he would uphold her independence, her right to work and have a life of her own, but he had gone back on his promises. Indeed he was going back on many things. He did not understand Karl Marx, who seemed to him to believe that the world belonged to organised industry rather than to peasants and fishermen living by nature's laws, so, although he had considered himself 'almost a communist,' he gradually lost faith in the socialist cause. He read the American anti-Christian lecturer, Ingersoll, and found him 'instinct with love, hope and faith in life'; he turned to Tolstoy's *My Confession*, and learnt how the unchristianity of the orthodox faith had led the great Russian to conceive a religion of his own. More and more Strindberg felt that only by becoming a complete atheist and explaining everything by natural causes could he escape from fear. It was impossible for him to believe in a kindly providence any longer, and the conception of an evil God was too terrible be borne. He cried out in panic that there could be no God, otherwise humanity was doomed. Yet, again and again, he was shaken back into belief in divine power by events he was unable to explain—-he could not deny the power of prayer, nor the validity of faith-healing. Indeed, when one of his own children was ill and he put his hands on her, he felt power flowing through him and watched fever and pain vanish. Yet he fought his way doggedly towards unbelief.

It did not escape Strindberg that Tolstoy—who, nearing sixty, was at this time engaged in renunciating his heritage— was considered by many people mad, and he himself now took precautions in case he were either actually to go out of his mind or be thought insane. He meant in either of these events to kill himself, but none the less he prepared a document explaining that 'as it would be scarcely surprising for a sane man to be driven out of his wits by seeing the world run by knaves and fools,' he wished if this happened either to be secretly poisoned by some skilful doctor, or else dispatched to the famous asylum in Belgium where, as he had read in the *Revue des Deux Mondes*, the patients were allowed freedom.

In spite of this strain, the move to the Hôtel Beau Séjour at Grez—'*chez* Laurent' to its patrons—was happy. The village, set in woods and water, reminded the Strindbergs a little, as the year advanced, of their summer home on Kymmendö, and this familiarity soothed his nerves and led him to write *The People of Hemsö*, a graphic and often humorous narrative of life in his beloved skerries, which proved popular both in Sweden and abroad. And in spite of his disillusionment, he added to his 'Utopias of Reality,' now giving the book the sub-title: 'Positive suggestions in the spirit of Saint-Simon.'

Now that the health of the whole family was improved, the nightmare shadows receded a little. Strindberg could swim and sunbathe and wander about the countryside with his little girls, while the company of the artists who gathered *chez* Laurent was a pleasant change from the staidness of the Swiss *pensions*. During the trial the Swiss Press had been hostile, and on his return Strindberg had found himself ostracised. Now these artists, coming out from Paris, gay, unconventional and cosmopolitan, took him to their hearts, and soon he and Siri von Essen were the centre of the circle. Evenings passed agreeably at one or other of the cafés; and soon they started a

107

cabaret for which Strindberg found time to write sketches with leading parts for Siri von Essen, and now once again they sang duets together to the accompaniment of his guitar. He wrote to his friends that 'things are going divinely well,' and Bonnier received the 'harmless' book with enthusiasm.

Presently two Danish girls arrived at Grez and were made very welcome by the Strindbergs. The elder, Sofie Holten, was both a painter and a journalist; she had shared a room with a cousin of Siri's while studying art in Paris, and as a further recommendation she was a contributor to Edvard Brandes' new periodical *Politiken*, for which Strindberg was anxious to write. On her side she was fascinated by the fine head and lion's mane of the notorious Swedish author, and asked to paint him. Soon he was sitting for his portrait, and at the same time making plans to take the artist on a bicycle tour, so that he could write articles about French peasants and nature, which she could illustrate. Sofie Holten pointed out in amusement what a scandal it would cause if she were to go off with the celebrated Swedish misogynist, and Strindberg had to content himself with enlisting her aid in equally urgent plans for the translation of his works into Danish and those of the Brandes brothers into French.

This friendship delighted Strindberg, and he was also interested in the younger girl, Marie David. She was only twenty and came of a well-known Jewish family, but her upbringing had been irregular, and she knew much of life for her years. Her parents had been unhappily married and had finally separated, the mother taking the two youngest children, whose paternity was in doubt (Marie herself believed that Georg Brandes was her father), to live with her in Naples where, before they were grown up, the mother died of tuberculosis. Marie David became a medical student and then gave up medicine in order to write. She had lived alone in Paris, was thin, pale and striking, wore her red hair short, held her own in all discussions and drank a great deal of wine. In fact she was an emancipated woman, but unlike many others she was neither a snob nor a prig. She was generous and gay, if a little hectic, and was popular *chez* Laurent, specially with the young women, all ardent believers in sex-equality. Marie David took this equality entirely for granted

108

and brought a fine irony to bear on the Swedish author's views. What point was there, she inquired, in advocating co-education and equal opportunity when he showed clearly that he thought woman's place was the kitchen or the nursery? She found Strindberg old-fashioned and stupid and was impervious to his charm, and he could not help admiring her effrontery—he was always impressed when a woman stood up to him. On the other hand Marie David was not indifferent to Siri von Essen's beauty, and thought it monstrous that she should be forced into exile, away from the theatre that was the passion of her life. Was this the freedom Strindberg preached—that his own wife should renounce her art to sit here, the servant of his moods, and be given a part in a cabaret like a treat for a child?

Encouraged by Marie David and her other friends, Siri von Essen made a new bid for freedom, with the added argument that finances were now so precarious that her earnings were really needed, but Strindberg would not hear of her suggestion. To continue her career she would have to go back to Sweden, and he could not go back. The second volume of *Married* was out, and Personne, a well-known lecturer, had published a pamphlet on *Strindberg Literature and the Corruption of Youth*. The public had turned against him; he must remain abroad, and he was convinced that if Siri went back and took the children with her, he would sink. This life of the family, this sense of himself renewed in his children, was his only salvation, his life-line, his umbilical cord. He insisted that she should stay and promised to redouble his efforts to make money. A Parish publisher had commissioned him to write a book on Stockholm society for a series on European capitals—Strindberg believed he knew enough of the language now to write in French—and this book and other work should soon bring in money.

So Siri von Essen remained at Grez and comforted herself with her friends, and specially with Marie David, who understood her frustration so well. Strindberg's quick eye soon noted a subtle change in his wife; she was taking more trouble with her appearance—she had the unmistakable air of one who is out to please. When he looked at Marie David now he saw her as the materialisation of one of his own fearful imaginings, and he was gripped by a terror greater than any he had known. He had refused to let Siri go back to Sweden; what if he were to lose her this way instead? Marie David had even insinuated herself into the affection of the children who called her 'aunt.' Seeking a refuge from pain Strindberg plunged deeper into animosity, whereupon new suspicions rose to torment him further. What did he really know of his wife? He had fallen in love with a madonna and discovered a wanton; he was sure now that she had had lovers of both sexes, before and since her marriage. What if the children were not his? What if he had been cheated of his only earthly happiness and his sole hope of immortality? What proof had he that any one of these three children whom he loved so dearly was his own?

One fear woke another, plunging him back into the terrible helplessness of childhood—the fear of loneliness, of people, of dogs and the dark. He veered again towards death as the only respite from his anguish, but now, perhaps because he was thinking so much of death, his past returned in vivid detail. He began to understand how great a part his unrequited love for his mother had played in the tragedy of his marriage, how he was doomed to seek his mother in all women, and to hate them because his heart was buried in her tomb. Now too, in the light of experience, he could see the significance of his blank background, his lack of a place in the social system. As a contribution to human history, Strindberg made up his mind that before he died he must write his own story.

Neither volume two of *Married* nor his other stories brought him royalties, for he was in debt to Bonnier. Strindberg reflected wryly that Personne, the author of the anti-Strindberg pamphlet, and Bonnier, whom Personne compared with a procuress or a receiver of stolen goods, grew rich, while he himself remained a beggar. When he finished *La Société de Stockholm*, he was met by fresh disappointment; the series was unsuccessful and the publisher returned his manuscript. It was no use approaching a Swedish publisher with this censorious work, so together Sofie Holten and Marie David began to translate it into Danish, but soon decided that the book was equally unsuitable for Denmark. Strindberg's plans to make money had entirely failed and he was forced to borrow; he begged Edvard Brandes to dispose of the Danish rights of all his works for a few hundred kronor, but Brandes succeeded in getting him some help without this drastic measure.

The Danish girls' visit came to an end, and Siri's grief at parting from Marie David was undisguised, but all Strindberg could see was fresh hope of saving his marriage. He decided to try Switzerland once more. Siri did not complain; she was bent now on avoiding scenes, and to this end she no longer read what her husband wrote. As she watched him with a knowledge of his psychology widened by the opinions of others —Sofie Holten for one had discovered the sweet kernel in the prickly husk—Siri saw that Strindberg was becoming ever more clearly two separate personalities. One part of him hated and distrusted her; through his brother Axel he had started a network of inquiries about her past, and had even gone to Copenhagen himself to look for evidence of her guilt. He would leave her suddenly, vanish for days together without a word, and then come back, fall at her feet and implore forgiveness. When he was away his suspicions withered and his love revived. Fear of his own deficiency as a lover made him write cynically of love-making and declare that the birth of a child was all the satisfaction a decent woman should expect from the sexual act, but if returning from one of his trips he found his desire for his wife renewed, his whole life was transfigured. Edvard Brandes, himself newly married, advised the Strindbergs to separate as they were evidently getting on so badly. Strindberg replied that now that he had 'cleaned his home of the hellish modern women who for a time had made his marriage insufferable,' he was 'living the most agreeable family life imaginable—with never a hard word'; and in one of these rosy periods, when he had just come back from Vienna and his dark side was dormant, he wrote a happy romantic tale which was immediately printed in a Danish magazine.

Thus, dizzily swinging between love and hatred, doubt and faith, Strindberg poured out his autobiography in the form of a long detailed novel, but as he wrote the urge to express himself dramatically returned. He could compose long descriptive passages, but where essential character was concerned, he must create figures larger than life and, through their concentration, more powerful than living people. Moreover he was sure that it was the duty of an author, however grim his message, to avoid being tedious.

The trend in France following Zola and de Maupassant was to present truth undisguised, and Strindberg now began to think out a form of tense domestic drama in which to manifest the vital war of the sexes. Two Swedish painters in Paris, man and wife, who had each submitted a picture to the Salon, gave him his theme of woman's vain but dangerous attempt to usurp man's place. And so, for the first time since writing *Lucky Peter's Journey*, more than four years before, late in 1866 Strindberg set to work on a play. He called it *The Marauders*, for the husband said to the wife: 'It's strange how you want to maraud and plunder what we have battled for while you were at your cooking.' Bonnier had had enough of the woman question and declined the play, so Strindberg went on with his autobiography, composing at the same time on his bright side another novel of fishing life, while on his dark side he conceived a violent tragedy. Whatever anyone else might think, Strindberg was convinced that his new conception of drama was sound.

Paternity had been for him a profound experience. He had felt his wife's pregnancies in his own bones and blood and recognised that he was more consciously a father than were most men—in this respect he had achieved the greater awareness for which he was always striving. When it dawned on him that possibly the children were not his, he was poisoned at the very root of his being, and although at times he seemed cured, the poison continued to act and spread. He worked his way back through every phase of his life with Siri von Essen to that first pregnancy on account of which she had recalled him from Paris. Was that first child his—that child which had died at birth? But was it dead—had that infant really died, or had she been simply hidden away by an unnatural mother who did not want her theatrical career jeopardised? Money trickled through Siri von Essen's fingers. What had she done with it if she had not been paying for the maintenance of that forsaken child? Strindberg wrote to Stockholm for a copy of the death certificate, but it did not come. He opened Siri's letters and set traps for her, but still found no point of certainty. He was consumed with doubt, and this was the most terrifying thought of all, that perhaps he would never find out the truth, never meet the enemy face to face, but be haunted for the rest of his life by hidden, mocking shapes.

Was his wife demon or angel? While he groped through the fogs, she walked with the dignity of innocence; when he flung himself weeping at her feet, she took him back and folded him to her breast. Ah yes, she liked him to be weak, she liked him to be a sickly helpless child! She thought he was sick. More than once she suggested that he should see a doctor, but he understood the meaning behind her words. She believed he was mad; she was planning to have him shut up. He studied the literature of insanity and watched his own symptoms; he consulted a Danish alienist and was furious when the doctor refused to give an opinion unless he had the patient under long observation. But one thing was quite clear to Strindberg: whatever his wife and his so-called friends might think, his brain was clearer and stronger than ever before. He had never been more sure of his talent. He determined to crystallise his agony and create a drama in which the intolerable sufferings of a father blazed out to the world.

CHAPTER NINE

1887–1889

It's as if I'm walking in my sleep, as if life and imagination fused
Letter to Axel Lundegård, Copenhagen, November 1887

WHEN IN the spring of 1887 Strindberg began to write *The Father*, he and Siri both knew that their marriage was finally doomed. She did not need to read her husband's words to perceive that the dark side was winning, and Strindberg could no longer see Siri von Essen for the appalling image of his own creation—Laura, the man-eater, who first destroyed her husband's heart and then his mind and finally his body, who told him that as he had now fulfilled his regrettably necessary functions as begetter and bread-winner, he must go.

Strindberg knew that he must go. He wrote to Stockholm to file a petition for divorce, but was informed that while both parties were domiciled abroad no action could be taken. And so, together still, yet utterly separated, the couple lived first at Lindau in Bavaria and then in Copenhagen. He slept and worked in one room; she shared others with the children and nurse. He ceased to call Siri von Essen his wife, took her nowhere and did not pass on the invitations that old friends such as the Brandes sent her. She was his housekeeper and had been his mistress, that was all; if he had to refer to his marriage he spoke of it as too ludicrous an affair to be taken seriously. It was better to forestall ridicule and do the laughing himself.

He brought all the strength of his repressed dramatic urge to bear on *The Father*, whittling the theme down to stark bone. The concentrated force of Greek tragedy was in his mind, and he saw his hero as a modern Agamemnon, with a trace, too, of Othello. Iago murdered Othello without sword

114

or dagger by awakening his own deadly suspicions, and guilty
or not Desdemona aided the murder. She was a fine example
of woman's instinct to destroy her man, and Strindberg
originally conceived the wife in his play as such a figure, unconscious of her fearful destiny. But as he wrote, his hatred
dominated, and in the end he created Laura conscious of her
crime, analysing it, more in the manner of the hideous pair
in *Thérèse Raquin*, which had left a strong imprint upon his
mind.

As model for the Captain, the Father, Strindberg chose a
type of German he admired—a cavalry officer with a kindly
disposition and a love of the classics—but before long he had
forgotten all models. Life and writing fused; Laura became
Siri and Siri was lost in the woman who poisoned her husband's
mind by suggesting that the child he loved was not his own,
and then tricked him into evidence of insanity, until at last
he was utterly helpless, her captive in a strait-jacket. This
was how Strindberg now saw himself, and he wrote out the
agony of his uncertainty.

LAURA: And as to your suspicions about the child, they are quite
groundless.
CAPTAIN: That's the most terrible part of it. If there were any founda-
tion for them, at least one would have something to catch hold of,
to cling on to. As it is there are only shadows that hide in the
undergrowth and thrust out their heads to laugh. It's like fighting with air or . . . with blank cartridges. The deadly reality would
have roused resistance, nerved body and soul to action. But, as it
is, my thoughts dissolve into mists and my brain grinds in a
vacuum until it catches fire.

Strindberg's admiration for Zola encouraged him not to
soften the horror of the action, yet compassion broke out in
him—and nostalgic memory:

. . . When you were young, Laura, and we used to walk in the
birch-woods, . . . glorious, glorious! Think how fair life was, and
how it is now. You didn't want it to become like this, nor did I. . . .

The moment *The Father* was finished it was snapped up by
the publishers and translated into Danish, German and
French, and not many weeks passed before the *première* was
announced at the Copenhagen Casino. Strindberg was in a

state of acute nervous tension: the critics were too much interested and the publicity too good; news of the projected divorce and also of Strindberg's visit to the alienist had reached the Danish papers, and these facts, combined with rumours of his madness, composed a lurid portrait of the author.

His reply, however, was already planned. He had now written four volumes of his autobiography—*The Son of a Maidservant, Fermentation Time, In the Red Room* and *The Author*. The fifth volume, on which he was at work, was to tell the true story of his marriage. He was writing it in French so that it would be sure of a public. *Le Plaidoyer d'un Fou* would show that he was not quite the fool they took him for.

Meanwhile, although he no longer considered Siri von Essen his wife, before they moved to Copenhagen he wrote to her relatives there, warning them not to receive her perverted friend Marie David. He was still exchanging friendly letters himself with Sofie Holten, but he was determined that Siri von Essen and Marie David should never meet again. He could not endure to think that these women shared a happiness from which he was excluded.

The Danish translation of *The Father* had been made by the Swedish author Axel Lundegård, a young admirer to whom during the stress of production Strindberg turned both for comfort and advice, and who was distressed by the brilliant author's hysterical state and his isolation from his wife. When, on December 12th, 1887, two nights before the *première*, Strindberg was gripped once again by a nostalgic longing for death, it was to this young man he wrote his last bidding. 'It is possible that in a fit of romanticism I might take myself off. I do not know. . . .' He gave exact directions for the disposal of his works, but his first injunction to Lundegård was to reinstate his wife by drawing a veil of obscurity over everything—for the sake of the children 'who have given meaning to my life.' At the end of this long letter he explained:

I don't know if *The Father* is an invention or if my life has been so, but I feel that at a given moment, not far off, this will be revealed to me, and then I shall crash either into insanity from agony of conscience or into suicide. Through inventing so much my life has become a shadow life—I seem to be no longer walking on earth but swinging without gravity in an atmosphere not of air but of darkness. If light falls into this darkness I collapse crushed.

Queer thing, in a dream often recurring at night, I feel myself flying, without gravity, find it altogether natural; at the same time all sense of right, wrong, true, untrue is lost to me and it seems that everything that happens, however unusual, must happen. . . .

When the first night came Strindberg managed to drag himself to the theatre and watch the audience, amazed, shaken, shocked by the awful human drama played out upon the stage. Hunderup, the theatre's new actor-manager who took the leading part, had done his work well and Strindberg's macabre figures lived. There was a horrifying tension in the house when the strait-jacket came into play, and Strindberg scarcely knew how it was that his own limbs were free.

Some of the critics protested against the play's violence, but one and all acknowledged that its author was a genius. The play was at once put on in Stockholm, but the Swedish audience was outraged. People walked out to demonstrate their disgust, and after the ninth performance the play was withdrawn. Mingled with Strindberg's annoyance was satisfaction at feeling himself too honest and strong for his smug countrymen—besides it was always a disadvantage in one's own country to be in advance of the times. He was writing for those robust enough to face the truth—and he sent off a copy of *The Father* in French translation to Émile Zola. The eminent French author greeted Strindberg as a colleague; he had certain criticism to offer—the social setting was not clear enough, the nameless 'Captain' and the other characters did not give him the complete sense of life he demanded; but none the less Zola affirmed that *The Father* was one of the few dramatic works which had really moved him, and he offered to write a preface for the French edition.

This recognition was all the more sweet to Strindberg as when, after the publication of *The Red Room*, which earned him the title of 'the Swedish Zola,' he had first read the Frenchman's novels, he came to the conclusion that Zola had already done all that he had in mind to do himself, and that he was therefore superfluous. But now he had created a dramatic form of his own and was accepted as a

117

playwright; already he was working on another 'naturalist' drama of a similar kind—*Miss Julie*—and for this he wrote a preface expounding his theatre theory.

Managers demanded farce, as if the joy of life consisted in being idiotic, but Strindberg explained that he himself found the joy of life in the attempt to understand its tense and cruel struggles. He did not think that there was anything really new in the subject-matter of *Miss Julie*—it was simply a study of one aspect of evil and offered no solution. But, while acknowledging his debt to the brothers de Goncourt and other naturalist playwrights, he felt that his method of faithful reproduction was particularly his own. Ever since writing *Master Olof*, in order to be true to life he had given his characters mixed motives, changeable personalities and the irregular speech of thought. There were no tricks in his work —he noticed the interest in psychology of the younger generation and intended the audience 'to see the wires . . . to examine the box with the false bottom, to handle the magic ring and find the joints, to have a look at the cards and see how they are marked.'

For his views on *décor* Strindberg now turned towards the Impressionists. His first reaction to this school of painting had been one of bewilderment, but now he sympathised with its fight against artificial realism. He conceived scenery that would aid instead of hindering imagination, and worked out his theories of production in great detail, hoping soon to have a theatre of his own in which to put them into practice.

More stimulating even than his first letter from Émile Zola was his first letter from Friedrich Nietzsche. Georg Brandes had been lecturing on this new prophet, now wandering in sickness and solitude from one European health resort to another, and Nietszche's work came to Strindberg as a revelation.

'Buy yourself a German modern philosopher called *Nietszche*,' he wrote to Heidenstam. . . . '*Everything* to read is there. Don't deny yourself this pleasure. N. is a poet too.' And as he read he continued to send his friend eulogies of the stimulating philosophy of the superman. Now Georg Brandes described Strindberg to Nietszche as 'Sweden's one genius, though like most geniuses a trifle mad,' and Nietszche

118

responded by assuring Strindberg of his, Nietszche's, un-equalled genius, and asking his advice about the translation of his works.

... Such as I am, the most independent and perhaps the strongest mind living to-day ... it is impossible that the absurd boundaries which an accursed dynastic nationalist policy has drawn between peoples, should hold me back and prevent me from greeting those few who have ears to hear me. ...

The Strindbergs by this time were existing in a kind of materialised nightmare. Through a gypsy woman, whose son was employed there, they had heard of cheap rooms in an old castle at Holte not far from Copenhagen, and had settled down in the greatest filth and discomfort with a mad Countess who played a hurdy-gurdy, the gypsy steward who practised hypnotism, his fifteen-year-old sister who made advances to Strindberg and then accused him of seducing her, and a pack of untrained dogs. From the midst of this extraordinary *ménage* Strindberg wrote back to Nietszche in Italy, telling him that in *Also sprach Zarathustra* he had without doubt 'given man-kind its most profound book,' but by no means supporting his wish to be translated into 'our Greenland language.' 'Why not into French or English?' he wrote. 'You can judge our intelligence from the fact that people want to shut me up in an asylum on account of my tragedy.' But he warned Nietszche, too, that it was impossible to find a French translator who did not improve on one's style according to the conventions of rhetoric and so rob it of originality. He enclosed one of his own articles in French to show how he himself had now acquired 'a witty boulevard style,' and offered to do the translation himself, if Nietszche would be patient and not mind considerable expense, since he was penniless and had a family to provide for, and also would have to do the work 'as a poet, not as an artisan.' On second thoughts, Strindberg did not think Nietszche should bother about England; the country appeared to be given over to women, 'a sure sign of deca-dence,' and was only concerned with 'a library for girls of good family—Currer Bell, Miss Braddon and the rest. ...'

Strindberg's letter delighted Nietszche and so did *The Father*, which the author sent him in French translation,

119

though he did not approve of Zola's preface. It amazed
Nietszche to find his own conception of love-hatred so power-
fully portrayed, and he at once told Strindberg that the play
was destined for André Antoine's Théâtre Libre. 'Simply
demand this of Zola.'

Nietszche was right. *The Father* was exactly the kind of
play André Antoine was looking for. This young business man
with a passion for the stage gave all his spare time to amateur
acting, and he had now conceived it as his mission to purge
the Paris theatre of romantic artificiality and substitute for it
the real life Zola called for 'with its shiver, its breath and its
strength.' To this end Antoine had taken a large room in the
Place Pigalle, called it le Théâtre Libre and gathered a group
of enthusiasts about him. Already it had become the rendezvous of the Paris *avant-garde*, and Antoine saw that *The
Father* would be a valuable addition to his repertoire.

Thérèse Raquin, Zola's own stage version of his novel,
Tolstoy's *Powers of Darkness*, and plays by the brothers
de Goncourt, Émile Fabre, Villiers and de Maupassant were
among Antoine's first selections for his theatre of revolution,
and Strindberg was proud to join such company. Ibsen's
Ghosts was also on Antoine's list, but Strindberg hoped that
The Father might steal a march on 'the Norwegian blue-
stocking.' He had come to the conclusion that *The Wild Duck*
was a cynical description of his, Strindberg's, marriage and
implied that he, like the photographer in the play, had taken
money from his wife's former lover, and that the first child
had been another's. He thought of Ibsen now, therefore, not
only as a foolish advocate of woman's emancipation, but as a
dangerous personal enemy, and here was a chance to outstrip
him, as his rival had not yet had a play performed in Paris.
For the rest the Théâtre Libre was after Strindberg's heart;
he had dreamt of a theatre where art and experiment rather
than greed and vanity were the motives, where the bourgeois
and the conventional were banned and the response of the
intelligent not drowned by the catcalls of the philistines.

He readily agreed to write more plays for Antoine, but
instead of going to Paris to join his group, where he feared to
find himself again oppressed by other people's aggressiveness
—he himself could only strike with his pen, and in personal

120

contact remained timid—Strindberg continued with the project of forming an experimental theatre of his own—a Scandinavian Théâtre Libre. He was established now in Denmark; the brothers Brandes had ridiculed Personne's pamphlet in the Danish Press and proclaimed their friend a moralist. His books and plays were translated into Danish, German and French, and there was immediate interest in everything he did. He was recognised as a leading Naturalist, although in fact his conception of dramatic character was larger than life. He intended his own theatre, besides Antoine's, to perform *Miss Julie*, with Siri von Essen in the part of this decadent woman for whom no end was possible but to take her own life with her lover's razor. And now, while trying to raise funds, he wrote a group of cynical one-act plays with his 'Independent Theatre' in mind. First came *Creditors*, a tragicomedy of two husbands and a siren, then *Pariah*, a male dialogue based on a friend's short story, next *The Stronger*, a sketch of two women, only one of whom spoke, and finally *Samum*, a brief tragedy of the Arabian desert. It seemed to Strindberg that these plays with *Marauders*, now ironically renamed *Comrades*, and his two big tragedies made an excellent repertoire with which to open a theatre. Besides playing the leading parts, which, he felt, suited her all too well, Siri von Essen was to translate material from the Théâtre Libre and manage the business.

How she was to do all these things, Siri could not imagine, but she welcomed any chance to return to the stage. Above everything now she wanted her freedom, but while she was still tied by law to Strindberg, only acting could make her life tolerable. She thought that they had already reached the lowest point possible in the union of two human beings, but since the correspondence with Nietzsche, Strindberg was even more difficult to live with. His talk was full of blasphemy —he proclaimed Christianity a religion for 'women, eunuchs, children and savages' and flaunted his contempt for Jesus Christ in the hearing of the children. Siri had no strong conviction of the deity of Christ, but she had passed on to her children the simple beliefs of her own childhood, and she was shocked when, in answer to his four-year-old son's question if God could see in the dark, Strindberg answered, 'No, but

Pappa can.' Siri detested the very name of Nietszche, who encouraged her husband to think he was God, when he could not even provide properly for his family. The children went about in rags, yet she and Ebba must wash and stitch and press to have the master's clothes immaculate, and she must slave to give him the kind of food he liked; otherwise he was ill or made a scene.

But even while on the one hand he wondered if he were a superman, and on the other tried to explain everything in terms of materialism, Strindberg's sense and fear of the supernatural remained, and his imagination was now further stimulated by reading the work of Edgar Allan Poe. He recognised so much of himself in Poe's work that when he discovered that the American had died in 1849, the year of his own birth, he began to wonder if he were not a reincarnation of this writer, or if at least Poe's genius had not been transmitted to him by cerebral vibration. The idea was tempting, and Strindberg now saw his life as a sinister mystery very like a Poe story. His wife sometimes appeared an old bent witch, brewing potions—he had agonising headaches again and wondered if perhaps the plot was to poison him instead of shutting him up as insane. When finally the gypsy steward threatened to shoot him, Strindberg fled from the castle, but returned shortly to an hotel at Holte, and turned the summer's strange experiences into a novel—*Tschandala*. His greatest preoccupation, however, was still with Nietszche, and from here he wrote to Edvard Brandes:

... my spirit life has received in its uterus a tremendous outpouring of seed from Friedrich Nietszche, so that I feel as full as a pregnant bitch. He is the man for me.

In the same letter, after discoursing on all his theatrical plans, Strindberg added:

Frightfully nervous, and mild persecution mania after stormy days and sleepless nights. Walk about with revolver and *mankiller* to protect my blond boy from the gipsies' kidnapping plans. ...

Strindberg had of late received from Nietszche agitated incoherent notes, which none the less had such a wild ring of self-exaltation—as for instance in the signature 'Nietszche

Caesar'—that he had taken his words as a jest. But now Georg Brandes informed him that this was no jest; it was the madness which Nietszche's friends had long feared would be the outcome of his megalomania, and indeed news soon came that the philosopher had been sent to an asylum. Mingled with Strindberg's deep compassion for the giant whose brain had broken under the strain of genius was sheer panic. He had been impressed by Nietszche's self-esteem, but he recognised its abnormal proportions, and now saw it mirrored in himself. Nietszche had infected him with his own vainglory— how then should his mind withstand the further infection? It already felt like 'an overcharged Leyden jar.'

All literature now appeared to Strindberg to treat of two subjects alone—woman's infidelity and madness—and usually of both. Bacon's wife deceived him and his frenzy stained the pages of Shakespeare. It was said that Guy de Maupassant suspected his mother of adultery—and now his brain too was giving way. At the asylum at Gheel there was a man who thought he was a Rothschild—but who, Strindberg asked himself, was to prove that he wasn't? Who was to say that he or Nietszche or any other man was really mad? This was the way he too would end. All of them, every one of them who tried to find and follow truth would meet in Gheel—yet nothing would be proved.

Only about his theatre project could Strindberg be rational, and all that winter, while he stayed at an hotel and Siri and the children lived with relatives, they laboured to get together players, premises and backing. In March 1889 they opened the Scandinavian Experimental Theatre, but after single performances of *Miss Julie* and *Creditors* in Copenhagen and Malmö they abandoned the project. Not only had they insufficient funds, but the business was too nerve-racking. In addition to the inevitable stress of a theatrical enterprise, as soon as Strindberg saw Siri working with other people he was again overpowered with jealousy and suspicion. It was clear that she no longer loved him, then she must love another, others—she must love and have loved others.

He wrote bidding her give up the stage again and leave the money-making to him. It would only take four weeks to write one of his rustic novels which was sure to make money, and more would be forthcoming from plays and other work. But Siri had had enough; her health and her spirit were broken and she only wanted to be left alone. Sadly, yet with the elation he always felt when he turned his face homewards, on April 1st, 1889, his son's fifth birthday, August Strindberg returned alone to Sweden. Except for the few weeks of the trial he had been away six years.

CHAPTER TEN

1889–1893

My children are my idée fixe

EVEN NOW the beauty of the Swedish summer did not fail to melt Strindberg's heart; the islands called him and once again he found refuge in a fisherman's hut. He was generally disliked now by his own countrymen, yet he drew strength from his native soil, and living here alone as in his student days he believed he would find peace. He wrote to Siri that this was how he wanted to live—as a monk and a hermit—that thus away from them, he would provide for the children by his work, and he and she could still be friends. Yet before he reached the end of the letter he had broken into abuse, called Siri an evil woman and commanded her to get out of his life. As soon as he had posted it he was in anguish and wrote another summoning her back. He considered the family an organic whole and to cut off his wife and children was to amputate his own limbs. 'Come back to me with the children and I will protect you.' When she did not answer, despair mastered him and he wrote again, describing his desire to take his own life; when still there was no word he warned her that unless she returned at once he would get himself a new wife and new children—and a week later he wrote: 'Siri, I am dying bit by bit and still I cannot hate you.'

Except for a few notes about purely practical matters, Siri von Essen kept silence. Over and over again she had taken her husband back; now her feeling for him was dead—she could not react to any of his moods. When he fled from the castle at Holte she had consulted a lawyer, and now she was only waiting for her freedom. She was in correspondence with Marie David about her future; all her friends urged her to return to the stage, but she was no longer certain if she could.

For one thing her health was precarious, for another she must keep some kind of home for the children, and even if these difficulties were removed there was a further obstacle; she was too old for young parts now and too young for old ones. Her chance to become a great actress was over, and she thought it might be wiser to earn her living by teaching dramatic art and translating plays from the French. After a while she took the children back to Sweden, and Strindberg flitted ever more fitfully in and out of their lives, until at last he went away and came no more.

The children understood that now a more fundamental change had occurred in their lives than usual. They were well used to moves and journeys—'train' was the first word young Hans had learnt—nor was it a novelty for their father to be away. But they felt that this going was different; they knew that their mother was unhappy and unwell, and that although Pappa was generally so gentle with them, he was not always kind to Mamma. And when presently Siri told Karin, the eldest girl, that Pappa was not going to live with them any more, the mind of the eleven-year-old child was filled with relief. Although Strindberg was kind to all children, yet the nerves of his own were overstrung when he was at home. They were happier this way, and happier still when one day in the middle of winter, while the little wooden house stood deep in snow, Marie David came driving in a sleigh, looking so like a young man in her fur coat and cap that Ebba actually flew to her mistress with the news that a gentleman was calling. Siri von Essen, desperate for money—Strindberg constantly promised sums that were not forthcoming—had written to her friend, now living once more in Paris, asking for a loan. In reply Marie David came herself and roused the morose household to gaiety. She had *chic*, and with her furs, her crocodile-skin cases, her silver-topped jars, her short red hair and exotic Danish accent, she was like a fairy godmother to the children, while to Siri von Essen she was the friend who with her generous, unquestioning love brought her happiness at last.

Dejectedly Strindberg returned to Stockholm to pass the long winter alone. The city was growing and becoming rapidly modernised; it no longer felt like home, and he had lost touch with many of his friends. Even Verner von Heidenstam, who had been his faithful ally, had brought out a pamphlet condemning Naturalism, and Strindberg felt that his own country had no further use for him. He sat in his old café drinking absinthe and succumbing to the misery of his thoughts. Sometimes he believed that his voice was failing from lack of use—when he looked in a mirror the eyes he saw were those of one in solitary confinement. He was utterly defeated. Even his injunction to Siri von Essen to keep Marie David out of the house so that his children should not be polluted was ignored. He missed them painfully, and to think of Marie David taking his place in their lives was torment. He made arrangements to leave his possessions to his unmarried sister Elisabeth, so that they should be safeguarded for his children and not fall into the hands of Siri's friend, but this precaution brought him little comfort. When good weather returned he wandered from one part of Sweden to another, collecting material for a book on Swedish nature. Nature alone was true, although he now saw all her activity as a vain attempt to check the inevitable process of degeneration. Still she was beautiful, and alone worthy of his love, and once again he took up his brush and painted her portrait. He worked strenuously at the technique of this art and gradually evolved a style of his own, with a vigorous dramatic quality that was also capable of great tenderness. Painting gave relief to his overcharged brain, and presently his industry was rewarded by an exhibition of his landscapes in a Stockholm gallery. Like his writings about nature, this work contained nothing to horrify or to wound, although sometimes the rocky cliffs so faithfully portrayed, when turned upside down revealed the profile of the painter.

The last act of his life with Siri von Essen must now be played. Each knew that the end had come, yet neither would give in. She claimed her freedom on grounds of her husband's mental instability, cruelty and desertion, but it was Strindberg who finally petitioned for divorce, and declared that she was unfit to bring up his children. He lived in lodgings now in a provincial town—his main contacts with human beings soul-destroying interviews with his lawyer and humiliating interrogations by the Church Council. The thought of losing the children haunted him; he could not sleep and he had no idea how to get hold of any money. His Naturalist plays had been well received in Berlin, although *The Father* was now banned, but the contracts were always so contrived that of all concerned the author got the smallest share of the profits. Even if he were to write again, clearly he could not depend on his pen to support his children, so he wrote to his brother Axel and certain of his friends about finding work. Should he become a journalist once more, or take a commercial examination and try to get a post on the strength of his foreign languages?

The case came up soon after Strindberg's forty-second birthday, and in his sick mind merged with memories of that first divorce through which Siri von Essen had been set free from Baron Wrangel. The proceedings then had so revolted Strindberg that he had fled to Paris as from a heap of offal. Now he must endure a worse stench; the intimate details of his life with Siri von Essen were exposed without reticence or mercy. They who had loved one another—and at moments he knew that he loved her still—fought like a pair of wounded beasts. Siri von Essen was determined to have the custody of the children. It was as if one of Strindberg's own tragedies were performed in the Court of Justice.

On the 24th March 1891, August Strindberg and Siri von Essen were granted a one year's judicial separation, pending the decree absolute, the wife keeping the children and the husband contributing to their maintenance. The last curtain had fallen and Strindberg had lost everything he loved. He could not get the children out of his mind, and to ease his grief composed a melancholy phantasy in which a blacksmith, whose three beloved children had died, travelled the world with Don Quixote, Sancho Panza and St. Peter, who showed him that on earth there was no heaven—but only its gate called death. He wrote *The Keys of Heaven* mostly in verse, and it contrasted strangely with the Naturalist plays that had poured from his pen for the last five years.

When, three years before, Strindberg wrote *Le Plaidoyer d'un Fou*, he had believed he was ready to die. As far as possible he had put his affairs in order and had sent the revealing manuscript to his cousin Oscar Strindberg, for posthumous publication. Now that he had nothing left in life, he found he did not want to die. His despair was so absolute that it became a satisfaction. He was curious to see how far fate could carry her persecution, and he greeted each new misfortune with malicious pleasure. He felt that to endure so much he must be a giant among men, a notion confirmed by the fact that the few men who still supported him were themselves giants, such as the Brandes brothers, Björnson, Lie and young Knut Hamsun.

The desire for a theatre of his own had not left Strindberg, and new plans were afoot. With this incentive and the stimulus of complete cynicism he returned to the Naturalist vein and dashed off half a dozen biting one-act plays—*Debit and Credit, The First Warning, Facing Death, Mother Love, Playing With Fire* and *The Bond*. In all these plays he portrayed the horror and futility of his own life, and the last was the scene of his divorce. But the theatre did not materialise, and Strindberg found himself in a welter of unplayed and unpublished scripts. Suddenly he found that he had written himself out—that he had been robbed not only of his children but of his talent. He was finished with domestic strife, with literature and the theatre.

Two things alone interested Strindberg now—science and evil. As the last shreds of goodness had been torn from him, he was determined to delve down into evil, to discover its power and use it, and he wanted at the same time to explore matter for himself. He considered that scientists had imposed materialism on the world without themselves knowing enough about it. They took things at their face value— accepted, for instance, certain substances such as sulphur and gold as elements, without sufficient proof that these substances could not be further reduced or split, and he considered the scientific attitude towards supernatural phenomena defeatist. In his writing August Strindberg had exposed truth; now he had no more to say, he would discover truth instead.

But to research he must have money, and so far his attempts to find work had failed. He thought if he could get abroad again it would be easier to earn; he contemplated becoming a hall porter in a hotel or playing the guitar in a variety show, but he had not even money for the fare. He had already sold or pawned most of his possessions, including his precious Swiss

129

camera; now even his books were going in order to buy food, and Siri von Essen's alimony often fell short.

The homeland which, in spite of his condemnation, he yearned for in his years of exile became a prison in which he relived his youth. But in the skerries, as he could afford no apparatus, once again he concocted devices for scientific experiments from junk thrown away by the cottagers, and old ambition woke. Before ten years had passed, he assured the few friends with whom he still kept in touch, he would be a professor and a member of the Swedish and French Academies. And even if he wrote no more himself, he saw his will active in another writer. *Hedda Gabler* was on in Copenhagen, and as soon as Strindberg read this play he believed he had fathered it. He considered the character of Ejlert Lövborg feeble—how could one believe in the talent of a man who shot himself for so slight a cause? But it was clear to him that Hedda Gabler herself was a close relative of Laura in *The Father* and Tekla in *Creditors*, and when, a little later, *The Master Builder* appeared, the connection with his own *The Secret of the Guild* seemed obvious. 'See now,' he wrote to the young Swedish author Birger Mörner, 'how my seed has fallen in Ibsen's brain-pan—and germinated. Now he carries my semen and is my uterus. This is *Wille zur Macht* and my desire to set others' brains in molecular motion.'

It was many months before means came to leave Sweden and then they came distastefully. While in Copenhagen he had come to know the Swedish writers Ola Hansson and his wife Laura Marholm, and had used a novel of Hansson's as the theme of his one-act play *Pariah*. Now without his permission, this couple, who were living in Germany, published one of Strindberg's letters to them in a Berlin paper, with a note explaining the author's plight. Strindberg was in no position to refuse the financial aid this action brought him, and he also accepted the Hanssons' invitation to stay with them at Friedrichshagen, but he was ashamed of such indirect begging. However, his prospects of making money in Germany were reasonably good.

He had now succumbed to the temptation to send the autobiographical work *A Fool's Defence* to a German publisher, partly to make money, partly to counteract the prevalent

notion that Siri von Essen was a martyr who had been married
to a monster. He knew that it was an evil book and that by
publishing it he was committing an outrage, not only on Siri
but on his own heart, but this knowledge only strengthened
his resolution. He had done with good and such an act fed his
perpetual sense of guilt. He enjoyed the irony of sending Siri
von Essen money advanced on this book which she had not
read, but which would shortly expose her to the world. Still,
at times, his perfidy disgusted him. Then he was glad that he
had forsaken letters for science, that he would no longer have
any occasion 'to use his own wife as a rabbit for his vivisec-
tions or to flay his friends and offer the skins for sale.'

At Friedrichshagen he surrounded himself with scientific
tomes and plunged into study, but it was not easy for him to
live with other people, however friendly. He had a sense of
being watched, and he was particularly suspicious of his hostess,
who showed a keen interest in the last letters he had received
from Nietszche. The thought of that brilliant spirit shut away
in an asylum was never far from his mind; Laura Marholm
had begged help for Strindberg—she had hurt his pride, and
now he was not sure that she had no part in a conspiracy to
prove that he too was mad. In any case he needed more
privacy for his work and more freedom for his temperament,
so in the winter of 1892 he moved in to Berlin.

The routine of research irked him as much now as in his
young days as a medical student; he had a profound respect
for fact, but no patience with systematic analysis and classifica-
tion, and it seemed absurd to go over ground well covered
before. Fact for Strindberg was not something to rest upon,
but a challenge to go further, and any boundary was an invitation to cross it. He ignored the accepted limitations of science;
beyond chemistry was alchemy, beyond astronomy astrology,
beyond the natural the supernatural, and all must be explored.
In his sparsely furnished room with its big easel, its piles of
books on the floor, its table bearing chemical apparatus instead
of manuscripts, he carried out experiments of his own devising.
He aimed at proving that sulphur and nitrogen, which
chemists assumed to be elements, were in fact compounds,
and he was also exploring the nature of gold; but although he
felt the urge to make these experiments, he was conscious at

the same time of waiting for a revelation. This might or might not come through the medium of another person, but in any case now he wanted company, so long as it was of his own choosing and he could escape at will. He had been alone too long; he wanted wine and warmth and music to help him forget his broken love, his lost children and the frozen hours of winter.

In his rôle of devil Strindberg let his hair grow wilder even than before, cultivated a small Mephistophelian beard, wrapped himself and his guitar in a voluminous cape and sought oblivion at Zum Schwarzen Ferkel, a tavern off Unter den Linden, made famous by Heine and Hoffman and enjoying a libertine reputation. Hither came Knut Hamsun, eminent among young Norwegians, and Adolf Paul, the Finnish author, Dagny Juel—nicknamed Aspasia—a fascinating Norwegian with whom half the circle was in love, Stanislav Przybyszewski, a Polish writer known as the world's most melancholy alcoholic, and many other writers and artists of every nationality.

Strindberg found himself at once the centre of attention. Champagne flowed from bottles whose tops were sliced off by canes, brandy was drunk like water, ribaldry and wisdom mingled until the long hours of the night gave way to dawn. He was surrounded with disciples and admirers, poets made verses in his honour, women offered him their bodies—here was the excess, the sense of sin and power that he craved. He played the Don Juan; it amused him to refute his reputation as a woman-hater, he insisted always that he was a woman-lover, and in any case women loved *him*, but though he posed as a roué, he did not carry his conquests far. He had a fleeting passion for Aspasia, but he still shrank from casual relations with women, partly on account of his fastidiousness, partly because he was unsure of himself. If he were to have sexual satisfaction it could only be through another marriage, and he already believed that one day, when means permitted, he would marry again, although he feared such an action would be an infidelity to his children.

Adolf Paul became his close friend, but the habitué of Zum Schwarzen Ferkel who interested Strindberg most was Stanislav Przybyszewski. The Polish writer regarded life as a prank of the devil and the soul as a sexual phantasy, and he was a keen student of perversion, insanity and such phenomena as hallucinations and the splitting of the personality. Once more Strindberg experienced a magnetic pull towards another's mind, although the Pole's emotionalism embarrassed him. At one time he would cover Strindberg's hands with kisses and at another offer him the freedom of his mistress. It suited Strindberg better when Stanislav expressed his feelings by playing Chopin on the tavern piano until the whole riotous company fell into a sentimental trance.

Yet, although such demonstrations made Strindberg blush, for while enjoying his fame he was still personally shy, his views were expanding. He declared himself sick of dissecting character, but his interest in human emotion and behaviour was as strong as ever, and Berlin gave him fresh opportunities of study. Homosexuality was prevalent, and he saw the stupidity of dubbing as unnatural, emotions which quite clearly nature had created. Too little was known about this aspect of love for the views of moralists or alienists to bear any weight, and as far as he could see the only aspect of the subject which could be usefully discussed at present was its effect on the preservation of the species. The masculine woman appeared to him the product of the present false civilisation; she was not in herself a good specimen of humanity and she inevitably attracted the effeminate man. In the whole sex question the only thing that Strindberg was sure of was that man must grow strong again. There could be no new age, no good future at all for the human race, until man learned once again to approach love honestly without the pipe-dream of false sentiment. He must discover in love a source of strength instead of allowing it to weaken him.

CHAPTER ELEVEN

1893–1894

*I love her, and she loves me, and we hate each other with a wild
hatred, born of love*

INFERNO

IN JANUARY 1893, nearly a year after his divorce was made
absolute, at a big literary party in Berlin Strindberg met
Frida Uhl, a young Austrian journalist with ambitions to
become a writer. One of her dearest wishes was to know the
famous Swede and she set to work to captivate him. She had
big dark eyes and a sympathetic manner, and soon, in reaction
to long loneliness and silence, Strindberg was struggling in his
imperfect German to tell her about the two things uppermost
in his mind—his scientific and metaphysical research, and the
loss of his children. His love for them was the only emotion
he trusted; they had become his angels, fair beacons in an evil
world. 'Let my children know that their father never gave
them up,' he wrote to his cousin Gotthard Strindberg. 'Let
them speak kindly of their father without speaking ill of their
mother.' Bitter though he was about Siri von Essen, Strindberg
did not want the children polluted by evil thoughts of either
of their parents.

Frida Uhl, herself emotional, encouraged Strindberg to talk
of the children, and when he showed her the photographs
which he always carried, declared herself quite in love with
the fair-haired Hans in whom she saw so much of his father,
and suggested that when he had a home of his own again
Strindberg might at least have his small son to live with him.

Strindberg was touched though also a little alarmed by the
concern of his new friend. Frida Uhl gushed in a way foreign
to his Northern nature, and also, young as she was, showed a
decided inclination to manage him—but he could not resist
sympathy. Before long the Flying Dutchman cape was aban-

doned, and in conventional attire with a flower in his button-hole and a stiff hat balanced on his lion's mane, August Strindberg was calling on Frida Uhl in her daringly modern bachelor-girl appartment. Presently he was explaining the secret of the guitar to her—how its charm lay in the fact that it could never be tuned exactly—and playing her his own melody, the fragment he had composed for *Samum*. He took her to see his favourite contemporary picture, Böcklin's *Isle of the Dead*; he accompanied her on walks and to theatres and restaurants and watched himself once more giving his soul into a woman's keeping—aware of the peril but unable to resist the pleasure.

Frida Uhl played him cleverly, extolling her freedom, denouncing marriage bonds, lauding the joys of spiritual love. He could not help admiring her independence and the way in which she earned her own living as a newspaper corres-pondent; but sometimes, as when for instance she tried to pay the bill at a restaurant, his masculine pride was outraged and he determined to dominate her. He was uncertain if he were really attracted by her. From the day he had first caught sight of Siri von Essen in a mist of blue veils her beauty had captivated him—he could see it still—but some-times Frida Uhl looked ugly; sometimes she received him with ink on her fingers like an unattractive schoolgirl, but she could also bewitch him with pretty clothes and perfume.

After so much hatred it was seductive to feel himself loved once more; it awoke his belief in his own goodness, his hope of a second springtime. He showed Frida Uhl the best of him-self and felt this best growing; he recognised this as what people called 'the ennobling influence of love,' yet he knew that he was not in love with Frida Uhl, but only unable to do without a woman. Frida Uhl weaned him from Zum Schwarzen Ferkel and his new friends; he joined her circle of young intellectuals, and believed that without her he would sink back into intolerable loneliness. This, he suspected, was how she wanted him to be—weak, helpless, in her power; here again was Laura of *The Father* and Omphale. He saw that his only defence was in his own love—he must be strong; he must love this woman more than she loved him, do the wooing himself and win her by his virility.

When he kissed her she spoke of a magical current, and he believed then that they were intended to marry. His belief in telepathy and in his own power to destroy his enemies, heal the sick and make the weak strong, was steadily growing, and he intended Frida Uhl to aid his investigations. She was careful not to disparage any of August Strindberg's ideas, but she hoped that he would return quickly to drama. *Miss Julie*, banned in Denmark, delighted Berlin, and its preface had proved him a leader of new theatre.

Creditors was in production at the Residentz Theatre, and Strindberg had become a famous figure in literary Berlin. Clearly the way was open for growing success as a playwright —and Frida Uhl was ambitious both for him and for herself. But what Strindberg now most wanted to create was gold— he had already shown his young friend the glittering results of his experiments—strips of parchment bearing flakes of a gold-like substance which proved him on his way.

Nevertheless success in the theatre was dear to him, and he was galled by having so many works still unplayed. Frida Uhl saw clearly that the great Swede needed somebody to take care of his affairs.

The first time he proposed, she refused—declaring that marriage would stifle them and destroy their love, but once he had made up his mind he would not be thwarted. More than the dark ice must crack this spring—August Strindberg would be reborn with a young bride at his side.

As soon as they were engaged he was troubled. He would have to write to Siri von Essen and assure her that the children would lose nothing by his new attachment—he had already made it clear to Frida Uhl that there was no question at present of Hans leaving his mother. He would also have to inform other relatives and meet Frida Uhl's family, and the question of money would dominate once more. Frida had warned him that her father, Court Councillor Friedrich Uhl, Editor of the *Wiener Zeitung*, might not look favourably on his prospective son-in-law's finances, and as she was not yet of age she could not marry without parental consent. Nothing therefore was more natural than that she should tout Strindberg's manuscripts to editors and publishers and in general keep an eye on his concerns, yet he watched her behaviour with growing apprehension, suspecting that the disorder of his affairs gave her a sense of superiority, and that her pity for his loneliness was already changing to contempt. Presently he wrote forbidding her to concern herself any longer with his business. 'We shall see if our love cannot live on its own fire without this horrible nourishment.'

So he contemplated their love and their hatred growing side by side. They could no longer exist apart; when she went to Munich for a few weeks he plunged first into dissipation at Zum Schwarzen Ferkel and then was laid low by illness, and Frida Uhl rushed back to fill his attic with spring flowers and encourage him to dream; yet he was sure that this very dependence on each other bred mutual hatred.

Frida Uhl's parents had long ceased to share a *ménage*— the Councillor lived in apartments in the Hofburg and his wife spent most of the time at her father's estate in Moravia —so Maria Weyr, the married daughter, was used to playing mother to her younger sister. Before this infatuation for the Swedish dramatist, Frida had believed her heart broken by a married man, so Mitzi, as Maria Weyr was called in the family, was quite prepared to deal with the new entanglement. It was soon clear to her, however, from Frida's letters that, whether the family approved or not, her sister's marriage to August Strindberg was the only alternative to a first-class scandal.

As it turned out, their mother, Maria Uhl, who lived in a visionary Swedenborgian world of her own, was delighted at the news of the engagement, for misguided as she found some of Strindberg's views, his love of nature revealed his true soul to her, and she looked forward to becoming the mother-in-law of such a man. The Councillor, too, offered fewer objections than his daughters expected; to begin with, rumours of the engagement had already reached the papers, and then he also was not without admiration for the famous Swede, although he declared that he would rather give a laurel wreath than a daughter to the author of *The Father*. *Creditors* was to be produced in Vienna, and the Emperor had promised to attend the *première*, but Frida persuaded Strindberg not to go. She doubted the success of a meeting between her father and Strindberg, and did not breathe freely until Mitzi arrived in

157

Berlin, bringing her sister's dowry and birth certificate and Councillor Uhl's written consent to the marriage. It remained now for Strindberg to obtain the certificate of his divorce from the Swedish authorities, a task which he entrusted to his brother Oscar—the second brother on whom the mantle of the father had fallen, and who managed the family affairs including the trusteeship of August's children. In answer to his letter Siri von Essen wished her former husband well, and now the way was clear for a wedding in Heligoland, where the English minister dispensed with banns and did not object to marrying divorced persons.

Even so, the betrothed couple could not get through these last weeks without shattering breaks and exhausting reconciliations. Without love Strindberg had nearly perished, but now that it had returned, jealousy came too with a host of dark and desperate memories which he was not clear if he had lived through or created. Ghosts of the past assaulted him, and on the eve of the wedding journey he found himself in a Berlin street face to face with Carl Wrangel. His old friend, himself married to Sofia In de Betou, wished him luck, yet Strindberg felt his words more as a curse than as a blessing. Whatever he did he could not elude the past and his destiny.

He was glad that Mitzi was the only one of Frida's relatives he need meet at present, for it embarrassed him to think of playing the deferential son-in-law at the age of forty-four. In mock of the situation, and because Frida's sister took so seriously on her young shoulders the functions of Bride's Mother, he called her Mother-in-law, but although this made Maria Weyr—almost twenty years his junior— feel ridiculous, her first impression of Strindberg was favourable, and she hastened—with the penetrating Uhl intelligence, intensified by personal feeling—to describe him to her husband.

. . . Strindberg is at the bottom of his heart a most noble nature, gentle to the point of weakness. But he has a very sad life behind him, which often misguides him, and once he has formed an opinion, he sticks to it. His health is excellent, he has no bad habits. . . . In order to keep his personality intact he reads only works of science; as far as novels go, only Balzac and the French psychologists. He is unfit to deal with managers and publishers, his nerves cannot stand

138

it. As a result, he earns almost nothing. He has piles of manuscripts, stories, plays; he is the hardest worker in the world, but he is no business man. . . . Whenever he's not writing he paints—just as well as he writes. He has tried sculpture, too, and plays the guitar; there is nothing he can't do. He's the man to turn a desert island into a Paradise, but he is also the man to perish in the midst of civilisation out of sheer helplessness, shyness, fear of mockery. He doesn't understand fun, rarely jokes, continually believes himself persecuted and despised. He cannot walk on the shady side of the street. He speaks eight languages, including Chinese. He does not speak them well, but he has them at his command in writing—with the one exception of German, which he finds extremely difficult; nevertheless, he has got it into his head to reform the German language and drives his translators to despair.

He lives here in a small hotel, owns nothing but a trunk, has left all his furniture to his first wife, cannot make himself familiar with the idea of any permanency, never knows if he has any money, or how much he has. He goes to bed at nine o'clock, gets up at five, lives on almost nothing: vegetables, fish, claret.

He blushes like a young girl, at anything, and that lends his face a bewitching beauty. His mouth and his eyes, anyhow, are wonderful, the latter are as blue as a bright sea. There is much grey already in his hair and there are cruel furrows in his face—he is a man of fatal destiny. He goes on his knees before a flower, he can starve but will buy a pot of flowers. When he has got hold of an idea he can be savage with men, but he dares not even contradict a girl. . . . He will not know to-morrow what he has done to-day; nor does he remember what he has written. He works as in a trance; no sooner is something on paper than it vanishes from his mind. As a contrast the future is always present with him, he is brim full of ideas and plans of what he is going to write.

Being happily married to another man made it easier for Mitzi to deal with Strindberg's moods; she smoothed over difficulties and urged Frida to use *la main douce*, although she doubted the wisdom of this marriage. However, it could not be stopped, so she helped her sister to get her trousseau. Their mother wanted to give her daughter heavy handwoven underwear from the family linen closet, but the girls were out for flimsy garments of Parisian design; Frida had discovered that her fiancé liked lace and perfume and all the frou-frou of femininity. The marriage was front-page news, and Strindberg enjoyed this novel kind of publicity, but Maria Weyr, who was to chaperon the bridal couple to Heligoland and represent the family at the ceremony, could only relieve her feelings by further descriptions to her husband of their strange brother-in-law to be.

. . . It is impossible for you to imagine, and no more could I ever have imagined, what an astounding human species the people are among whom Frida now lives. They are most unnatural, unwholesome, eccentric, queer and odd, nothing but talent and not a spark of common sense, it is unbelievable. Strindberg towers high above them but he would be apt to drive an ordinary being like myself insane. I have never in my life met such a man before, there isn't the like of him—thank God! I shall not be able to stand it much longer. He weighs on my nerves like lead. At first he seems far better-looking and more attractive than in his pictures and there are moments when he looks much younger; but his face will abruptly change to that of an old man when, as often happens, he starts to brood all of a sudden and entirely forgets in the middle of a sentence that anyone is listening. He manages to remain absorbed in his thoughts for a quarter of an hour at a time, not saying a word and not hearing what is said to him. I can never shake off the fear of seeing him suddenly go insane. At the same time he more and more impresses me as a great genius. It sounds like a gruesome fairy-tale when he talks of his last winter in Sweden, when throughout the long nights he gave himself up to scientific experiments. It is terribly strenuous listening to his talk. You almost see how his thoughts work and rush ahead, and he can't catch up with his speech and suffers martyrdom. Half of what he says you must really guess. He also paints; there, too, he is a law unto himself, naturalistic symbolism he calls it. He finishes a picture in two or three days, he paints surprisingly well considering that he never learnt to paint. He is so full of talent that he doesn't seem to know what to do with it. But his is not a joyful way of creating. It is more like the savage impulse driving a murderer to his crime. To me he is uncanny. I cannot understand Frida, nor how she dares entrust her future to the hands of such a man. But these two can no longer be separated; on the contrary I must do all within my power to marry them as quickly as possible. I am afraid his love for her is mere passion; as an intellect she is not his equal, nor will any woman ever be. He does not seem to demand that either, his opinion of woman being the lowest possible. . . . Her love for Strindberg, as a contrast to his, seems utterly of the mind; she admires, nay, she idolises his genius. I do not believe she would ever dare embrace him if he did not permit or demand it first. God alone knows how this will end in the long run. My confidence in this marriage in these circumstances is very limited and I fear results. Frida, in her divine idiocy, expects from him heaven on earth. . . .

So the day came—a sunny May morning with the blooms of the chestnut trees in the Linden for wedding candles, as

140

the cab laden with luggage rolled down to the station. They had decided to stay a while in Heligoland, and in any case they had no home, so all their personal belongings travelled with them, including Strindberg's enamelled footbath, his basket of chemical apparatus and his green canvas bag of manuscripts and notes.

In spite of all the preparations, Strindberg had not yet received legal proof of his divorce, and they were six days on the island before the wedding could take place. It was the simplest possible affair, with Maria Weyr and a couple of pilots as witnesses. Then Mitzi took the next boat home, and Strindberg was alone with his bride.

They took rooms in one of the little white villas let by the fishermen in summer-time, and once again Strindberg put into practice his belief in marital privacy. They must each have their own room and be at liberty to come and go and lock the door; they must have time to think about one another, to relish each fresh meeting and not take love for granted.

Birds, flowers, sunshine and sea made a perfect setting and love swept away his fears. Once more Strindberg was in tune with nature and Frida found him a joyful and romantic companion. But after a few weeks his spirits flagged. He tried to write a novel, but it did not go well and he and his wife seemed to have nothing of interest left to talk about. It was as if through their very love they neutralised each other.

Letters from England determined their next move. They heard that William Heinemann, who was Ibsen's English publisher, was interested in a volume of Strindberg's poems in translation, and Justin Huntly McCarthy, the son of the historian, had translated *The Father* into English and written a long article about it in *The Fortnightly Review*. Now J. T. Grein, a young Dutchman with an admiration for André Antoine's Théâtre Libre, was starting an Independent Theatre in London, and asked permission to produce *The Father*. He already had on his list Browning, Zola, Ibsen and an interesting young Irish playwright called George Bernard Shaw. August Strindberg would be in good company and Grein urged him to come to London.

The news excited Strindberg, but at first he declined to go. He wanted to woo back happiness in this island refuge with

141

his bride. She, however, felt that a change was needed; in this seclusion he brooded over his lost children—he told her once that only a man felt true maternal love. And in any case they could not afford to miss any opportunity to make money—and London suited her ambitions.

A midsummer of sweltering heat found the honeymooners therefore sharing a brass-bound double bed in lodgings at Gravesend to which they had been recommended by the skipper of the boat. They were rescued from this plight by J. T. Grein, who offered them his Pimlico flat with his friend Bobbie Jeffreys as hostess, while he himself went abroad, but this hospitality did not outweigh disappointment. Grein was eager to produce *The Father,* but Strindberg had left the arrangements too late for it to be included in the first season's programme, and William Heinemann had gone to Italy without leaving any instructions about Strindberg's poems.

The heat continued, and much as Strindberg loved the sun, the London sultriness brought a nostalgia for the Baltic breezes. Nor could he abide the English fare Bobbie Jeffreys provided, and although the sights and smells of Pimlico recalled Charles Dickens, the great city alarmed him too. At Hamburg, on the way over, he had had an attack of agoraphobia which rooted him to the spot in surging traffic, and he felt that at any moment this paralysis might seize him again. In addition to the creatures of flesh and blood with whom his shyness and bad English made contact so difficult, he saw London peopled with ghosts, and now his own past made a fresh assault upon the present. He had made Frida Uhl swear that she would never read *A Fool's Defence,* but when without warning a copy of the German edition arrived, she opened it and read.

After this, although they did not confess it even to themselves, Strindberg and Frida Uhl had no hope of real happiness together. His soul was naked to her, black with the poison of hatred, yet still tormented by love. And in the fearful portrait of the wife, whom August Strindberg had first embraced and then pilloried before the eyes of the world, Frida Uhl saw not only Siri von Essen but herself. Now she was embraced—when would she too stand in the pillory?

The season was ended, the theatres closed and the people

142

the Strindbergs most wanted to see had gone away. There was no sense in staying longer in this unsympathetic city, but Frida did not want to leave. She had finished her education at a convent in Hampstead, knew English well and loved London. Besides, in spite of his injunction not to meddle with his business, they both knew that Strindberg was incapable of managing his affairs himself, and Frida thought she might do better for him alone. She had always had a secret inclination towards the stage, but she switched her ambition now towards the founding of a Strindberg Theatre. They had planned for this in Berlin, but the work already done by Grein might make London a better place to begin. Frida Uhl had imbibed all Strindberg's ideas of theatre reform, in which the love of the amateur and the student was to triumph over the greed, vanity and conservatism of the profession. She was eager to have a hand in this modern movement, and she was not hampered by shyness.

So, after less than three months of marriage, the couple parted. Strindberg joined a group of friends at Sellin on the island of Rügen, among whom was Adolf Paul, the Finnish writer who had been his shadow at Zum Schwarzen Ferkel, and with whom, to his relief, he could at last speak his own language again. He worked at a treatise on sulphur and cooled himself in the sea from the still blistering sunshine, while in London Frida Uhl awaited the return of Messrs. Heinemann and Grein, and wrote to the manager of the Imperial Theatre in Vienna, imploring him to produce another Strindberg play, or at least to announce this intention and so rouse the interest of other managers.

Meanwhile the couple corresponded stormily on waves of desire, anger and repentance. Pride would not allow them to admit that the marriage was a failure, and Strindberg devised extraordinary means of saving the situation. 'Do not let us be too intimate,' he wrote, and harped on the theme that her pity for him had turned to contempt. 'Let us start all over again, wiser by experience.'

The need for money now outweighed every other consideration. Frida's dowry was nearly spent, and Siri von Essen, living in Finland with Marie David and wearing her hair short as a banner of independence, demanded the arrears due for the children's maintenance. A popular Swedish newspaper had pirated *A Fool's Defence* on the pretence that it was unprotected German literature, so Strindberg's name was further blackened in his own country without him being any the richer. When an invitation came from his mother-in-law to visit the Uhl home at Mondsee, where her husband was to join her for the rest of the summer, Strindberg had no will to refuse. Maria Uhl's letter calling him 'son' and signed 'Mamma' spoke straight to his perpetual need. Only a mother could have compassion that did not turn to contempt.

He had not, however, anticipated the strangeness of being treated as a child again, and so discovering that he had in fact never grown up. Rebellious though he was, his weakness at once responded to parental influence and put him in the power of his new relatives. His mother-in-law gazed at him with the eyes of a seer and told him she had known him long before his coming; his father-in-law took him fishing, let him carry the rods and inquired about his prospects. The Councillor also wired peremptorily to his daughter to come and join her husband, but before she arrived, although he too had urged her to come, Strindberg fled from this new pressure.

They found one another again in Berlin and took a couple of large rooms in a *pension*. Frida Uhl continued her journalism and Strindberg resumed his chemistry and his esoteric studies. The urge to write had returned in force, but there were no human shapes in his new drama. *Antibarbarus* was concerned with the nature of sulphur, with the theory of transmutation applied to minerals and the belief that all is in all. As he worked, his consciousness developed and the confines of man's intelligence vanished. He went through in the present what became another's future, and he learnt to throw himself into a kind of trance in which ideas took form from the subconscious. Occasionally he even experienced the complete departure of the spirit from his body, and returned to life exhausted but inspired.

Frida was alarmed by these manifestations and, as she was pregnant, the constant smell of chemicals affected her disagreeably. Her condition could not fail to wake his tenderness and pride, but she was less pleased; even though a little money was now trickling in from books and plays, she could not see

144

how with Strindberg's commitments they were to support this child, particularly if her own career were interrupted. Besides, she was not a good housewife and did not see how they were to manage a home. Her untidiness irritated him, and she could not tolerate his ill-smelling test-tubes and retorts. Sulphur so dominated their lives that she had come to think of it almost as a person, as her rival. Nietszche had finally destroyed Strindberg's first marriage. *A Fool's Defence* and sulphur were destroying the second.

That book gave him no peace. Not only was he haunted by the knowledge that Frida Uhl had read it, and that it must also have reached the eyes of Siri von Essen, but it was suddenly denounced in the Press by 'A German Mother,' and the author was charged under the new law Lex Heinze with immoral writing. That to begin with was a gross insult—to have the name of Strindberg coupled with that of Heinze, the name of a pair of procurers whose complicity in a murder had started Berlin's new drive against vice. To have to face court proceedings again, and this time in a foreign language and a foreign land, was alarming, not only because thoughts of imprisonment once more tormented Strindberg's imagination, unlikely though it was in the case of a Swedish subject, but because he saw in the event the relentless turning of fate's wheel. Everything was happening again, and it became steadily more difficult for him to separate the present from the past.

By Christmas time the Strindbergs were in financial straits, and in view of her condition Frida thought it wise to go where good living could be had without expense. Accordingly they set out for the family estate in Moravia, where Frida's mother was living with her parents. Not satisfied with turning Strindberg into a child again, fate now decreed that he must revert to grandchild, but all the same the adventure pleased him. He was enchanted by the wide wild plain through which the Danube drifted in snow-covered blocks of ice, and he at once made up his mind to investigate the gipsy population and find out how much of the old Romany language these tribes had preserved. The establishment of Frida's grandparents at Dornach astonished him. The house, vast, white and austere, dominated the countryside, and Dr. Cornelius Reischl and his wife, once a celebrated Viennese beauty, dominated family, servants, vassals and guests alike. The old man, retired from a successful career in law and commerce, had bought this vast estate chiefly for its hunting, and day after day he would come home laden with game. The old lady supervised the dairy, in which every cow had her milkmaid and every maid her man, and the gardens provided an abundance of vegetables and fruit. Accustomed as they were to frugal fare, the Strindbergs found it difficult to eat enough to satisfy their host. This, Strindberg observed, was their punishment for having complained of the manna the Lord provided. Now like the murmuring Israelites 'they were stuffed with the flesh of quails until it came out of their nostrils and was loathsome to them.' Even the army of cats and dogs which pervaded the house could do little to reduce the superabundance of food which overflowed from the pig troughs, while outside the gates ran hordes of hungry gypsies.

Now Strindberg had space for his laboratory and many amenities of study. Besides the local flora, fauna and mineral, there was an extensive library which, on the death of a creditor, Dr. Reischl had unwillingly acquired. He seldom opened a book, although when rheumatism kept him from hunting, he read the periodicals sent him from Vienna by Frida's father and expounded their contents at meals. Strindberg was courteous to him and did not thrust forward his own views. He was touched by the aged couple, who had built their mausoleum in the garden and tended its plants as if to their own memory. In the evenings he played chess with the old man and was careful to let him win, and for the rest neither grandparents nor mother-in-law intruded on his privacy. Frida was properly looked after and Strindberg pursued his examination of natural and supernatural phenomena.

Such peace could not last. He was always thinking about Siri von Essen, and whether his immediate emotion was one of love or of hatred, he transferred it to Frida Uhl. Soon his fear of persecution woke again; he believed that she tampered with his mail and that his enemies were active. When he wrote to his eldest child, now nearly fourteen, inviting her to come and share this princely life with him, Karin wrote back asking him to send money so that her mother and the other children could also share in his good fortune. He had no money and the fear that the children had come to hate him gnawed at his heart. Now the case against *A Fool's Defence* was being prepared in Berlin and as a preliminary Strindberg was required to report to the local police. Dr. Reischl was outraged; he had already begun to mistrust this foreigner, who spent his nights photographing the moon by a system of his own, and trouble with the police confirmed his suspicions— such a thing had never been known in the family. Strindberg protested that as a Swedish subject he was immune from this jurisdiction, but the old man continued to rage, and presently Frau Reischl informed Strindberg that he must leave the house. As, however, Frida refused to stay without him, her grandmother presently offered them a small stone cottage in the garden.

'Das Häusel' was a romantic little dwelling on the river bank, and they accepted it gratefully, although for the time being Strindberg had to return to Berlin to arrange for his defence and also for the publication of *Antibarbarus* which had been translated into German. If his enemies were at work, so at least were his friends, and on the very day of his departure he put into Frida's hands a volume entitled *A Book about Strindberg*, which had just been published in Sweden. Among others Björnsterne Björnson, Jonas Lie, Justin Huntly McCarthy, the Brandes brothers and Knut• Hamsun had joined to tell the world about him. Knut Hamsun wrote:

August Strindberg is the most important author of his country, perhaps of our times. He is a supreme genius, a brain on horseback, charging his own way, leaving all others far behind. He is a live challenge to everyone and everything and belongs everywhere. He is the heaven-sent event in Nordic literature, the man who has imbued it with new life. He is a hero burning with sacred fire, a worshipper of beauty, yet ready to sacrifice it without hesitation in the cause of humanity. He is a seer, shedding light upon the future and piercing the shadows of the present.

He is a fighter against evil powers, one who would fain banish misery from the world. He is a radical reactionary who wants to cut short the false path and go back to make a new beginning, who will progress no further with over-development, but wants man to return to the primitive instinct, to retreat from hyperculture back to nature, until the straight way lies plain and unobstructed before his eyes. . . .

But Berlin had gone over to the enemy. Strindberg's lawyer was pessimistic, Zum Schwarzen Ferkel had become com-

mercialised and lost its charm, his friend Stanislav Przybyszewski had deserted his mistress and children and married Aspasia,
with whom Strindberg himself had once found solace. Aspasia
was now having an affair with another of Strindberg's friends,
and he suspected that both men were out for his blood, while
his disciples had taken all he could give and gone their way
forgetting him. He presented his samples of 'intermediary
gold' for analysis, but the authorities would not give a
definite opinion; he did not claim that he had made gold,
but only that he had proved the transmutability of metals.
Copper had been the main ingredient of his experiments, but
in his golden flakes there was no trace of copper. The analysts
allowed this, but would not admit that it proved anything.
Strindberg returned to Dornach disheartened and found 'Das
Häusel' a paradise.

The grey stone cottage had a cloistral look—the absence of
wallpaper delighted him—and he chose for himself a narrow
white-washed room that suggested a monk's cell. The walls
were so thick that he could stand pots of flowers inside and
outside the window, and here he arranged his books and was
at peace. He dashed off some bright canvases as a welcome to
the coming child, and in long quiet hours roamed the marsh-
lands by the river, watching the heron and gathering rare
flowers. As he sat silent and still in his monk's cell with a
medieval cap on his head and a short brown pipe to smoke,
birds came hopping to his table to be fed. He knew the
tastes of each one and the notes of all, and just how these
notes differed from those of their brethren in other parts of
Europe.

Plant life was now Strindberg's special interest. He had put
into the garden every species of flower and vegetable that
could endure the climate, and he tended their growth with
the utmost care. He believed that the organism of plants was
closer to that of animals than was commonly supposed, that
the process of nature was always the same and only its in-
tensity varied, and he made a minute study of the nerves of
plants and their reactions to stimulants and narcotics.

In much the same way he watched his wife as the time for
her confinement drew close. He was more than ever interested
in this crisis of creation, and he could not bear to think that

148

woman's part in it was unmitigated pain. To avoid such an intolerable suggestion he disbelieved everything that women told him, but with Frida he hoped to find proof that in the final agony was joy. Throughout the grinding hours of labour he tended her with an intuitive knowledge of her needs, and at moments she seemed to respond to his suggestion that her pain was indistinguishable from pleasure.

But the birth of a little girl set no seal on their happiness. The child cried incessantly, nurses and relatives came and went, all quietness was at an end, and presently the question of baptism provoked another conflict. Strindberg had long been attracted towards the Roman Catholic Church, whose decorative ritual was such a glowing contrast to the chill rites of Pietism, and which gave due adoration to the mystery of the Virgin Mother. He had no objection to his child being baptised in the Catholic faith, but as neither he nor Frida was a believer, and he was technically a Protestant, they saw no reason for haste. They had chosen the name of Kerstin and the religious ceremony could wait.

The child continued to cry abnormally; the servants whispered that the foreign gentleman was an atheist, and one woman declared she had seen the devil in the garden. Before long Dr. Reischl stipulated that the child be baptised or the family leave Dornach, and Maria Uhl, aware that the idyll in the cottage was breaking up under the strain of noise and diapers and constant interference, tried to persuade Strindberg to comply with the old man's wishes. Then he and his family might be received again in the mansion, and perhaps later find a home at Mondsee.

Strindberg replied by letter:

Dear Mother-in-law; We Protestants are tolerant and pretty easy-going in matters of creed, but we do not sell our faith, still less our children. This time you have judged me wrongly. Since we are now exiled and I cannot make any source of income before the autumn if I stay here, and as I am unwilling to burden the house with my presence now that the child has come, I shall go out into the world for a while to earn my bread, so that I can fulfil my obligations to my family.

I have one other motive for departure, with which you will no doubt concur, the fear of bringing another child into the world, which would effectively seal our ruin. . . .

149

He would go—but where? *Antibarbarus* had come out in Berlin, but had scarcely been noticed even with hostility; the scientists had decided to ignore him. His thoughts turned again to Paris. *The Father* and *Miss Julie* had each had a success at the Théâtre Libre, and now *Creditors* was to be performed with Lugné Poë, founder of the Théâtre Nouveau, in the leading part, and Herman Bang, the Danish dramatist, directing the production. It looked as if Paris was the place for Strindberg, and there he could always find friends. Leo Littmansson, for one, his fiddler friend of the Red Room days, was living in Versailles, and to him Strindberg now addressed himself:

> We shall soon be fifty and have danced away our milk teeth and should be thinking of our end. But I can't help it, I must laugh when I look at Life and her tricks, damned nasty tricks at times.
> That's why I write to you again to ask whether you're alive and kicking and would like to have me to stay somewhere near you this summer as in our old Kymmendö camp. I want to learn French, as well as a Swede can.
> Truly I've grown damned important; there's a bust of me in the Finnish National Museum and two full-length waxworks with a tremendous bush of hair and picturesquely tramp-like clothes. . . . I've been hissed in Naples, produced in Rome, judged worthy of an auto-da-fé by Sarcey in Paris, etc.
> I've been married twice and remain a monogamist. Have unmasked the whole Universe.
> . . . Do you know anyone who would correct my French a bit without manicuring my prose and pruning my claws? . . . I'd be in Paris now if I had the fare. . . . The difficulty is that my law suit in Berlin begins to look bad, while in the university town of Göttingen they threaten me with arrest for heresy. As you see, my life is still as stormy as ever. There have been fair intervals, enchanting idylls, but at times it's hellish torture. I am often weary of it. I have had everything I wanted of life and much besides. . . .
> . . . We must see if my pictures won't sell in the Scandinavian Club. . . . They can go cheap, about 100 francs apiece. . . . The amusing thing is that I was the first to paint symbolic landscapes and now the whole pack of realists have turned with the wind.

News came from Paris of the great success of *Creditors*, but still there was no money. The child was ill and now illness gripped Strindberg again. He had always been prone to an eczema on his hands and work with chemicals brought them out in a septic rash. On top of this he developed a sore throat and feared that he had caught an infection from the hateful dogs that overran Dornach. But Leo Littmansson received his letter kindly and sent him the new French books on transmutation he had asked for, and in spite of his ill-health and the discomfort of the cottage, Strindberg continued to write a book of essays and to pour out confidences to his old friend.

. . . This, you must know, is the position. My marriage is about to be dissolved. The cause: much the same as the first time.

All women hate Buddhas, maltreat, disturb, humiliate, annoy them, with the hatred of inferiors, because they themselves can never become Buddhas. On the other hand they have an instinctive sympathy for servants, male and female, beggars, dogs, especially mangy ones. They admire swindlers, quack dentists, braggadocios of literature, pedlars of wooden spoons—everything mediocre.

And women's love: see *Creditors*.

English physicians have recently established that when two children of a family sleep in the same bed, the weaker draws strength from the stronger.

There you have marriage: the brother and sister bed.

Just try to understand, as a woman she was bound to hate me as soon as she had read my writings. As my wife, she loves me. An intermittent current with alternating effect. . . . 'My beloved wife who hates me.' Hatred and love! All is one. The same source of energy. Sometimes positive, sometimes negative electricity. But one and the same.

What fate now awaits me, I do not know. But I feel 'The Hand of the Lord' upon me. Some change is coming, upwards or straight down into the bowels of the earth. Who can tell?

I am once more a victim of superstition. I hear the voices of crows at night in my garden and children weeping on the further shore of the Danube; I dream of days gone by, and have a longing to fly in some warmish medium, neither air nor water . . . to have no more enemies, neither to hate nor be hated any more. . . .

Prison might have some attraction, but what comes before—brutal lawyers, probing my soul and asking questions I will not answer—No!

That Nietszche's brain should have gone to pieces is no more astonishing than that a wooden garden tub should fall apart when the roots in it spread too luxuriantly. In my childhood we once had to circle a wooden tub in which a syringa was growing with bands of iron. But it burst in spite of them.

151

It was autumn when fate decreed that Strindberg should go out into the world once more. He had come with his wife to Dornach in a sleigh; he left in a paddle steamer alone. Chugging up the Danube in the dusk, he saw the lighted windows of the cloistral cottage where he had communed with the birds and flowers and waited for the new life that had sprung from his own, and for a moment disillusion was forgotten. He felt himself tied so strongly to his wife and child that he was tempted to plunge overboard and return to them—return to the past from which he could never escape. But as the steamer drew him inexorably away from this chapter of his life, he felt the bond between himself and Frida Uhl 'stretch and stretch until at last it broke.'

Even so, he could not let her be. As soon as he reached France he found that Leo Littmansson had arranged to sell some of his pictures and was translating his new essays into French, that *Le Plaidoyer d'un Fou* was coming out, that Henri Becque and other famous members of the present *chez* Laurent circle were eager to know him, and that Lugné Poë was arranging for a production of *The Father* at the Théâtre Nouveau. Strindberg's incurable optimism soared and he invited Frida to join him, then changed his mind and informed her that he was coming back to Dornach. At one moment Paris enchanted him, at the next it filled him with dismay; at one moment he gloated over his freedom, at the next he was weeping for loneliness.

Presently Frida came to Paris, leaving the now thriving baby with a wet-nurse, but Strindberg felt that she had come less to see him than to pursue her own career, or if to see him then as a spy rather than as a comrade. Women, he had decided, never appreciated man's efforts, but only his success, and if success came they were jealous. His wife was seeking commissions for articles and translations, although now that she was a mother he thought she should give up all but a little desultory writing. He was sure that, like Siri von Essen before her, Frida Uhl was jealous of his brain and his fame. Her revenge was to try to make him look like a fool—with the pretence of furthering his affairs, she even carried on flirtations with his business acquaintances. When she was summoned back to Dornach by her grandmother, he exulted—yet still he flooded her with letters, analysing every emotion and suggesting countless contradictory solutions of their problem. When, because he had failed to let her know that he had gone to Dieppe, he had no letters from her for six days, he fell into a rage; when she sent him pictures of 'Das Häusel,' he reproached her with rousing his homesickness.

Of one thing alone he was more certain than ever, that love and hatred were indissoluble, and that all writers who tried to portray love as an emotion unrelated to hatred were false prophets. And gradually his hatred won until he wrote to his second wife:

What is the use of a comedy of love, since we hate each other? You hate me from a feeling of inferiority; I am a superior who has done you nothing but good; and I hate you as an enemy, because you behave like one.

If I wanted to go on fighting you, I should have to use the weapons of your decadent morality, but I won't do that. So I'm leaving you —and going never mind where. As soon as you're alone, deprived of the urge to humiliate me, your energy will desert you too. Your strength is rooted in cruelty, you need an eternal victim to play the part of the eternal fool. I don't want the rôle any longer.

Look for another man. Adieu!

P.S. . . . I was bewitched into a marriage in which I've been treated as a beggar, worse than a servant, and have fallen so low that my children curse me. . . .

CHAPTER TWELVE

1894–1896

Inferno

ON DECEMBER 18th, 1894, *The Father* had its première at the Théâtre Nouveau, a grander affair than the performances sponsored by André Antoine two years before in the Place Pigalle. Philippe Garnier, the star of the Théâtre Libre, was in the name part, and Lugné Poë, who was responsible for the production, played the pastor. Zola was there and Sardou, Prévost, Henri Becque, Rodin and Gauguin, in fact everyone who was needed to make the evening a Paris occasion. Ever since he began to write plays, August Strindberg had dreamed of such a moment as the peak of ambition for a Scandinavian playwright. He had truly arrived—but he was not there. He sent the company a letter of thanks, begging them 'to excuse the stranger . . . a sick man to whom retreat and solitude are necessary.'

In the morning the papers rang with his fame, and the great Swedish author was warmly invited to stay and make his home in France. Paris caught fire with the notion of woman's inferiority and all the smartest jokes were on this subject. Strindberg was the hero of the moment, admired, envied, exploited. Even the Berlin prosecution had failed—his star had risen indeed. He carefully scrutinised his own reactions and found indifference; he was no longer interested in literature or the theatre—truth and drama lay for him in the six little porcelain crucibles he had purchased with money 'stolen from himself.'

He had proved to his own satisfaction that sulphur contained carbon, and he was concerned now to prove that hydrogen and oxygen were also present. He had discovered too that mercury was a compound, and he believed that this metal

154

could be used in the production of gold. He read that chemists at Oxford had agreed to the presence of a hitherto unrecognised gas in the atmosphere, which could be separated from nitrogen in a way that he had foretold in his *Antibarbarus*. Without doubt his researches were proceeding along the right lines; he must break up everything until at last he found the single origin of all matter.

He lived now in the Quartier Latin; across the road from his small hotel was a home for the deaf and dumb, and from his window he looked into the garden where mute children, 'silent as flowers,' spoke by signs and smiles. He was close to the Luxembourg gardens and walked there contemplating nature; he roamed among the old bookshops of the Quartier, and at night was drawn moth-like by the lights of the cafés to sit once again drinking the green comfort of absinthe. But when he made his experiments he drew down the blinds and locked the doors; he was jealous of his secrets and some of his practices were too unorthodox to admit inquiry.

His poverty was a grinding humiliation. After ten performances in Paris *The Father* had gone abroad with the Théâtre Nouveau; Strindberg heard that other plays in its repertory were admired in Sweden, and that the King had given Lugné Poë the medal *Pro Litteris* as a reward for promoting Scandinavian literature in Paris, but he himself had received exactly three hundred francs from *The Father*. It seemed that managers, translators, publishers and editors were united in a plot to cheat him, and the only way out of his intolerable position was to renounce money altogether—to ignore both his commitments and his dues. To allow himself to be cheated was to confess his weakness, to renounce money of his own free will renewed his self-respect. Let the devil take his royalties then and leave him his honour—he would no longer be a dupe but only a beggar.

So he worked on in his little room, forgetting in his enthusiasm to take care of his delicate hands. He made the fireplace into a smelting furnace, and soon his hands were bleeding and blackened. When the pain grew so severe that he was forced to notice it, sometimes he thought of it as the price of truth, and sometimes as a manifestation of the unknown powers which for years had frustrated all his efforts.

He still called himself an atheist, yet every day he was more conscious of powers he could not explain in terms of chemistry.

In his unkempt sick state he shunned all company and repelled every advance, but when Christmas Eve came he could bear his loneliness no longer. Christmas was a family festival; a year ago at Dornach he and Frida had smuggled a little tree up to their own quarters of the big house and celebrated in secret, and wherever they were he and Siri had always contrived a Swedish Christmas. Now Frida was at Dornach with the baby Kerstin, and Karin, Greta and Hans were in Finland with the two women. He had faded from their lives. Demands for money were the only communications he ever had from Siri von Essen, although she was now the directress of a dramatic school for young ladies. As for Frida Uhl, they still wrote to one another, for he must hear about each stage of the child's development, and also he could no more resist the waves of sentimentality that from time to time submerged him, than he could control his hideous rancour. Cruel or kind, golden or black, he wrote his thoughts to Frida—and she replied, but none the less the rift between them could not be bridged. She showed her scepticism of his experiments, and he let her know that she was replaced—in fact by solitude and science, but he implied that her rival was another woman.

So now loneliness drove him to join in a Scandinavian Christmas and melancholy drove him out again—to drink his absinthe in solitude and flee from the revellers in the streets as if from pursuing Furies.

His hands grew worse, his arms swelled, he could not dress himself properly or go out, and he was quite without funds. News of his plight spread through the Swedish colony in Paris, and with the help of the chaplain, Pastor Nathan Söderblom, money was collected and arrangements made for him to go into the hospital of St. Louis. On the way Strindberg stopped the cab in order to buy two linen shirts and wondered if he were purchasing his shroud. Death seemed to be close at hand.

He found himself in prison, in the hideous company of the maimed and sick. At table, on account of his bandaged hands, he had to accept help from 'creatures lacking a nose or with a cheek that had begun to rot'; he had to keep company with others whom he believed to be criminals escaping gaol through graft. And for. this fearful asylum he was expected to feel gratitude to his fellow countrymen and to society. He was not even sure that it was on account of his inflamed hands that they had brought him to what was largely a mental hospital. However, he was nursed by an aged Sœur de Charité, of the Order of St. Augustine, who 'wore the costume of the dead because she had never entered life,' and though she 'distributed poisonous medicines so that he toasted in arsenic a death's-head who pledged him back in digitalis,' she was gentle and called him 'my child.' To use the precious name of Mother was balm to his heart. 'The mere presence of this *mère* comforts and soothes me,' he wrote to Frida. '*La douce chaleur du sein maternel*, as Baudelaire calls it (I think it was he), does me good.'

Frida offered to come and look after him and he was touched, but he could see from her letters that she still conceived a life with him of her own shaping. He had chosen the other way of liberty and science, and he told her not to come.

In February 1895 he left the hospital with his hands still bandaged and resumed his former life. The analysts confirmed his finding of carbon in sulphur, and Strindberg decided that the time had come to make his discovery public. *Le Temps* accepted an essay which led to requests for further scientific articles, and he was invited to use the analytical laboratory at the Sorbonne for his researches. This privilege, however, he did not enjoy, for both professors and students were hostile to the morose middle-aged foreigner who had given up his proper career to trespass in their province, and they showed their scepticism of his amateur experiments. His unkempt appearance increased his timidity; he trudged like a tramp past cafés where when *The Father* was produced, only two months before, journalists had clamoured for an interview. When he had satisfied himself of the presence of oxygen and hydrogen in sulphur, he decided to run the gauntlet of the students' scorn no more, and in the privacy of his room he turned his attention to the production of iodine from the by-products of coal.

Strindberg still found painters the best of drinking com-

157

panions and was at home in many of the studios of the
Quartier, and now his neighbour Paul Gauguin urged him
to write a note for the catalogue of his forthcoming exhibition.
Strindberg answered the request 'with an "I can't" or more
brutally with an "I won't,"' and explained his refusal in a
long letter.

I can't understand your art and I can't like it. I can't get any grip
on your art (which this time is entirely Tahitian) but I know that
this admission will neither surprise nor hurt you, for it's clear that
you gain strength from others' hatred. Your personality finds
pleasure in the antipathy it arouses—the price of being left in peace.
If you were admired you would have followers who would regulate
you, classify you, give your art a name which within five years the
young would use as a by-word for an out-of-date art, which they
would do their best to make more old-fashioned still.

I myself have tried, have made the most determined effort, to
classify you, to fit you in as a link in the chain, to trace the history
of your development, but in vain. . . .

No, Gauguin is not shaped from Chavannes' rib, nor from
Manet's, nor yet Bastien Lepage's. Who is he then? He is Gauguin,
the savage detesting the encumbrances of civilisation, something of a
Titan who, jealous of the creator, in his spare moments makes his
own small universe, the child breaking his toys to bits so as to make
other toys out of them, the one who resists and defies, declaring that
he sees the skies as red, not like the masses as blue.

And now it occurs to me that since writing myself warm, I have
begun to get a certain grip on Gauguin's art.

The modern writer has been accused of not describing real characters, but of *quite simply* constructing them himself. *Quite simply!* Bon
voyage, Master; come back to us and look me up again; perhaps by
then I shall have learnt to understand your art better, and be in a
position to write a real foreword to a new catalogue . . . for I myself
am beginning to have a tremendous need to be savage and create a
new world.

The whole of the letter was printed in Paul Gauguin's
catalogue.

Knut Hamsun, who was also living in Paris, now came to
Strindberg's help. The appeal on behalf of Strindberg that
he sent to the Swedish papers was ignored, but the Danish
Politiken published a letter signed by Hamsun, Jonas Lie and
other famous Scandinavians, and now Hamsun wrote off to
Adolf Paul, the Finnish writer who like himself had first met
Strindberg at Zum Schwarzen Ferkel.

Strindberg is very badly off. . . . He is living here on a most in-secure footing, writing an article from time to time which perhaps some paper prints and perhaps not. He is badly paid—he only got forty francs for his last article on sulphur; his translator kept twenty francs, so only twenty francs was Strindberg's share. He is in debt and has been living on credit the whole time and does not know how long he will be able to remain where he is.

He lacks clothing. Now, in winter, he goes about in a light green summer suit and he is embarrassed. He feels he cannot call on anyone, not even on publishers, in his present state.

I thank you personally for being willing to intervene on his behalf in Berlin. You tell me he has a grudge against you. But I scarcely know anyone against whom he hasn't a grudge. He doesn't like me either, he says my personality is too strong for him. It's hardly pos-sible to have anything to do with him. But I don't mind and I see that you don't either. In spite of everything he is August Strindberg.

It ought to be made possible for him to live as he chooses. If he wishes to write masterpieces—all right. If he wants to dabble in chemistry, all right. If he wants to do nothing at all, all right. The man has done so much good work and is of such importance that he ought to be allowed to do as he pleases.

We were going to dine together one evening and were looking for a place. We stopped in front of a little restaurant with no par-ticular pretensions where other people going in were also shabby. But Strindberg said: 'No, it's too well lighted for me here, it's too bright. Let's go somewhere else.' He didn't say it in a complaining tone, he simply stated it as a fact. 'Here it is too bright for me!' And yet this was none other than August Strindberg! I cannot forget the impression it made upon me. Do something for him if you can—

KNUT HAMSUN

Money poured in and Strindberg was furious; once more his honour had been attacked by interfering fools who would not allow him his voluntary poverty. He wrote to the Scandinavian papers protesting that the appeal had been launched without his knowledge or consent, and directed that any donations should be sent to his children in Finland. He wrote to the Deutsches Theatre in Berlin, which was arranging a per-formance for his benefit, declaring that he was not interested in this charity performance, but that if it made any money it should be sent to his child in Austria—news which threw his father-in-law into a towering rage. The Court Councillor had just celebrated his seventieth birthday in Vienna with much dignity and pomp, and now people would hear of a charity performance in aid of his daughter's child.

Strindberg did not pay his debts or thank his benefactors—indeed he wrote to Knut Hamsun 'keep your thirty pieces of silver and let us be done with one another for the rest of our lives.' Yet as spring broke he found himself strangely happy; money continued to trickle in from an invisible source and he ceased to resent it and looked on it as manna dropped from heaven. He was able to buy books and scientific apparatus—even a microscope with which to discover life's inmost secrets. At the same time chemists, industrialists and occultists approached him with bribes and flattery. *Le Temps* published his article on iodine, and a representative of 'the world's largest manufacturers of *Iodures Hydroquines*' called on him, waving a cheque for one hundred thousand francs. The suggestion was that Strindberg should take out a German patent for his synthetic iodine and both he and the manufacturers grow rich. Strindberg was not tempted; he had quarrelled with Frida Uhl before now when she had suggested that he should sell his 'intermediary gold.' Such discoveries belonged to humanity and not to himself—he would not bargain over something vouchsafed him by higher powers—and in any case he distrusted commerce. He was more impressed by a letter from Paul Sédir, the disciple of Papus, master of the occult sciences in France, hailing Strindberg as 'a God of the Dawn.' He sent such letters on to Frida Uhl to show her how he was succeeding in spite of her scepticism, and still from time to time he wrote affectionate notes and told her that he was coming back.

Parallel with his scientific studies, he delved deeper now into the occultism to which so many artists were turning in reaction to realism, and soon he found everything charged with mysterious meaning. He looked on St. Louis as a kind of patron saint—St. Louis of the hospital, the Sorbonne and La Sainte Chapelle—'from suffering, through knowledge to repentance.' He meditated the words, but he was far from the humility of repentance; his ego continued to feed on every experience and swell unchecked. Now that he believed he was guided by an unseen hand he could bear his loneliness. 'It was as if he had died and been born into another world where none could follow him.'

As he roamed about the Quartier, the names of the streets

caught his eye. Rue Alibert—was not Alibert the name of the graphite the analysts had found in his sulphur? Rue Dieu— why Dieu when the Republic had washed its hands of God? Beaurepaire—a fine resort of criminals. In the window of a dyer's shop his own initials were displayed on a silver cloud and over them arched a rainbow. *Omen accipio!* He remembered the words: 'I do set my bow in the cloud, and it shall be for a token of a covenant between me and the earth.' He observed the golden cross on the dome of the Pantheon touching the clouds and felt his feet winged with happiness. As he walked between budding chestnut trees to the Luxembourg garden gorgeous with summer, nature belonged to him—he had divined the secrets of creation.

He was now at work on *Sylva Sylvarum*, a pamphlet setting out his botanical theories. He must destroy the ignorant classifications which had been so long accepted and let people see into the life of the vegetable kingdom; he must demonstrate that all is in all and that plants too contain and yield the primary substance that is the essence of existence. But Strindberg could not stop there; he had to use his secret knowledge further. He rejoiced that he was free of women, but he wanted his wives to love him still and call him back; the thought came suddenly that the sickness of a child—the slight sickness of a child exaggerated by an anxious mother would bring this call. His occult studies had taught him what to do.

As soon as he used black magic, Strindberg had a sense of foreboding, and as the days passed he was convinced that the unknown powers had turned against him. His invisible source of money dried up; the proofs of *Sylva Sylvarum*, which he was having printed at his own expense, arrived in utter confusion, and when at last they were finished, the printer's bill was so heavy that he had to pawn his microscope to meet it. Nevertheless he felt that with this work 'he had solved the riddle of the Sphinx.'

His landlady presented the bill, three pianos played continuously in the rooms next his, nails were hammered into the wall beside his bed, and there was a din above that brought down pieces of plaster on his head. He complained to his landlady, but she declared that she heard nothing, and

161

Strindberg fled, leaving his possessions behind him as he could not pay the bill.

His refuge was the Hôtel Orfila, a *pension* for monks and students to which he was guided, first by finding a treatise by the eighteenth-century chemist Orfila confirming some of his own theories, and then by seeing this man's monument in the churchyard of Montparnasse. Evidently the spirit of Orfila wished him well, for no women were admitted to this hotel, and he was now inclined to believe that the intolerable piano playing had been the revenge of some Scandinavian ladies he had slighted. The Orfila was run by an amiable Abbé and promised peace. On his first night there, Strindberg read the Book of Job and was comforted. If the Almighty had handed him over to Satan to be tried, this was a mark of His confidence.

Presently he began again to make gold. So far, although transmutation was proved, his intermediary gold vanished when put to certain chemical tests. Now his eyes were directed to the letters 'F.S.' crudely marked on a wall, and after first thinking that this was a sign that Frida Strindberg loved him still, he came to the conclusion that the letters were a chemical symbol—'Fer-Souffre'—iron and sulphur must be the secret of making gold.

He borrowed money to buy apparatus and would not be deterred, although in the crucible he saw a skull with glittering eyes, the coals burned into grotesque figures and everything in the room assumed weird shapes. When he grew too frightened, he fled to Madame Charlotte's crêmerie to drink with the artists, or to the Brasserie des Lilas for a solitary glass of absinthe. 'Ce Strindberg,' once such a dandy, was now a well-known freak of the Quartier.

Outside his window it was summer—he heard the voices of young girls beneath the trees—but within himself was unending autumn. He read Job and the Lamentations of Jeremiah and contemplated the approach of old age. He must press on with his investigations; he would not have lived in vain if he could prove that the accepted division between matter and spirit was an illusion. He now challenged every orthodox tenet about earth, moon and stars—with the result that he was elected a member of two astronomical societies.

One day his sister Anna von Philp, visiting Paris with her

162

husband and son, called at his monastic retreat. Strindberg was excited to see one of his own blood again after so many years, and at once showed the visitor his gold, but Anna von Philp saw that her brother's nerves were in pieces, and when she invited him to her hotel, one glance at her card showed him that he could not go. The von Philps were staying on the right bank, and for a long time now Strindberg had found himself unable to cross the river.

For the sake of his health, and particularly of improving the state of his hands which had never properly healed, Strindberg now agreed to visit his old friend Anders Eliasson, a doctor at Ystad in the south of Sweden, but he found his homeland alien, and he was certain that his mental state was under observation. He was homesick for the Quartier where he could be alone or mix in congenial company, and after six weeks he returned to the Pension Orfila, with the intention of applying for a job in the Jardin des Plantes to aid his studies in natural science.

In the review of *Sylva Sylvarum* in *Initiation*, the paper of the occultists, Strindberg found himself referred to as a fellow countryman of Swedenborg's. In his undergraduate days, he had dismissed this philosopher as crazy and had scarcely given him a thought since. Now in the arcades of the Odéon he picked up Balzac's Swedenborgian novel *Séraphita* and found himself enthralled. Nor did he fail to notice that the very day on which Swedenborg entered his life was the anniversary of the prophet's death; moreover, it was Palm Sunday— Swedenborg had brought him the palm, but whether of the victor or the martyr, Strindberg did not yet know.

Séraphita filled him with a nostalgia for heaven and a contempt for the impure earth and its inhabitants. He now saw himself as a righteous man, whom the Almighty was testing and whom the purgatory of this world was fitting for a higher sphere, but this comforting notion was upset when he received a letter from his children in Finland telling him that they had been very ill. The date of their illness corresponded with his experiment in black magic, and he was badly frightened. Strange phenomena continued and he began to wonder if he were not in the power of the Devil—the making of gold had always been taboo.

Presently in a house near the *pension* he heard someone playing Schumann's *Aufschwung*, and was at once certain that the pianist was Stanislav Przybyszewski, who in the days of Zum Schwarzen Ferkel had called Strindberg 'Father' and 'Master' and kissed his hands. For a long time now he had believed that the Pole was his enemy, partly on account of his former intimacy with Aspasia, and partly from jealousy of his superior mind to which he considered Przybyszewski owed much of his own development. Strindberg had already seen the treachery of this man in many of his misfortunes; he believed that now, as the Pole's attempts to rob him of the means of subsistence had failed, Przybyszewski had come to kill him. In mortal terror Strindberg 'reversed the spear' and willed his enemy's destruction; at once he felt like a murderer and both gloried in and feared his evil conscience.

The same tune continued at the same hour each afternoon, and Strindberg inquired of the artists at Madame Charlotte's crêmerie, to whom the Pole was well known, if he were indeed in Paris. The answers were contradictory and evasive, but signs and portents convinced Strindberg of his presence, and he continued to sharpen his will and rally the forces of his hatred. He read the Old Testament now with the sole purpose of invoking Providence on his side and stimulating in himself the vengeance of the Psalms. 'Make haste, O God, to deliver me,' he prayed. 'Let them be turned backward and put to confusion that desire my hurt.' The mercy preached by the New Testament seemed to him mere cowardice.

Presently the music stopped. Shortly afterwards Strindberg heard that Stanislav Przybyszewski had been arrested on the charge of murdering his mistress and their two children. His first sensation was one of relief; then came horror and amazement. Was it possible that the Pole's terrible crime was the direct result of his, Strindberg's, will to hatred and revenge? Had he in fact become a wizard? He had seen a man shudder when he laid his coat upon the other's shoulders; he had felt again and again his power over others. Przybyszewski was shut up, but what of the unknown powers? He was pursued by small misfortunes and saw them all as part of a planned persecution; he was convinced that his latest friend was a *Doppelgänger*, and his own personality grew confused.

164

The weathercock on the cross of Notre Dame flapped its wings telling him to fly northward; a pine-clad landscape appeared in the zinc bath of his alchemy, the Pole star beckoned to him, and pansies with children's faces signalled to him to go away. But to flee would be to confess himself beaten; Strindberg stayed therefore and went on with his essays in Natural History—*Jardin des Plantes*. His brain was as good as ever, and his friend Torsten Hedlund had promised to publish this book. Hedlund was a Theosophist, who had already foretold for Strindberg a future full of suffering and glory, and he was one of the very few people in whom Strindberg now confided. Hedlund had come to his aid more than once both physically and spiritually, and now he was bent on getting his distraught friend to accept the doctrine of Theosophy and to recognise Madame Blavatsky as its exponent. Strindberg read the books Hedlund sent him and found much to agree with and more that enlightened him, but he was not prepared to join any sect, and least of all one led by a priestess whose chief concern was 'to outdo man and usurp the altar of the Saviour.' In November 1895 he wrote to Hedlund:

About theosophy I hesitate to commit myself. It's supposed to derive from Buddha and I was educated by three Buddhists, Schopenhauer, von Hartmann and lastly Nietszche. Perhaps therefore we have points of contact. Madame Blavatsky's appropriation and degrading of the matter made me suspicious of it. As a Buddhist I am, like Buddha and his three great disciples, a woman-hater, just as I hate the earth which binds my spirit because I love it. Woman is to me the earth and all its glory, the bond that binds; and all the evil of the worst evil I have seen is the female sex. The hindrance, the hatred, the low calculation, the crudity, above all the inhuman threat to a spirit that wants to grow, to rise. The instinctive meanness as Schopenhauer the master says: To love a man—to debase him in his own eyes and lift him up in the eyes of the world to meet the needs of her own vanity. That instinctive dishonesty: it is she—she in her illnature and stupidity—who has made him, if in spite of everything he becomes something. What could she give who had nothing? He took where there was nothing, for he created out of nothing.

There are lovely delusions, O Lord, all too lovely! But shall I never learn to kill my flesh? It is still too young and fiery, but let it burn itself out. And completely. But the spirit! Consumed perhaps too.

If everything is one, the flesh too is justified. No, I answer myself, and so the whole edifice topples down.

I'll never get out of this. A bachelor's life seems to me pretty
dirty. Family life is best, but!! but! dirtier still when one stirs it
up. Outside it—absolute degradation where the beast is encountered.

In the main, Strindberg accepted the doctrine of reincarnation, but he strongly resisted what appeared to him the central
tenet of Theosophy—the killing of the personality. He himself
made no distinction between the ego and the personality, and
he saw his whole life as a struggle to preserve his individuality
from outside influences. Why should he now seek to destroy
it? This kind of suicide did not attract him.

Przybyszewski was released for lack of evidence, and in the
fierce heat of July, Strindberg lay on his bed holding an un-
corked phial of potassium cyanide and reading *La Joie de
Mourir*. As the poisonous fumes mounted he felt the volup-
tuous approach of death, but believed his time had not yet
come.

The students departed for the summer vacation and the
pension was empty, yet the room next Strindberg's appeared
to be occupied, and the visitor's movements corresponded with
his own. When Strindberg sat writing at his desk, so did the
stranger on the other side of the wall, when he moved his
chair, the unknown did the same. When he went to bed it
was a signal for the other to follow suit and like himself to turn
over the pages of a book, put out the lamp and breathe deeply
in preparation for sleep. Now the last remnants of self-
possession deserted Strindberg. His limbs ached and he
believed that Przybyszewski was discharging poisonous gases
through the wall. He thought of giving information to the
police, but was held back by fear of being thought insane.
Then he felt an electric current passing through his room—
and fled.

He hid in an hotel close to the Jardin des Plantes, and
from here described his fearful experiences to Torsten
Hedlund. Then a lull came in his sufferings; the roses, his
favourite flowers since childhood, were in full bloom in
the Jardin and refreshed his soul; he slept quietly at night,
and in the daytime went on with his work. From stones,
through plant life and the animal kingdom he had explored
until he reached man, and found behind man the Creator,
who developed as He created, who designed and rejected,

resumed plans that had failed, and often made extraordinary leaps, so that the scientists had to fill in the gaps.

This peace, and the clear condition of his brain, convinced Strindberg that he had not suffered from delusion, but had in fact been threatened by enemies whom his flight had foiled. Presently he felt confident enough to send his address to the Pension Orfila and resume contact with the outside world. At once the persecution began again; an old man 'with grey and wicked eyes like a bear's' continuously carried mysterious objects into the room adjoining his, and from above came the sound of file and hammer. He believed that his enemies were once more constructing their infernal electric machine, and then a wheel began turning over his head.

Now he had no doubt that he was condemned to death, but he was uncertain whether, after all, the Pole was his executioner, or if others who knew that he practised the black arts had decided he must die. He thought it possible that the police, believing him to be an anarchist, had devised this way of getting rid of him. In any case he was resolved now to meet his destiny. His papers were in order and no ties bound him to earth. He wrote to Hedlund once again—'We'll see if this is my last letter'—and asked him in the case of his death to claim his body:

. . . for I consider it a punishment to be cut up in the anatomy room and for the concierge to sell bits to the shops. The cheapest is cremation (50 francs). On the other hand I've had a childish desire ever since my youth, quite inexplicably, to be buried in Montparnasse. This costs 500 francs, but could no doubt be got from Bonnier in advance for my collected works. I do not want to lie in Swedish soil, for it is damned, and I do not want my grave fouled by enemies.

Don't you realise that Sweden is the place of the exiles, of the damned who must sit and watch how the world is run without their advice being heard? The land of the non-adult, the disenfranchised, the muts.

Hence the demoniacal hatred, the jealousy, the clawing; devils intent on tormenting each other. . . .

In the Jardin des Plantes Strindberg took leave of his true friends—the birds and beasts and butterflies, the stones and trees and flowers, the snakes and fishes, while the words of *Séraphita* echoed in his mind: '*Adieu, pauvre terre, adieu!*'

He prepared himself for death, but he felt no remorse for

his sins; he was sure that he was not responsible for his unhappy life. Nor need he fear hell in another world, since he had gone through a thousand hells on earth. He had been born with a nostalgia for heaven, as a child he had wept for the ugliness of life—he had sought God and found the Devil. In his youth he had borne the Cross of Christ, but he had always denied a God who ruled over slaves, fawning on the master with the whip. He was convinced of his own righteousness.

That night he was awakened by the sensation of a pump drawing out his heart and lifting him from the bed. He heard the clock strike two, then an electric current struck his neck and pressed him to the ground. He rushed out into the garden, and the next day fled to friends in Dieppe.

When he saw the horror in his hostess's eyes, Strindberg looked at himself in the glass. He was dirty and unshaven, his cheeks sunken, his hair grey, his eyes wild, but beyond all this there was an expression in his face that brought horror also to himself—an expression of evil. Now he knew that he would be driven hence too by furies. In this fair home were all the things he had once hoped for—married love, happy children, goodness, beauty—he was dazzled by the radiance of it all. Here was Paradise, but he was a damned soul.

He thought that if there were to be a further manifestation it would come at the same fateful hour of the morning, and when, as he sat reading alone in his room, two o'clock came, he flung open the windows, bared his breast and dared the enemy to strike. Once again a force like an electric current suffused his body and struck his heart. Although he could scarcely breathe he remembered the compass on his table. It was unmoved; this could not then be natural electricity. He rushed downstairs and flung himself on a couch, but another discharge struck him like a cyclone. Now he fled in panic from room to room, hiding in one place after another, but everywhere the furies sought him out. When at last he returned to his room, dawn was breaking and in the silence he heard the bell for the Angelus. He opened the breviary which he had bought one day in Paris, along with a rosary to ward off evil spirits. '*De Profundis clamavi ad Te, Domine!*' he read, and comforted sank prostrate on the bed.

The next day Strindberg left for Sweden, to stay once again

with Dr. Anders Eliasson. In the clear light of morning he was anxious to know if his experiences could be explained by natural causes. If his friend in Ystad diagnosed a nervous derangement that could give rise to such amazing delusions, he would take his word for it.

On the way he stopped in Copenhagen and called on Georg Brandes, sending in his visiting card, now printed in this manner:

AUGUST STRINDBERG

Former Amanuensis at the Royal Library of Sweden. Holder of the Imperial Russian Geographical Society's medal, Member of the French Astronomical Association, of the Paris Dramatists' and Composers' Society and of the Alliance Française.

In the course of conversation, to Brandes' embarrassment Strindberg offered to help him destroy his enemies by the simple use of black magic.

The moment he saw Anders Eliasson he was filled with suspicion. The doctor was in debt—and he was ambitious. Strindberg was sure he wanted him shut up or dead in order that he might steal the secret of making gold. The shape and material of the bed in which he had to sleep suggested instruments of torture, and he also feared poison by one of the drugs it would be so easy for the doctor to administer. The cold-water cure he was forced to undergo did not improve his health; the choking current came again and he wondered how much longer it would be possible for him to endure.

Eliasson was inclined to attribute some of his patient's mental distress to religious mania. In any case he thought the Bible and Breviary unsuitable reading in his present condition, and he removed them from his room, leaving instead Victor Rydberg's *German Mythology* as a soporific. Strindberg opened a volume at random and read words which became engraved upon his mind in letters of fire:

As the legend relates, Bhrign, having outgrown his father's teaching, became so conceited that he believed he could surpass his teacher. The latter sent him into the underworld where, in order that he might be humbled, he had to witness countless terrible things of which he had had no conception.

August Strindberg was in hell on account of his own overwhelming pride—he must at last believe it.

CHAPTER THIRTEEN

1896–1899

Light after darkness. New productivity, with faith, hope and charity regained—and absolute certainty

FROM THIS moment Strindberg's life was changed. His afflictions continued, but he saw each ordeal as a penance, a step on the road to Damascus. He believed that it was now God's will that he should cease to explore life's secrets and to win unlawful knowledge, but he could not refrain from sending Torsten Hedlund one final essay on synthetic gold. He wrote to him from Ystad on August 18th, 1896:

> The last crisis I have been through I have not described to you, but I shall do this in a book—a novel if you like to call it that. I believe that we are closer to one another than hitherto—but—but . . .
>
> I am therefore renouncing my scientific studies, but as a memento I beg you to print these three pages I am sending you—in 100 copies, so that I may be saved from 100 letters on the same subject—to answer enquiries, and also that I may have a proof that I was not mad when I believed that I made gold.

A letter from Frida suggesting that he should go to Austria and see his little daughter determined his next move. Frida would not be there; she was obtaining a divorce and going to stay with Maria Weyr in Vienna, but his mother-in-law, who was living not far from Dornach, was willing to receive him.

Strindberg saw this as the first stage of his penitential pilgrimage. He had to spend a night in Berlin, and his drive through the city was a *via dolorosa* of bitter-sweet memories. Here he had been reborn in the second springtime of his life, here he, Adolf Paul and Stanislav Przybyszewski had explored each other's minds and vowed eternal friendship in the pursuit of truth. All had ended in bitter hatred.

He made the last part of the journey by carriage through the orchards and meadows of the Danube plain. Sunk though he was in melancholy he felt more at home here than in his native land. The flow of the river that knew so many foreign regions suited his vagrant spirit, yet here for a while he had rested—he had planted trees and a child had been born to him. This was for him a mother country.

The meeting with his small daughter was one of the most poignant moments of his life. He had left an infant six weeks old and came back to a little girl of two and a half—this was Faust's return to earth, but purer and more tender. 'To love a child was for a man to become a woman, it was to feel the heavenly joy of sexless love.'

But his happiness was brief; at table when he touched Kerstin's hand to help her, she drew back and said, 'He hurts me,' and another time she pointed at an invisible figure behind her father's chair, cried out 'The chimney sweep!' and screamed with terror.

Maria Uhl believed in the child's clairvoyance, and before long Strindberg was talking frankly to her and her sister of his sufferings. At once they prescribed the protecting arms of Catholicism and the visionary wisdom of Swedenborg. They were amazed to find that all Strindberg knew of his great compatriot was what Balzac had disclosed in *Séraphita*, and hastened to repair his ignorance.

In his groping, impressionable state, the teaching of Swedenborg sank deep into Strindberg's mind and magnified the reflections roused by the *German Mythology*. Without doubt he was in hell, and the only path to salvation lay in pursuing the demons to their dens within himself and destroying them by repentance. The fact that Swedenborg had gone through torments similar to his own, before he had been vouchsafed his revelations, strengthened Strindberg's resolve to tread the stony path, but the struggle with his pride was by no means over. Ambition, according to Swedenborg, was the first stumbling block of the heaven-bent soul, but had he, Strindberg asked himself, ever striven for fame or tried to impress the world with his attainments? Did he not despise wealth? Had he not sworn that if he acquired riches from the making of gold they should be devoted to the welfare of

171

humanity? And as for the holiness of wedded love, had he not sought it all his life? He must be doing penance for sins committed in a previous existence—and it was the higher souls who had to go through the fiercest hells.

Thus still he nursed his pride, although he continued to be beset by fears and subjected to every kind of disturbance, including sometimes the 'electric' current. His mother-in-law pressed for his conversion to the Catholic Church, although Swedenborg ruled that men should not give up the religion of their fathers; prayers were said for him, beads told, and a vessel in his room filled with holy water by the priest himself to avert the nightly visitations of the demons. But although Strindberg was swayed by the faith of the Catholics with whom he was surrounded, and attracted by the ritual, he had a certain loyalty towards Protestantism, and at the same time no prayers seemed quite such a protection against evil spirits as the Dalmatian dagger with which, on occult instruction, he stabbed at the invisible figures creeping up on him. Nor did this practice prevent him from seeing himself as Jacob wrestling with God.

He now feared that the Theosophists, as he had refused to join their ranks, had become dangerous enemies, and a worse terror was that he would be arrested and charged with witchcraft—'the sin which even after death cannot escape punishment.' He made a jest of the fact that Pasteur died the day after the publication of *Sylva Sylvarum*, but he was not quite sure that the events were unconnected. And when, just after the appearance in *Initiation* of an article of his own, criticising current astronomical theory, the head of the Paris Observatoire and Sweden's most eminent astronomer both died, and the death of others concerned in the same work followed, Strindberg's dread increased—both that these deaths would be laid at his door, and that he would himself become a victim of Theosophist magicians.

He made friends with his little daughter, but only at the expense of peace and privacy. Even his solitary walk, at that early hour of the morning in which he still felt a harmony with nature and a happiness that could flare into ecstasy, was sacrificed that the child should not be hurt. He restricted his movements and his thoughts to match those of the toddler

172

which exhausted him, but remembering how he had willed sickness on his innocent children, he accepted this too as part of his penance.

During these months in Austria his mind was greatly confused and leapt illogically from one group of ideas to another, but in this very confusion, as in the fecund disorder of nature which he had so often observed, his new life was generated. Light glimmered at the end of the tunnel; he turned his face towards it and his extraordinary powers of recuperation began their work.

Guided still by signs—he recognised the landscape that he had observed in the zinc bath, both in a Swedenborg description of hell and in a Moravian view—at the beginning of December 1896 he returned to Sweden believing that at last his exile was ended. The urge to write about human life—and his own life—had returned, and he thought often now of *Master Olof*, that masterpiece of his youth which had brought him so much disappointment. He had written the play in a frenzy of doubt, but in the epilogue he had gone beyond doubt and declared God to be an evil power. His endeavour to find truth had been unremitting and sincere, but for this sin too he must atone. God was relentlessly pursuing him; he longed to be defeated by the Almighty, but still to keep his honour.

Lund, the small university town of southern Sweden, which Strindberg had never liked, considering it a come-down for a man from the north to live there, was the next station on his penitential pilgrimage. Here he was met by many facets of his past—old friends, old enemies, creditors, students to admire him, professors to denounce him. Doctors argued over him, the pious prayed for him, and there were others who encouraged him once more to touch forbidden knowledge and renew his sense of power. Stark on his morning walks loomed the lunatic asylum, reminding him of Nietszche, of his sister Elisabeth whose mind was failing, and of his own peril. But however eager the doctors were to explain his experiences in terms of paranoia, no one could deny the lucidity of Strindberg's brain; he set to work now on an exhaustive study of Swedenborg, comparing this writer's hell with those described by Dante and by the Greek, Roman and German mythologists, and Swedenborg's higher man with

Nietzsche's superman. Meanwhile the pull of Catholicism increased; he missed the little chapels and monasteries of Austria, the inspiring churches and cathedrals of France, and saw the cold tyranny of Protestantism as a punishment imposed on the barbarians of the north—an exile, a Babylonish captivity. His Catholic bent was increased by reading *Comment on devient un Mage*, by the poet playwright Sar Péladan, which showed that a man could have supernatural power and yet be an advanced soul and a good Catholic. He would now write his own *Inferno—The Diary of a Damned Soul*—and give an objective account of his own torments which had not ceased, but had lost much of their terror since Swedenborg became his Virgil. He recognised them as symptoms of the state called by Swedenborg 'Devastatio' and aids to spiritual catharsis, and he discovered that he was by no means so singular in his experiences as he had believed. As he came to know people in Lund, he found one after another who had fearful visitations; there seemed to be an epidemic of the supernatural in the town, and sometimes Strindberg even exorcised another's devils. His own demons would, he believed, be finally sought out and slain in their dens by the writing of *Inferno*. When that was accomplished he once more contemplated a monastic retreat where he would be received into the arms of the Mother Church.

Gaunt and grey-haired he wandered about the streets of Lund, and to those who remembered him in earlier years it seemed that the fire had gone out of him, although his eyes shone with vision. He now wore a mantle of monkish cut and colour—he always suited his dress to his changing rôles—but this was not altogether penitential garb; although he had chosen the path towards God, he was not yet prepared to renounce his own will. He still had a 'familiar,' an old friend who was something of a Satanist with whom he could discuss the underworld—and this friend also cultivated the appearance of a monk. Nor; for all his first resolution and the advice of the doctors, did Strindberg give up alcohol, for he slept better and his dreams were sweeter when he drank. Besides, the company at the Tavern was congenial whereas at the Blue Ribbon Café he found himself surrounded with miserable malicious faces. He had grown even more sensitive; he felt soft, uncovered, so that he shrank from rough contacts, and alcohol gave him a cloak against the biting winds of human existence.

In this state of hyperæsthesia, Strindberg watched the return of spring to his native land—the taking down of the double windows all over the town, the cracking of the ice, the discarding of clothing, heavy with winter care, the return of birds and flowers to the forsaken earth. The suffering of Passion week, followed by the festival of Easter, filled him with trembling adoration. He was conscious of life in every stick and stone, every substance of the universe; he felt the breath of the azoic, heard the voices of the dumb and watched the movements of the inanimate. He was aware when another human being, however far away, touched his fate; he felt both the joy and the pain of others. Even another's death agony and release from suffering by death was experienced by him. He felt himself of all times and all places and looked on his soul as a somnambulist which left his body and travelled in other worlds.

In May he wrote a letter which was addressed to the small Kerstin:

Dear little glow-worm,
    You glimmer in the distance. . . .
    But, dear child, wasn't it your birthday during these last days? Yes, it was. So take my good wishes, child. Unfortunately I cannot send you anything else.
    I am tired out with writing, but glad too that I can write. My book is called *Inferno*. Hell does not flourish without Beatrice, but I have really made a start.
    It is beginning to be green here but it is still chilly. I must not leave Lund.
    On the first of May the students had a great celebration and I was invited. I wore a white student's cap with a black peak and a gold and blue cockade. I felt as if I were young again, and drank punch with the students.
    When is your picture coming? I am longing for it.
    Tell Grandmamma that many strange things are happening here. Nearly everyone is convinced that higher powers have come back to inhabit the earth. I know only one person who does not believe it, and he has already been punished. Something new is on the way. Mankind is quaking with fear. Swedenborg is right, and he alone explains everything that is happening.
    Péladan is the Catholic occultist who is seeking reform; his book

How one becomes a Magician, is the best and finest book a Catholic can read. Péladan is a white prophet, not black.

When I have published my *Inferno,* I shall very likely go into a monastery: Frères Saint Jean de Dieu; helpers of the sick.

It has come to this.

Farewell! Greet Grandmamma's mother, Grandmamma and Grandmamma's sister. Mamma will not wish for any greeting.

PAPPA

Lund 4 May 1897

As he did not expect to find a Swedish publisher for *Inferno* he wrote it in French, for the better chance of having it read at least in manuscript. He had kept a diary of his travels in the underworld, and now he expanded his entries and reviewed them in the light of Swedenborgian revelations—with the same thoughts always echoing in his mind: 'if he had read the Prophet before he would have understood.'

Yet still he hungered for more assurance, for a faith that was proof against all probings. The universe swayed under his feet; he yearned for the fastness of the rock of ages. When he heard that Mrs. Annie Besant found Catholicism compatible with Theosophy his inclination towards the Church increased, for although he was opposed to the Theosophist priestesses, he was open to every influence that pressed in the direction he wished to go. He was still disinclined for the dogma and the obedience which would be imposed on him, but the desire for a refuge was stronger than his reluctance. When a crow on the housetops flapped its wings and flew towards him, reminding him of the weathercock on Notre Dame des Champs, and a ladybird crawled southward over the finished script of *Inferno,* Strindberg followed their instructions and packed his bags.

Now in wondering melancholy he revisited scenes of torment and of revelry. No more for him the artists' bacchanalia; he was concerned with prayers and services, with crucifix, rosary and holy water. The Luxembourg garden became a temple of his meditation, and he saw it as the holy city of St. John's Revelation. He read Thomas à Kempis and Haubert's *Temptation of St. Anthony,* Chateaubriand's *Le Génie du Christianisme,* and came for the first time on Huysmans' *Là Bas* and *En Route.* He marvelled that this Frenchman,

176

born just a year before himself, should have gone through so much of the same agony—and been like himself reborn, and he saw in *En Route* further proof of the suffering caused by occult power in the hands of evil men. When he read Allan Karder's *Book of Spirits* he was again attacked by the mysterious current and took this for a warning that such books were forbidden to him who had chosen the road to the Cross. And sometimes there was a ticking inside his coat, right over his heart, as of a death-watch beetle counting the seconds to his death.

Although *Inferno* was finished, its impetus carried him further. He was not quite out of the tunnel, and he had to accomplish his release both in his life and in his writing. He called the new book *Legends*, and this too he wrote largely in French, although *Inferno* had at once been bought by the Swedish publisher Gernandt and, since the author refused to make a Swedish version himself, was translated into his own language by his friend Eugène Fahlstedt.

In the first part of *Legends* Strindberg described his life in Lund and, besides outlining his further occult experiences, gave free vent to his contempt for the town and his annoyance at being ridiculed and ignored. Once he had written this, he breathed more freely, and he now introduced into the book an essay on the soul, which had already appeared in *Initiation*, explaining its somnambulistic state and the way in which it contracted with fear and swelled with happiness. He recounted his dreams, gave reasons for his belief in *Doppelgänger*, reviewed his studies of Swedenborg and ended the volume with a section called *Wrestling Jacob*. The more he thought about Jacob, wounded in the hollow of the thigh but standing up fighting with the Unknown until the breaking of the day, the more clearly he saw himself. Strindberg too now cried out to his God 'I will not let Thee go except Thou bless me.'

He got in touch with the Swedenborg Society in Paris and visited the chapel, but it did not please him, and since reading *Versa Religio* he felt Swedenborg's influence weakening; the book savoured of professional religion with which Strindberg was not concerned, and he found the time had come to take affectionate leave of the master who had

177

'frightened him like a child back to God.' Although he would never again lose faith in the guiding hand he must continue on his journey alone. The Abbé of the Belgian monastery which he had hoped to enter was apprehended for immorality —but in any case Strindberg's resolution to join the Catholic Church was waning; it was too irrevocable a step and the denominational bid for power disgusted him. Pietists, Catholics, Swedenborgians all claimed God as their own property and cramped Him with dogma; Strindberg must exchange protection for liberty and work out his own salvation. The Cross was not to him a sign that Christ had suffered for his sins, but an injunction to bear his own sufferings with patience. Nor was the Christ of his heart a tortured thorn-crowned man, but a child of light, the White Christ, the Advent child who smiled. He had had enough of darkness; his whole being yearned for light and at last his thoughts turned again to the theatre. As a happy omen *Master Olof* was now revived at the Vasa Theatre in Stockholm and had a success with both critics and public.

Strindberg had not written anything in dramatic form since the group of cruel one-act plays which poured from his pen at the time of his divorce from Siri von Essen. Now suddenly the whole world of his consciousness became theatre. The impulse to write of himself was as strong as ever, but he emerged from the peevish pettiness of self-justification into the dramatic art of self-revelation. He no longer relentlessly hammered out his experiences and opinions, but felt his way along with the new vision which showed his blindness, the new knowledge that taught how much more there was to know, testing his consciousness, using his clairvoyance, letting characters change, divide and double, scenes grow out of the beyond and melt again, events reveal their underlying action in fugue-like movement. He wrote of his own Road to Damascus, but he travelled incognito in the way of Everyman, and the Lady of his fate was nameless too.

He returned to Lund in the spring of 1898 with the first part of *To Damascus* finished, convinced that this was his finest work. *Inferno* and *Legends* were both in print, and the latter refuted the 'impression made by the former volume that the author had gone out of his mind. His descriptions of

178

Lund, however, gave offence, and friends asked him, for instance, how he came to portray them as continuously borrowing from him, when in fact the boot was on the other foot —to which Strindberg could only answer that whenever he had a pen in his hand the Devil entered into him. In his new work, however, he was watched over by an angel; he was supported by his 'creedless religion' and inspired by the return of his muse. When he looked in the mirror he no longer saw the evil which Swedenborg had shown to be the Devil within him. He was no longer possessed, but he connected his liberation with a sad event. The mind of his sister Elisabeth, eight years younger than himself, had now failed completely and she had gone into the mental hospital at Uppsala. Strindberg believed her to have taken upon herself his sins and the evil of the whole world; he felt himself in constant spiritual contact with her and she became a part of all his meditations.

In August he retreated for a short time to the Monastery of Maredsous, but was soon persuaded that he had no vocation and returned to Lund. He was no longer haunted, but he was heartbroken; without a woman he could not be whole, and his thoughts turned continually to Siri von Essen and to Frida Uhl who was Siri's shadow. He opened *To Damascus* with the street corner in Berlin which had been the scene of the second spring-time of his life, and in the opening lines of the play called his wife back to him.

In a slow-moving picture, composed from the landscape of his life with Frida and flashbacks to his former marriage, *To Damascus* unfolded—a morality play, a marriage drama, dream, pilgrimage, confession. Strindberg spoke with the voice of many characters, expressing thoughts that had once been his, living again through past experience, watching the action of himself—the Stranger, the Writer, and of his *Doppelgänger*—the Beggar, the Madman—listening to the inmost cry of his soul: 'I did not want to be made a fool of by life!'

In his clairvoyant state Strindberg shattered the closed windows of Naturalism and let in atmosphere, and beyond the human figures on his stage moved superhuman power. He wrote in easy flowing prose; the terseness had gone from his dialogue and the sharp edges from his scenes, and while using

Mendelssohn's Funeral March to give the atmosphere of tragic pilgrimage, Beethoven's fugal passages were the pattern of his composition. In his awareness of repetition in life, he ended part one of *To Damascus* back at the street corner on which the curtain first rose. The Stranger was now writing in the sand and receiving money which only lack of faith had prevented him from having before. Once more the Lady came and led him to the Church. 'Well, I can pass through it,' he said, 'but I shall not stay.'

Still Strindberg wrote on, giving the kaleidoscope a shake, so that from the same ingredients new patterns sprang. The penitential journey grew more painful—the Stranger would not bend so he must be broken; he made gold and his honours turned to dross, he was thrown into gaol and had the scum of the earth for fellows; the Lady bore a child and needed him no longer—mutual torture had been fate's only purpose in their meeting. Yet, at the end of the play's second part, when the Stranger, starting on his journey to the monastery, looked into the Lady's eyes, he cried: 'Come, priest, before I change my mind!'

As memory still lingered in Berlin, Strindberg now began a novel called *The Cloister* after the original name of the tavern which had become Zum Schwarzen Ferkel. This symbolic change into a black pig pleased his fancy, and free at last from fear he began to describe Przybyszewski, Adolf Paul and others of the circle, but while the book was still only a fragment, the theatre called him back. The Advent theme which he had touched on in *Legends* flowered into a mystery play.

This plot too was spun from his own past, but in *To Damascus* he had taken the first step away from the X-ray photograph of autobiography, and in *Advent* he went further. The grip of egomania was slackening, and he could see more in the mirror than his own face. In his adoration of light he made the Judge and his wife, who like Frida's grandparents grew flowers round their own mausoleum, fear sunlight as a symptom of their wickedness, while the children loved it as a friend. He conceived the White Christ as a child of light, and the Other One as the dark soul condemned to scourge sinners to the Cross, and he let the supernatural loose upon the stage.

180

Both parts of *To Damascus* were published by Gernandt towards the end of 1898, and as soon as he had finished *Advent*, Strindberg set to work on a play showing how a man proved innocent may still be guilty. This time there were no supernatural figures in the cast, but the whole theme of *Crime and Crime* was inspired by the power of evil. At last Strindberg had found a way to express the sense of guilt that had haunted him for twenty years, ever since the death of Siri von Essen's first child. The scene of *Crime and Crime* was the Quartier Latin with the Jardin de Luxembourg as the Garden of Eden from which the guilty couple, scourging each other endlessly in a treadmill of recrimination, were expelled. The playwright had deserted his mistress and child for *la femme fatale*, and as the child was an obstacle to their happiness they wished it out of the way—and it died. The father was suspected of murder, his career fell to pieces and, although finally cleared of suspicion, the Abbé still declared that as he had murdered in thought he was not innocent and must atone for his crime. With understanding and repentance a new life dawned for the playwright, and Strindberg wrote the last lines of *Crime and Crime* in ecstasy at his own deliverance. Until his pride was broken he had been unable to write more plays—now once again they flowed from his pen. 'To-night I will go to the Church and have a reckoning with myself, but to-morrow I shall go to the theatre.'

While refusing the limitations of convention, for this play Strindberg used conventional form with a dash of Parisian style, and turned out a polished tragi-comedy. At the same time he invoked the aid of Beethoven's Sonata in D minor to create the atmosphere of sinful thought, for this music always pierced to the core of his own conscience. And in order that no one should miss the invisible powers, he put *Crime and Crime* in the same volume as *Advent*, with which it appeared to have little in common, and joined the two plays by the single title *Under Higher Judgment*.

Strindberg had come back to the theatre, the love of his youth, and in Finland the seventeen-year-old Greta had decided to go on the stage. At Christmas time she wrote her father of this plan and he replied with a joint letter to the two girls:

Dearest Children,

It was kind to write me such a long letter for Christmas which is lonely here and not particularly gay. Now I'm really up to date about your affairs, both large and small. So you two, Karin and Greta, are no longer children, but young ladies, ready to go out into life.

As I don't take advice myself, I won't give you any; for you know very well yourselves what brings happiness and what unhappiness.

I offer you my services instead, and you know that I have contacts with the theatre and literature, so when the moment comes you can rely on me. The odd thing is that I thought it would be Karin who would want to go on the stage and Greta who would cling to house and home. But I was wrong, as you see.

I have now put aside everything else and occupy myself exclusively with writing for the theatre, so as to fulfil the promise of my youth as a dramatist. I've recently finished a serious phantasy in the style of Andersen's stories, and to-morrow I'm going to begin a drama of Swedish history. You can be sure therefore that I don't regret Greta's theatre career, for the stage is indeed my own art.

That once I deserted you is certainly in the eyes of the world reprehensible, but all the same I don't feel I have any right to repent of this, for I acted as if on the bidding of a higher power. And truly it seems now as if through this you were able to develop in greater freedom, freedom from my nagging and freedom from the hampering solicitude of parents who from the best of intentions try to shape their children's destinies to their own wishes. We certainly should have been at odds with one another at this stage, whereas now I trust that you look on me as a friend who will not force opinions on you or interfere with your souls, and on whom you can count if bad luck comes.

Best wishes for a happy New Year, and don't forget me.

Your friend

Lund 26 Dec. 1898   AUGUST SG.

On January 22nd, 1899, Strindberg's fiftieth birthday, telegrams poured in to his lodgings, many newspapers paid him tribute, a gala performance of *Master Olof* was given in Stockholm, and his old friend Verner von Heidenstam published a poem hailing the great writer who wore not stars and glory, but a martyr's crown of his own choosing. Although his views and his behaviour still shocked many people, Strindberg could have no further doubt that as a writer he was widely acknowledged, and as a sign of national esteem Hjalmar Branting, who had recently become a member of the Riksdag, proposed that he should be given a writer's grant. To this suggestion his old acquaintance wrote:

I have never been anything but a writer, and the tendency lately of us writers to want to be prophets and politicians has been I think to go outside our province. 'No programme' was my old motto and still is. The same liberty to grow that I desired for others I reserved for myself. It was quite by chance therefore that I worked in association with you as a friend of peace and universal suffrage, and you must not consider me a political person. Some people need religion, others don't. I must have contact with 'Jenseits' in order to get perspective and *lointain* in my paintings and I can't breathe in your physical vacuum.

As we differ in this, we must too in our views of life and everything. In regard to the purely practical measure you propose, namely of persuading the Riksdag majority to give me a writer's grant, I don't want to be the majority's or the peasants' poet any more than I want to be a Court poet. . . . So thank you again once more, but I must decline. . . .

Strindberg had studied Shakespeare's historical plays and tragedies with new appreciation, and now he once more resolved to put Swedish history on the stage. *Master Olof* had come to its own at last, but he could do better. In order to go behind the historians, who whitewashed and canonised every king and influential person, he plunged into the old chroniclers and story-tellers, and with a fine disregard for chronology lifted passages of dramatic promise from legends, myths and Edda. The audience for his new plays must have enough imagination not to bother with clocks and calendars.

For his latest experiment Strindberg chose the fourteenth century—the last epoch of the fated dynasty of the Folkungs, and filled his stage with kings and queens, guilty lovers, innocent children, flagellants and clowns, a strange diversity of beings moving in what he visualised as a giant game of chess—the white side and the black both played by the hand of the Almighty. And for the voice of the Powers, the voice that prophesied evil times, exposed secrets, told how the gentle King Magnus must atone for the blood-guilt of his crown and the crime of his forebears, he chose the figure of a woman—the Possessed. Insane according to common standards, this character lived largely in an unseen world, but although she communed with spirits, her consciousness of earthly life was greater than that of those who knew no other existence. Thoughts of insanity were never far from Strindberg's mind, but after his sister's mental collapse he believed

185

madness to be nothing more than a state in which the limits
of normal awareness were passed. The doctors now considered
him sane, and he knew very well that his brain had never
failed, but his ordeal had frayed his nerves; with his reason he
no longer feared, but his nerves did not listen to reason. A
stranger coming to the door or unexplained glances in a café
made him tremble, but although he could withdraw from
society, he could not withdraw from life. The more he shut
himself up, the more clairvoyant he became. He found himself in telepathic rapport with friends, relatives and enemies.
If a man in the neighbourhood went bankrupt he shared his
humiliation, if a woman was in labour he felt her pains.
Sometimes his consciousness widened to include whole nations,
to see the cripples and beggars of the world, and a new compassion for humanity mingled with his criticism. There was
so much intolerable suffering.

He finished his dramatic extravaganza *The Saga of the
Folkungs* in April 1899, and at once turned to the completion
of the Vasa cycle begun with *Master Olof*. Twenty years had
passed since this play was finally finished, and when the curtain rose on *Gustavas Vasa* twenty years had passed since that
wily king brought the young idealist to heel. Now Olaus Petri
—for as the King's Secretary Olof resumed the original form
of his name—was no longer the central character. The Odin-
like figure of Gustavus Vasa strode the boards, dragging in his
wake his epileptic heir Prince Erik, bred in hatred and finding
the whole world a madhouse. Strindberg brought all his
knowledge of life's complexity and all his skill to the moulding
of these characters. In his drama nothing should be left of the
lay figures, the lifeless images that strutted woodenly across
the pages of the histories. He would show Sweden that history
was made not out of deliberate wars and political programmes,
but out of moods and weather, out of fun and lust and irritation, out of all the common stuff of daily life. His men of
history—the women, except as mothers or maniacs, were
mere shadows—lived everyday lives with moods and minds
that changed, and they talked a robust colloquial Swedish,
beautiful or ugly as emotion dictated. This was Strindbergian
truth, to paint the Swedish Reformation in the stark colours
of faith, tyranny, treachery and passion, to ignore the bugbear

184

of anachronism, and seek out the human heart with the same ardour that he had sought for flakes of gold.

Summer overtook him as he wrote, and his mind strayed often to Kymmendö, perhaps, as he wrote to a friend, because in his present play Master Olof appeared as an old man, and *Master Olof* had been conceived on Kymmendö. In any case the lure of the Baltic islands in June was irresistible, and he agreed to join the von Philps out in the skerries at Furusund for the rest of the summer. His nephews and nieces were to be of the party, and he invited Greta to come and join them and make the acquaintance of her father. He felt an urge now to be on friendly terms again with his family.

He found Furusund 'the loveliest place he had seen in Sweden,' and he got on well with Greta, but even these distractions did not weaken his concentration. His play was more real than the life about him, and as always threads of his own life were woven into the pattern—even his painful irritation when disturbed while writing was expressed by Olaus. The mighty King, the man of blood and bone whom Strindberg had raised from the dust, rolled on—the Lutheran Reformer on whose palate the bouquet of Catholicism still lingered, the tyrant who was yet the loving father of his people, until at last his conjurer let him depart in peace with the ringing words: 'O God, Thou hast punished me, and I thank Thee!'

Gustavus Vasa seemed to its author an advance on *The Saga of the Folkungs* both in technique and characterisation, and seated in his timber shack with his favourite scenery to rejoice his eyes, Strindberg drove on with the last play of the cycle.

Now he could make gold with his pen, although still as a recreation he got out his chemical apparatus and gilded such things as the crook of his walking stick. In *Erik XIV* the unhappy Prince, now King, fluttered through the scenes on the rim of insanity, and about him Strindberg wove some of his inmost thoughts. 'You use that word hate so often,' Erik's old friend exclaimed, 'that you've come to see yourself as the enemy of mankind. . . . That word is a first manifestation of creative power, and you cast a spell over yourself with the incantation. Say love a little oftener and you will believe yourself loved.'

185

Indeed, in spite of the savagery and cynicism, tender shoots of love kept springing up in all these historical plays. The bloody tale of the Folkungs ended with the plague striking down the boy king and his little bride. 'Hush, now I want to go to sleep again; then my dreams will catch her. Oh how lovely to walk among the clover with one's sweetheart and listen to the larks up in the sky!' In *Gustavus Vasa* Prince Erik had caught a glimpse of heaven in the face of a flower girl and taken her for his love, although he hoped to wed the Virgin Queen of England, and in *Erik XIV* love cleansed the soul of a thorough-going scoundrel, who only feared that his jealousy might be roused. 'Erik, don't touch that chord, or the devil will descend into my soul, where I've just built a little chapel to the unknown God.'

The young people flirted in the long twilight evenings— Greta got on especially well with her first cousin Henry von Philp, the medical student—and busy though he was, Strindberg still had time to be gallant himself when an attractive woman crossed his path. His sentimental side woke, and there were children too in the party who roused nostalgia and were woven into Erik's lament: 'If only it hadn't been Whitsun Eve! That wakes so many memories . . . memories of the children specially. The best this miserable life can give.' . . . 'Death and damnation! Where are my children? Who has dared to touch the bear's cubs? . . .'

Even when the Vasas' day was over, the curse of the Folkung blood was not broken, and in the closing lines of *Erik XIV*, Strindberg's consciousness of life's terrible repetitions burst from the lips of a renegade courtier: 'Ah, God, it's beginning again!'

But for himself life was beginning again with a smile.

186

CHAPTER FOURTEEN

1899–1902

The higher phantasy has a greater reality than this actuality.
These banal accidents are not essential life. My whole life is a
dream

BITTER AS he had been about Sweden, 'the land of the non-adult,' this time Strindberg really had come home. The autumn of 1899 found him moving into his own capital and viewing it with refreshed and loving eyes. On his last visit Stockholm had not pleased him; in the years since his child-hood, there had been an outcrop of neo-Gothic houses, pompous banks and blatant factories, which with the police-men's new spiked helmets gave an impression that Sweden was becoming a satrap of Prussia. Now a gayer type of archi-tecture was springing up—houses washed in pale colour with balconies, bigger windows and light furniture of birch and oak. White façades, white boats and flying pennons decorated the water-fronts, and it seemed to Strindberg that Sweden had recovered from the industrial revolution. The younger generation was in love with the country and celebrated her in dance and song, and Strindberg saw these pleasant new fashions as the result of better social conditions. Nietzsche's influence no longer prevented him from rejoicing in Sweden's democratic progress, and as he settled into his flat with his writing-desk, his books and his piano, he found his roots steadily growing both as a Swede and a Stockholmer.

At the same time he was not drawn towards his fellow writers such as Heidenstam, Karlfeldt, Snoilsky and the two famous women, Selma Lagerlöf and Ellen Key. He still felt more at home among painters, and fond though he had always been of music his love for it had deepened. It was clear to him that Beethoven had reached greater heights than any other artist. He hung his death-mask on the porcelain stove and meditated on the Master as he worked, and for the sake of music he endured company. He still tried too, though shyly, to make friends with relatives and old acquaintances, but they seemed mere shades of the 'eighties and content to be so, whereas he must press forward into the new century. So most often he remained alone, and as in his young days looked in through lighted windows at the mystery of other people's homes—but with this difference. Then he had looked with envy, now compassion was added to his awareness. Behind the gay façades so many hearts had broken and would break. In spite of disillusion he was doing his best to make friends with life.

Just as Strindberg made this move back to his own city, a young Norwegian actress came to live there for the first time. At an audition earlier in the year, Harriet Bosse had been told that there would be an engagement for her at the Dramatic Theatre if she learned 'to speak like a human being.' She had spent the summer improving her Swedish accent and now the promise was fulfilled. She made her début as Louise in *Gringoire,* and she attended the *première* of *Gustavus Vasa* at the beginning of October, and the dress rehearsal of *Crime and Crime* a few months later. Straight from some months' training at the Paris Conservatoire, Harriet Bosse was not particularly impressed by the Swedish theatre, but she had never seen anything so inspiring as these plays of Strindberg's.

To Damascus was to be put on next, but the part of the Lady was not yet cast. It was suggested to Strindberg that in the current production of *A Midsummer Night's Dream* he would see collected all the female talent of Stockholm. Harriet Bosse was playing Puck, and in spite of the eyes which, he complained, always 'harpooned' him in the theatre, Strindberg remained standing up in his box, fascinated by this slender exotic creature. Through her manager he invited her to call on him; Harriet Bosse borrowed a black dress from her sister which, although too large, would she hoped make her look interesting, was received by a very spruce grey-haired gentleman, fêted with flowers, fruit and wine, and found herself cast for the Lady. Before she left, the famous author showed her specimens of the gold he had made, and begged the feather from her hat to use as a shaft for his pen.

The choice of an inexperienced *ingénue* for the difficult lead in *To Damascus* surprised many people, but Strindberg believed she had the qualities the part required. He intended something of the sprite in the Lady—elf, siren, wife and witch, drawing the threads of a man's fate through her fingers and knotting it with her crochet hook. There was a suggestion of the Oriental in Harriet Bosse's colouring and mould of feature which appealed to his imagination, and her Puck had shown poetic feeling, while at the same time she was young enough to be flexible. All the same he did not intrude upon her; from the day of their meeting in the spring of 1900, she did not hear from Strindberg again until the first night of *To Damascus* in the autumn. Then a bunch of red roses and a note awaited her.

Miss Harriet Bosse
As I shall not show myself in the theatre this evening, I want to thank you now for what I saw at the dress rehearsal. It was fine and beautiful, though I had imagined my character rather brighter, with just a touch of roguishness and more breadth.
A little of Puck—that was my first word to you and is my last.
A smile in the midst of unhappiness shows there's still hope, and the situation is seen not to be hopeless.
And so, good luck on the journey between thorns and stones. Such is the road. I only lay a few flowers on it.
                                        AUGUST STRINDBERG

Strindberg had now come to an end of his historical inspiration, and during the summer, in response to a request from a new theatre, had written a midsummer pageant of Stockholm in which he sang the praises of his city. The family gathering at Furusund had not, however, been such a success as in the previous year, partly because memories of Siri von Essen were constantly revived. His love for her had been the sweetest emotion of his life and its loss his greatest tragedy. Relatives who were always prying and advising stirred the devils within him.

How, however, his thoughts revolved round Harriet Bosse. *To Damascus* had a *succès d'estime* and she was considered very promising, but Strindberg perceived that the part of the Lady was really too mature for her, and he resolved now to write a play that would exactly suit the young Norwegian—

189

he believed that she could feel and portray the most subtle emotions of a kind usually only reached by music. Very tenderly he created the character of Eleanora, the Easter child, and gave her his mother's second name—which Poe too had used. The image of his sister Elisabeth was with him as he wrote, alone in her night-bound cell, suffering vicariously for the sins of her family and winning atonement for them all. He projected himself into Elisabeth and drew her, not this time as the possessed woman of *Erik XIV*, but as a gentle affectionate child of earth touched with the finger of God. He endowed Eleanora with his own hypersensitive and clairvoyant powers and added a spark of Séraphita's divinity, and he imbued her brother, Elis the schoolmaster, with his own jealousy and stubborn pride. *Easter* was a play of Passion Week—and before the hearts of the family could flower into Easter glory, they must be frozen, broken, scourged until not a trace of hypocrisy and pride remained.

His flat was dark. On November 3rd, 1900, he noted in his diary that the sun no longer came into his rooms, and the long northern winter once more stretched before him; but as he took his solitary morning walks, the sounds and smells of Eastertide defied winter, and memories of every phase of his life seeped into the play along with the smell of melting snow. *Easter* was set in Lund in that spring-time when Strindberg rose from the underworld with senses and supersenses quickened, but here too were his schooldays in Stockholm both as boy and master, here was the garden of the deaf and dumb in Paris, here were phenomena of birds and flowers gathered up on his travels for a book of miracles. Yet *Easter* had no panorama, only a single set of a middle-class living-room—but the room was a veranda made of glass, and the sun and the moon and the stars, the cracking ice and the melting snow, the first spring flowers and the homing bird were members of the cast. There were no completely super-natural figures as in *Advent*, yet the Beyond shimmered in the atmosphere, while Haydn's *Sieben Worte des Erlösers* sounded the great Passion theme behind the destinies of half a dozen people going through 'the school of suffering.'

When after a short run *To Damascus* came off, Strindberg sent Harriet Bosse another bouquet of red roses and the

HARRIET BOSSE IN 'EASTER'

manuscript of *Easter*. At first she thought that after the Lady, Eleanora would be easy to play, but when she studied the part she saw that she was offered another hard task. She had no doubt however that she wanted it. Strindberg bade her become 'our actress of the new century,' and was taking on her education. He sent her books in German, French and English, including Maeterlinck, Péladan and Rudyard Kipling —calling her attention specially to the dream theme of *The Brushwood Boy*. He wrote to her too of Eleanora's relative, Balzac's Séraphita-Séraphitus, 'for whom there could be no earthly love because he-she was *l'époux et l'épouse de l'humanité*.' He told her that this character was the symbol of the highest type of human being, foreshadowed in much modern literature and believed by some people to be on its way down to earth. Strindberg urged Harriet Bosse to remember that Eleanora was a child of God, and to avoid every stage convention of insanity.

She was bent on pleasing him—she studied languages so as to be able to read everything he sent her, and took piano lessons again because of his fondness for music—yet for all this new sweetness, Strindberg's mind now took a fierce backward twist. He was liable at any time to drop suddenly from bliss to blackest gloom, and now old memories racked him with an increasing pain that could only be assuaged by violent expression. He turned his back on the redemption of *Easter* and planned a *Danse macabre* with Saint-Saëns' music as accompaniment. He opened his heart to all the old poisoned streams of hatred, and at once was consumed with suspicion of his relatives and friends.

He wrote to his old friend Gustaf af Geijerstam, now literary director of Gernandts:

> I feel something sickly in your personality, which weighs on me and threatens to make me sick. I recognise, too, the threat in your actions which aim, even if with good intent, at interfering in my fate.
>
> You have tried, for instance, to rule my sympathies and antipathies, to decide what company I shall keep, force opinions on me and so forth.
>
> I am retiring, and I beg you not to communicate with me until I communicate with you. I'll risk your refusing to see me then. . . .

When Strindberg found that Ibsen had already used the *Danse macabre* in *John Gabriel Borkman*, he took *The Entry of the Boyars* as the tune for his own *Dance of Death*. He concentrated his sense of life's malevolence in the stone turret of an island fortress that had once been a prison. The walls were impregnated with hatred, the atmosphere poisoned all who breathed it. Once more the theme was married hatred and married misery, and Strindberg conjured up the savage skill of his Naturalist plays to draw a loathsome wife and, this time, a still more evil and treacherous husband. He composed this awful figure, this larger-than-life vampire Captain, who destroyed the peace of all about him as he staggered from one death throe to the next, from caricatures of many men including Geijerstam, and over them all he poured his own despair. 'Life was so alien, so contrary, so cruel, right from my childhood, and people were so cruel that I became so too.' And into Kurt, the Quarantine Master, returned after fifteen years abroad, divorced and robbed of his children, who first tried to save the doomed couple and then was infected himself with their poison, Strindberg slipped another of his selves— sensuous, well-meaning, weak. Even the young people at Furusund did not escape his pen; he was anxious about Greta's real opinion of him, and neither his conscience nor his suspicions let him rest. He twisted the budding love between her and her cousin to his plot and suggested that their fate too might lie within the vicious circle of their inheritance; then he saluted the brightness of their youth— 'How strange that flowers should grow out of filth!'

With its battering cynical dialogue, its silent nightmare action and the pounding of the *Entry of the Boyars*, *The Dance of Death* was a masterpiece of horror. Strindberg sent the script to Harriet Bosse who was astonished by this sinister work of the mind that had just shaped *Easter*—but already the same mind had sped on with a fairy-tale tragedy *The Bridal Crown*. Strindberg's muse would not now let him rest for a day, and her inspiration had bewildering variety. This time he must paint the lakes and forests of Dalecarlia, that region of Sweden so rich in tradition, from which Engelbrecht the Miner had risen against the tyranny of the Dane. The Dalesmen were an independent people, still using a dialect and costume of their own and keeping alive old customs and traditions. Strindberg was tired of analysing and propounding; he composed *The Bridal Crown* from the myths, songs and superstitions of the Dalecarlians, though the theme was one which, like married misery, never ceased to haunt himself— the murder of an unwanted child—this time by the mother in order that she might win the virgin's bridal crown.

He peopled the woods and waterfalls with sprites, and was so delighted with his goblin world that in *Swanwhite* he made freer still with fairyland. In January 1881 he had written his first fairy play in a glow of happiness because Greta had just been born, he and Siri had spent a happy summer on Kymmendö, and the Dramatic Theatre had at last put on *Master Olof*. Now, twenty years later, having pacified his devils with *The Dance of Death* and his conscience with *The Bridal Crown* which ended in repentance, his bright side again dominated, and *Swanwhite* was a play of roses, romance and white magic. All the same Strindberg still contemplated a retreat from the world in accord with the third part of *To Damascus*, in which he led the Stranger right inside the monastery where he must seem to die in order to be reborn—in fact, in February 1901 he wrote to Richard Bergh, the painter to whom he had been sitting for his portrait, for details of an Italian monastery:

Even if I don't retreat for life, I long to go in. . . . I believe my presence here at home is only an annoyance, a disturbance to other people's quiet work.

Now that I have fulfilled the promise of my youth and done my duty to my country, I think it would be becoming to disappear. I feel I almost owe it to public modesty to hide my unwieldy cumbersome personality. And let my work speak! Alone!

But as he wrote his fairy play, he was in fact bound closer to the earth each day, for the wheel had turned again and he had fallen in love with Harriet Bosse.

If he were to remain in the world he must have her beside him, and one evening in March, when she came tripping up to his flat, so young, so serious, so friendly, so modest, to say that after all he had better give the part of Eleanora to a more experienced actress, he told her of the greater part she had come to play in his life. She was not only his Easter child, but the Lady of his destiny, and she alone could decide how

193

his pilgrimage should end. He proposed in the simplest way he knew: he asked her if she would have a child by him.

Alarmed and deeply flattered, Harriet Bosse wrote her reply in Norwegian:

> If you believe the woman you created for the Stranger has the power to bind him to life by taking his hand and showing him all the brightness and beauty of the world, then it is not right for him to go into a monastery.
> But supposing she couldn't.
> How disappointed he would be if afterwards he found that she was not as gifted, enlightened and wise as he believed.
> If he found that her spirit was too small to bear the great weight of his. Don't you think this would ruin everything for him, that all his hopes would collapse and it would be even darker than it was before?
> And she! . . how she would suffer if she failed to reach the high goal . . . to reconcile him with his fellow beings in the way he hopes and desires.
> I can well imagine that small woman's glorious happiness if the Stranger—in spite of all her forebodings—just took her hand quietly in his and walked with her towards—the goal.
> And forgot the monastery.

He forgot the monastery. Once again he had chosen an ambitious young actress for his wife, and he believed, as sincerely as he had twenty-five years before, that motherhood was the crowning achievement of feminine nature and must therefore be the highest ambition of every woman. True, in the first days of his infatuation for Siri von Essen, when she was still married to another, Strindberg had assured her that she was not intended for the rôle of wife and mother, but in his heart he had never believed that a good woman could want more. Since reading Swedenborg, the works and fruits of love were more than ever symbolised for him in the mystery of procreation—and he also wanted to prove his virility. He knew that Harriet Bosse feared the loss of her freedom, but he assured himself that when the children came, 'the souls now waiting to be given life by their love,' she would be content. In the last part of *To Damascus* a little bitterness about Greta Strindberg had crept into the drawing of the Stranger's young daughter. The independent adolescent, 'a rose that had blown too soon,' could not mean so much to

Strindberg as the infant which 'lay like an angel in the
white veils of her cradle'—besides which Greta brought
him stinging memories. Like the Captain in *The Dance of
Death*, Strindberg now wanted to throw all past humiliations
into the sea, to 'cancel them out and pass on.'

But even after they were formally engaged, Harriet Bosse
continued to doubt if she could play the part, more difficult
than anything in the theatre, of August Strindberg's third
wife. And he continued to wear down her resistance.

Beloved,
    You ask if you can give me goodness and beauty in life. But what
have you not given me already?
    When you, beloved kind friend, came into my home three months
ago, I was sad, old, ugly, almost evil, without hope.
    And then you came.
    What happened?
    First you made me almost good.
    Then you gave me back my youth.
    Next you woke my hope of better things.
    Then you taught me the beauty of life—as far as may be, and the
beauty of poetry—Swanwhite!
    I was sad, you gave me happiness.
    What have you on your side to fear?
    You, young, beautiful, talented, and more than this, good, what
have you not to teach me? And you dare say you lack knowledge.
    You have taught me to speak in fair words, you have taught me
to think fine and lofty thoughts, you have taught me to forgive my
enemies, you have taught to respect the fate of others than myself.
    Beloved, who can separate us if it is not the will of Providence . . . ?

And, to allay her fears, he also wrote: 'Beloved, beloved!
Hear my cry, the Eagle's free, free, free!'

As a betrothal gift, besides a sapphire and diamond ring,
Strindberg gave Harriet Bosse *Swanwhite*, the first love play
of his life. Between its conception and its creation he had
become a disciple of Maeterlinck's—in 1894, when he first
heard of the Belgian playwright, Strindberg was blinkered
with realism and shied at anything outside his direct line of
vision; he was still trying, though vainly, to escape from his
fears through scepticism, and he distrusted what he heard of
Maeterlinck. Now, after enjoying *La Princesse Maleine*, he
turned to the author's philosophy, and found that it spoke to

195

his condition. Maeterlinck, too, had been influenced by Paris occultism; he too believed in dark powers, a supreme will and the communion of souls. As Strindberg had once written of *Thus Spake Zarathustra*, he now wrote to Emil Schering, his German translator, that *Le Trésor des Humbles* was the most important book he had ever read, and he translated passages of it into Swedish for Harriet Bosse.

She was his dove, his child, his mother. His eagle's wings would lift her above life's hardships so long as she drew him like a mother to her breast. At the end of *To Damascus* he dissolved the Lady into the Mother: 'In life I could never caress you. . . . Come, my child, I'll make amends for the wrong I did you, I'll rock you to sleep on my knees, I'll wash you clean. . . .'

Harriet Bosse must make amends for all the wrong done him. He could only be reconciled with mankind and with himself through a woman; he could only be washed clean by one with whom he could prove that 'Caritas, not Eros, is the God of love.' He wanted children, but he would have preferred them to spring 'like chaste Minerva from the head of Zeus.' He dreaded the transformation of the kiss into 'a surgical operation,' leading to 'anger, tears, contempt, blood and bandages.' These waiting weeks frayed his nerves, specially as he knew that many mocked at the match between the grey-haired author, twice divorced, and the actress thirty years his junior. Though he sang love's triumph in *Swanwhite*, he sounded its knell in the final scenes of *To Damascus*.

He was gallant and loaded Harriet Bosse with gifts and flowers, but if—outside the theatre—another man looked at her, Strindberg's peace of mind vanished. Before long he would only take her to a restaurant if they ate in a private room, and sometimes when she had dressed for a drive, he would suddenly dismiss the victoria and keep her indoors where none could see her but himself. On the stage the world was hers, off it she must have none but him. In his youth he had given his heart away to a vain and frivolous girl who thought she could act; through her true talent, her goodness and her beauty Harriet Bosse must wipe out that shame. He saw her as a goddess, wise and full of compassion—his whole life was becoming a dream and he created her rôle in that

196

dream. Yet, though he felt he was dreaming, his senses and his wit were sharp as ever, and startlingly new and vigorous language flashed from his poems and plays.

As on the occasion of his second marriage, the ceremony was delayed, for although it had been easy for Frida Uhl to obtain freedom, since her marriage had never been recognised by the Catholic Church, the Swedish formalities were not yet concluded. Strindberg wanted to follow the example of Master Olof and dispense with a ceremony. He suggested that on April 19th, Olof's Day, he and Harriet Bosse should pledge their faith outside Gustav Adolf's Church—before God and in the presence of witnesses—and then that he should pin a document to the door declaring their union valid. He let himself be dissuaded however, and on the first of May 1901 they were married in an orthodox way.

Strindberg did not allow his bride to bring any possessions from the flat she had shared with her sister ever since she came to Stockholm. She must come to him just as she was— to the new flat he had taken for them just as it was, and which in secret she found hideous. In spite of his appreciation of modern furniture, Strindberg's home was decorated in the fashion of the 'eighties with heavy mahogany, palms on pedestals and aspidistras. He did his best to make his bride's room fair; indeed he was so much impressed himself with the new carpet that he described it in the third part of *To Damascus*—'green as a summer meadow . . . light green like hope.' Here too he wrote of the evening when she came and 'the rooms were full of kindly spirits blessing us and our home' . . . 'the candles burned quietly in prayer and the flowers were lost in thought.' He could 'hear the poems coming,' poems which were all for her, for 'the white dove who, unafraid because she had never provoked the heavens, could give the frightened eagle peace.' But Strindberg's poetry could not give Harriet Bosse happiness; he was fighting the whole time to keep her from the world, and she, called by nature and the theatre, struggled the whole time to escape back into it.

Strindberg's energetic routine of work was unchanged by marriage. He added *Carl XII* and *Engelbrecht* to his histories and planned a drama of Christina, the Queen daughter of

197

Gustavus Adolphus who, jealous of the qualities of the other sex and lacking those of her own, played the man and played with men. One of the women artists at Zum Schwarzen Ferkel provided him with a model.

After some weeks he suggested to his wife that they should take a tardy honeymoon in Germany. Harriet was overjoyed, but when all the arrangements had been made and they were ready to start, Strindberg had an overwhelming conviction that the powers were hostile. He announced this in a brusque tone that allowed no argument, and then tried to comfort his wife with flowers and Rhine wine, Baedekers and books from abroad. All the joys of travel, he declared, without its discomforts; but Harriet Bosse, shut up in her green room, could find little comfort in grinding away at foreign languages. Strindberg had travelled so much, done so much, knew so much—now he only wanted to rest in his happiness. But she was young, for her the world was new—she cried a good deal, then went off to stay with friends in Denmark without him. Now it was his turn to weep. 'So many tears, so many tears, so many burning tears,' he wrote, and when this did not bring her back he followed her.

At Hornbaeck, on the Danish coast, they passed some happy weeks together. Strindberg was writing poems and contemplating a play which should follow 'the disjointed yet apparently logical form of a dream' more faithfully than *To Damascus*. He took no interest in the events of the day, never read a newspaper unless some dramatic headline caught his eye, and wanted no company but his wife's. He noticed with pride and alarm the admiration that his 'little Javanese' attracted on the beach, and wondered at his audacity in marrying her, believing that every other human being must envy him and plot his downfall. When finally a photographer took a snapshot of her bathing, he swept her off to Berlin where his happiness returned, for Harriet Bosse was pregnant. Now he had once again the strange and moving awareness of paternity and was sure that his wife would blossom into perfection.

But in spite of her condition, when they returned to Stockholm Harriet Bosse fled again. This time Strindberg did not follow, but only sent frantic letters pleading his cause.

198

It's not true that I'm selfish. I can't live without giving. I've always given, yes sacrificed. . . . Sacrifice a little of yourself for me, and I'll sacrifice everything for you.

In misery he worked at his play, rising at seven for his walk and returning to a morning of concentrated writing, but he could not sustain the effort for many hours or inspiration flagged, so the rest of the day dragged out in loneliness and fear. Everything was happening again; only music and alcohol could bring him comfort.

To begin with he called his dream play *Prisoners*, since this world which looked so fair was clearly either a prison or a lunatic asylum, then he changed the name to *Corridor Drama*, as much of the action took place in the corridor leading to the stage door of the Dramatic Theatre, where night after night he had waited for Harriet Bosse. In the corridor was a door with an airhole shaped like a four-leafed clover, and no one seemed to know what was behind it. This struck his fancy and he wove it into his plot—the cupboard containing the secret of existence, which proved to be nothing since out of nothing God made life. But his work did not satisfy him; his love had flown and taken his muse with her. Miserably he destroyed the script, but he could not destroy the idea and soon began to write the dream play again, calling it this time *The Growing Castle*, for now his fancy was caught by the domed roof of the cavalry barracks which he could see from the window of his study, flashing gold above the trees. Everything struggled upwards away from earth's filth—so, since everything was one, why not a castle too?

After he had been through 'forty days of suffering,' a period Strindberg noticed to recur often in his life, Harriet Bosse came back. He was very considerate—stopped smoking because it upset her, and planned for her diversion. He himself painted in the afternoons when he could not write, and occasionally modelled in clay. It occurred to him that modelling and piano-playing were the most suitable occupations for his wife while she was unable to act. Harriet Bosse acquiesced but without enthusiasm; she knew that her husband meant to be kind and she was trapped. Sometimes now he talked to her of Siri von Essen and never unkindly, but if they touched on 'the woman question' and she defended her sex, he would leave the room and she would hear him washing and washing his hands. As once unsuccessfully with Frida Uhl, Strindberg now made Harriet Bosse promise never to read *A Fool's Defence*, and to her he added the injunction never to play the part of Miss Julie or to give a daughter higher education.

Yet if Harriet Bose felt trapped, so did Strindberg. His spirit was dragged down by petty irritations—a curtain awry, a chair out of place or an imperfect cup of coffee could ruin his day, and mealtimes became an offence instead of a feast. He found eating horribly unromantic and wished people did not have to do it at all, or at least need eat only the fruits of the earth and not its flesh. He had never been so strongly aware of the inner conflict of heaven and earth. He could not live without human love; yet his third marriage was following the old pattern and he was lost in a limbo between the high plane and the low, unable to thrive on either.

He wove his lamentations into *A Dream Play* which contained both the *Corridor Drama* and *The Growing Castle*, and he brought a daughter of the Gods to earth to see if human complaint was justified. She was the Eleanora of *Easter* grown from child to woman, crossed over from the ante-room to heaven itself, but because of Harriet Bosse's looks this time she came as the Daughter of Indra, a Hindu goddess descending from the clouds to life-racked man. To her Strindberg gave his own agony of being earth-bound, his despair at life's limitations. When the Poet asked her what she had suffered most from during her time on earth she answered: 'From . . . living. From feeling my vision dimmed by having eyes, my hearing dulled by having ears, and my thought, my swift, luminous thought, bound down in labyrinthine coils of fat. . . . A brain . . . what crooked creeping channels.'

In his determination to free imagination from all fetters Strindberg dramatised his dreams, for in them, as he wrote in the preface to *A Dream Play*:

Anything can happen; everything is possible and probable. Time and space do not exist; on an insignificant groundwork of reality, imagination spins and weaves new patterns made up of memories, experiences, unrestrained fancies, absurdities and improvisations.

STRINDBERG ON HIS FIFTIETH BIRTHDAY

The characters split, double and multiply; they evaporate, crystallise, scatter and converge. But a single consciousness holds sway over them all—that of the dreamer. For him there are no secrets, no incongruities, no scruples and no law. He neither condemns nor acquits, only relates, and since on the whole there is more pain than pleasure in the dream, a tone of melancholy, and of compassion for all living things, runs through the swaying narrative.

This compassion too he gave to Indra's Daughter, so that as she passed from one earthly scene to another, again and again the cry was wrung from her heart: 'How human beings are to be pitied!' She was Strindberg's heavenly and female self, and his male earthly self split into three—first, the Officer imprisoned in the Growing Castle, so fair outside, so grim within, where he was forced to cart dung that he might yearn for heaven—the Officer who could never forget that as a child he was unjustly punished, and so was forced to confess that he too had caused another to suffer for his fault, who had to go back to school although he had taken his degree, who haunted the Corridor night after night, while season passed season until he was grey, as he still waited with his withered bouquet for his Romance who never came. Strindberg's second earthly self was the Lawyer, the young idealist, trapped and broken, mirroring in his own ugliness all the evil and suffering from which he scraped a meagre living, whose laurels vanished as he bowed his head for them, whose marriage with Indra's Daughter crashed—for all her divinity —on the rocks of domesticity. 'I paste, I paste!' the servant girl cried and continued to stop up every chink in the windows with her strips of paper, until the daughter of the heavens, inhaling the fumes of cabbage, gasped for air. She wanted purity and beauty, but such things were not to be had in the home of a poor man, and the one kind of beauty that cost nothing and which the Lawyer craved—orderliness—the Daughter of Indra did not give him. Even the child could not hold them together; love had failed. And finally there was the Poet— Strindberg's earthly self who was closest to the heavens, who took mud-baths in order to harden his skin against the stabs of life, and whose imperfect words, telling of man's plight, the returning goddess would interpret before the throne of God. Words which began, because now Harriet Bosse bore a child in pain which Strindberg could not identify with pleasure:

> *Why are you born in agony,*
> *why do you give your mother pain,*
> *when, child of man, you bring her joy,*
> *joy of all joys, a mother's joy?*

Of all the plays he had written, Strindberg liked *A Dream Play* best, his 'child of suffering,' fruit of the forty days when he believed that Harriet Bosse had already left him. There was more poetry both in form and language than in *To Damascus,* and although he was aware how words clouded and dragged down his thought, the play flowed from verse to prose to verse again and was filled with imagery. The servant pasted man up in his prison cell, the Lawyer twisted the squeaking door handle and with it the heart of love, the rich were tortured on the racks of the gymnasium—but the images were not all grim. A tormented earth stretched heavenward—the castle itself growing out of the manure, the huge hollyhocks climbing to the light, man himself ascending the ladder of suffering. By the legend of the divine Brahma, enticed by Maya, mother of earth, to propagate himself, Indra's Daughter explained the hell from which only suffering could set man free, and at the end of his dream Strindberg sent the Growing Castle up in all-purging fire, while as a symbol of faith, forbidding despair, the bud at its summit blossomed into a mighty chrysanthemum. If the old were destroyed, a new world would rise, and the golden age of the poet—the dreamer—might yet be reached.

CHAPTER FIFTEEN

1902–1908

Alone

MARRIED LIFE did not become any easier after the birth of Anne-Marie, and presently Harriet Bosse took her away to spend the summer in the country. It was Strindberg's habit to pace the flat in the evenings, and often in these last weeks he had carried the infant in his arms. Now his loneliness was all the sadder and he feared it might never end. He was depressed too about his work; he had written so many plays in the last years and had broken through into a wider sphere of experience and expression, but since the production of *Easter* the theatres had shown no interest in his experiments, and although he believed *A Dream Play* was the best thing he had written, he was tormented by the problem of fettering his imagination with words. When the Poet bade Indra's Daughter tell him her sorrows, she replied: 'Poet, could you tell me yours . . . ? Can your words ever reach as far as your thoughts?'

The more Strindberg's imagination grew, the more inadequate he found language—and for his plays more than words were needed. They must be bathed in light, clothed in form, dipped in music—but no theatre would help him. He wanted to see the Daughter of Indra living in Harriet Bosse's beauty, but the only work of his that the Dramatic Theatre would present next season was *Samum*, the drama of revenge in the African desert, written in violence at the time of his first divorce.

His dreaming spirit was abandoned and the ghost-ridden flat weighed on him. In poems and letters he told Harriet Bosse of his desolation. Once again she had taken the light with her.

He roams through empty rooms alone,
lighting up lamps and candles everywhere.
Down from the salon wall the portrait stares,
alien and cold. . . .
From room to room he tears in search—
searching for what cannot be found.

. . . The child holds me to life and to you. What our quarrels were about I don't remember. So they must have been bagatelles, due perhaps to over-anxiety about the baby and pardonable strain. I understood your regrets for your fleeting youth, but I hoped the child would give you youth again—as she gives it back to me. But no.
. . . My feelings for you and the child are entirely unchanged, although the dread of a divorce paralyses me. Judge then of my agony which had already begun before the child came, when you prophesied your departure. I thought first of all that I wouldn't allow myself to become too attached to the child, so as to suffer less later, but that was impossible. So now I am here.
Alone. . . .
Is your part in my life already at an end? Can there be an end to something we thought had no beginning? . . .

The answering letters were sorrowful but gave him little hope. She had warned him she might fail in the difficult rôle of his wife, and she had failed. But Strindberg had failed her too—he had promised her freedom and she found herself imprisoned. When she returned to town to start rehearsals for the autumn season, however, she was too busy to worry, and he loyally supported her in her work. Grieved though he was by the failure of their marriage, his belief in her talent was unshaken, and she welcomed his help. She read everything he recommended and listened eagerly to his advice; his faith inspired her and she was determined to become the great actress he believed her to be. The repertory offered her plenty of scope—during the winter besides Biskra in *Samum,* she played Ilka in *War and Peace,* Hedvig in *The Wild Duck,* and also Juliet. Strindberg identified himself with her in each part and was far too nervous to attend any first night. He spent the hours pacing the flat, waiting for telephone calls to tell him how the play was going. And the next day he would read the notices with her, wholeheartedly sharing censure and praise.

As far as his own work went, he could carry the dream sequence no further without the help of a theatre, so he concluded his cycle of Swedish history with *Gustav III* and drew a portrait of Luther in *The Nightingale of Wittenberg*. Now after writing seventeen plays in five years, of which only three had been produced and one or two more published without causing any stir, Strindberg's dramatic inspiration at last waned and he returned to the novel, the essay and the poem. For his stories once again he picked up old threads. *Fairhaven and Foulstrand*, place-names suggested by Furusund and its twin port and already used in *A Dream Play*, continued his collection of tales in which certain phases of his own life—and particularly of his marriage with Frida Uhl—predominated. *The Gothic Rooms* was the sequel to *The Red Room* and attacked society in general—he was still driven to frenzy by the slavery of man 'born under one set of laws and forced to live by another.' Where man was free Strindberg could judge him, where he was bound, reason was submerged in the torrent of his pity which drove him to a raw anger rebounding on himself. But although he still went back into the past for his material, he pushed forward in his exploration of the writer's art. These last years of passionate labour as a dramatist had brought him to a further consciousness of language—he had experimented in musical form, alliteration and word harmony; now he continued his research both in verse and prose and in the one overflowing to the other. He planned a volume of fugues and preludes, and in *The Gothic Rooms*, in spite of the swing back to Naturalism, he followed a fugal pattern of dialogue, while in *Fairhaven and Foulstrand* he included poems from his current volume *Word Play and Design*. He had come to believe that the essence of poetry lay in what Swedenborg called 'correspondences on different planes,' and that therefore metaphor was of the utmost importance.

He was not actually alone when in the spring of 1903 he wrote *Alone*, a meditative epilogue to *Inferno* and *Legends*, but he knew that solitude was closing in on him again, and while he described his former sensations, when after years of exile he returned alone to the capital, he was also preparing himself for a new isolation. He extolled solitude, bent on persuading himself that this was the best way of living, but again and again a lament broke from him, for he knew that he could neither live happily with another, nor be happy by himself. In this long autobiographical study in lyrical prose with some verse passages, he described the whole process of his writing, the descent into the street for the early morning walk when—according to his own inner state—he found himself in or out of tune with humanity and nature, and his return to the writing-table, when the energies he had accumulated, whether from peace or strife, never failed to serve his will.

. . . I live and I live the manifold lives of all the people I describe, happy with those who are happy, evil with the evil ones, good with the good; I creep out of my own personality and speak with the mouths of children, of women, of old men: I am king and beggar, I have worldly power, I am the tyrant and the down-trodden hater of the tyrant; I hold all opinions and profess all religions; I live in all times and have myself ceased to be. This is a state which brings indescribable happiness.

By the time *Alone* was published in the fall of the same year, his wife had moved into a flat of her own. At first the child was with her, and was taken each Sunday to visit Strindberg, but presently Harriet Bosse went on tour and Anne-Marie returned to Karlavägen to live with her father. There was no actual break; he continued to write his wife letters of great affection, always including minute details of the baby's health and progress. He did not reproach her, but he continuously lamented his loss, and gave to his grief not only his own voice but the child's. Even after they agreed to divorce, for he had always promised to give her back her freedom if the marriage failed, Strindberg and Harriet Bosse continued to see one another. This time there were no recriminations.

All the same, Strindberg's fresh disillusion through Harriet Bosse's failure, which she felt keenly herself, 'to reconcile him with mankind,' turned Strindberg over once again to his dark side. He appeared without rancour, gentle, melancholy, an ageing man devoted to children, flowers and music. He paid one of his rare visits to the theatre to see Greta Strindberg as Lisa in the revival of *Lucky Peter's Journey*, and admired both his daughter and his youthful work—his first play of light—but underneath his mask of resignation, fear and fury seethed.

206

In this condition he finished the cynical drama of *Queen Christina* and set to work on *Black Banners*, a savage assault on his fellow writers, thinly disguised as fiction. At the beginning of the novel he acclaimed Balzac, Dickens and Zola as the giants of literature, and from each he took some quality, but the venom was his own. His disgust at the grossness of living overflowed—the noise of men sucking in their soup while their heads ducked forward 'white and bare as bathers' bottoms,' the stench of sweat at the end of a dinner party, the sweat breaking out under the women's arms 'in landscapes and sea-views,' the refuse heaps, spittoons, commodes. . . . Against this background he painted a picture of Gustaf af Geijerstam whom he had already invited to get out of his life. He had once been a close friend, but for a long time now Strindberg had regarded him as an enemy who had threatened to write the story of his first marriage, who had pried and pressed on him and stolen his ideas. Geijerstam had served as one of the models for the Captain in *The Dance of Death*, but now as Zachris, the literary vampire, sucking the genius from men of letters by flattery, interference and treachery, he was a still more repellent figure. Yet into this monster who wept whisky from his bloodshot eyes, grimaced with gold-plugged teeth, picked with tobacco-stained fingers, Strindberg, whose habits were fastidious, infused much of his tormented self—almost as much as into Falkenström, the vampire's victim who dreamed beauty but could only see the hideousness of life. Jenny, the wife of Zachris, had driven him to perdition with her sadism and depravity, yet when she fled from him to a Lesbian friend, Zachris was tortured with longing.

Strindberg knew that the writing of this book was akin to black magic and, as he wrote, each vindictive sentence made him hate Geijerstam more and despair further of a world in which only swine could thrive—and to make out that filth was wholesome was to be a swine. He was sick, ashamed and frightened of what he had done, but none the less he determined on publication.

Neither Swedish nor German publisher would touch the book, however, and now he found himself compelled to write something that would bring in money. He turned again to history, but not to drama—theatre had once more closed her doors against his misery—and wrote a volume of *Historical Miniatures*, ranging from Moses to Napoleon. This he followed with a couple of long short stories *The Roof-laying Festival* and *The Scapegoat*, which took him back to commune 'with ghosts in a ghost house,' and brought his autobiography up to date. Anne-Marie was now almost his only flesh and blood companion. Relatives and nursemaids came and went with more or less disturbance to his dreams—only when they brought him music were his brother Axel and a few others certain of a welcome.

So the months passed, winters in the Karlavägen flat, summers on Furusund, still the loveliest place he knew, and gradually the comforting mantle of Swedenborg descended on Strindberg again. In June 1906 he began to write *A Blue Book*, a testament of philosophy dedicated to his master which would explain everything, including *Black Banners*, and show that he had not altogether failed. One thing he was still quite sure of—that he knew how to make gold, and he now sent Harriet Bosse the formula to use after his death.

In the spring of 1907 everything happened at once. *Black Banners* found an eager publisher in Björck and Börjesson, who prophesied that the book would be a scandal and a bestseller. The Swedish Theatre arranged to put on *A Dream Play*, and plans to found a Strindberg Theatre materialised. This last event not only plunged him into a whirl of affairs, but started him writing plays again at furious speed. He had read of Reinhardt's Kammerspiel Haus, and now he determined to write chamber plays for his own intimate theatre. It was new and stimulating to have no doubt whether his work would be produced.

For about a year now Strindberg had known the actor-producer August Falck, and it seemed to him propitious that this young man with an enthusiasm for his plays should both share his Christian name and also the surname Strindberg had taken for himself in *The Red Room*. Besides, Falck had not only given *Miss Julie* its Swedish *première* during his last season, but had written Strindberg an excellent production plan for *A Dream Play*. Now August Falck was determined to found a Strindberg theatre.

208

While Falck energetically sought a building and backing, encouraged by the scepticism of the Press and the enthusiasm of the young, Strindberg started on his *Chamber Plays* in a style of modified Naturalism, and at the same time crystallised his views in a *Memorandum to the Intimate Theatre*. He pointed out that after the impetus given to Theatre by Naturalism, there had been a lull, until with the turn of the century Reinhardt opened the Kleines Theater, and now had taken a further step forward with his Kammerspiel Haus, thus bringing the idea of chamber music into drama—'intimate treatment, important theme, meticulous treatment. . . .'

But although these thoughts inspired Strindberg's mind and he hastened to put them into execution, his soul was dark, for now Harriet Bosse had slipped out of his life for ever, and with her had gone Anne-Marie, his youngest, his last hope of happiness—how could he of all men keep a child from its mother? In *Storm*, the first of the chamber plays for his Intimate Theatre, Strindberg used his own new tragedy.

Black Banners came out in April 1907 and roused more indignation than anything he had written since *Married*. 'August Strindberg, how dared you?' one Göteborg paper wrote, and it looked as if this time he might be prosecuted for libel. Yet Falck noticed that, in spite of the scandal, Strindberg was released by the book's publication. The devils were out, and while he worked with enormous speed at *Storm*, *The Burned Site*, *The Ghost Sonata* and *The Pelican*—Falck used to sit sometimes in the room outside the study and tiptoe in and pick up the sheets as they fell to the floor from the Master's hand. At the same time Strindberg added paragraph on paragraph of philosophic reflection to *The Blue Book* until it ran into a second volume. Björck and Börjesson not only offered exceptionally good terms for the *Blue Books*, but agreed to print the volumes with red margins and capitals like a missal.

This was a time altogether of acute tension, for on top of the incalculable difficulties of starting a theatre, from the moment *A Dream Play* went into rehearsal at the Swedish Theatre—with Harriet Bosse as Indra's Daughter, putting a fresh strain upon his nerves—Strindberg's domestic arrangements failed. In the course of a few weeks he had six housekeepers, each worse than the last, and was often reduced to doing everything for himself and 'living on scraps for the pigs.' He recognised these ordeals as attempts by hostile powers to arrest his work, but this did not make them easier to bear. Nor was his beloved *Dream Play* a success. His director, Ranft, was not daring enough, and the best that could be said was that it was an interesting experiment. After twelve performances it came off.

Nevertheless, financially, Strindberg was better off than usual, for many of his earlier books had gone into a cheap edition, and his wide range of subjects, vivid language and untiring support of the underdog, won him many followers. This encouraged Falck, when in June they found premises which they could transform into the theatre of their vision, to borrow up to the hilt, but even so, by the time the whole place was elegantly fitted out, they were touting Strindberg's pictures and pledging his *Occult Diary* against the rent.

But come what might, at last Strindberg had his own theatre and reproductions of Böcklin's *Isle of the Living* and *Isle of the Dead* on each side of the proscenium arch declared its policy. Falck had formed a company of keen, intelligent young artists—he was himself playing leading parts besides directing—and *The Pelican* was chosen for the Intimate Theatre's opening play.

Strindberg did not go to many rehearsals, but he saw Falck every day and repeatedly warned him against being old-fashioned and too realistic. In the evenings, when the work of the day was done, the elderly writer and the young impresario relaxed together over 'a great whisky-drinking' which soothed the nerves and set the fancy free. Strindberg also smoked incessantly in these days and wanted Falck to do the same. Once, when through a cold the young man lost his voice and could scarcely be heard on the stage, Strindberg sent him an urgent message: 'Smoke, boy! The Hindus cure all complaints with tobacco.'

During these evenings, Strindberg talked to Falck about Harriet Bosse and his desire to help her in every possible way —sometimes he still wrote her love letters and sent wistful notes to Anne-Marie. He also told his young friend of the powers which ruled his life, and even occasionally demonstrated his alliance with them by willing a watch to stop or performing some other harmless piece of magic. His days were still guided by portents, and he had in the flat a stuffed owl which he believed to be related to his powers. Sometimes he would send it down to the theatre, but then again he would feel an urgent need for its presence and demand its immediate return. Once he had fought against belief in the supernatural as the refuge of fools, now he saw it as the privilege of the most intelligent. The death-mask of Beethoven was his symbol of man's highest achievement and a figure of Buddha kept before his eyes the image of God.

The Master in *Storm* was engaged in settling his accounts both with life and with people and in savouring the sweetness of memory. Strindberg clung to the fairest memories of Harriet Bosse to save him from further wreck, but as *Storm* progressed her figure darkened. The fear that she might marry again and give his child a stepfather was new agony, and in the last of the chamber plays melancholy gave way again to rage. The Mother saw herself as a pelican, tearing her own breast to feed her young, but Strindberg saw her as a vampire, eating the meat and giving her children the bones, freezing them to save money for her lover. As in *A Dream Play* he ended with an all-purging fire, but this time no compassionate goddess ascended to heaven—only a criminal mother leaped to her death.

In *The Burned Site*, 'opus 2' of the series, Strindberg worked out the awareness that had grown steadily throughout his life of fate's repetitions and the linked destinies of men. In each event he traced an earlier action, in each character another from the past, and he carried this theme over to the third, most intricate and original of the chamber plays— *The Ghost Sonata*, first called by the theosophical name *Kama-Loka*. Now once again Strindberg used the dream idiom in which everything was possible and probable, but to the vision of a poet he added the technique of a skilled Naturalist.

Utter exposure of life's most shameful secrets was the theme of *The Ghost Sonata*. In the glass veranda of *Easter*, through the eyes of Lindkvist, the Creditor, Strindberg had portrayed the pitiful attempts of human beings to keep up appearances and protect their pride. Piece by piece he had

211

broken their stubborn spirits, but only so that in the end they might find happiness—after the ice the thaw, after the rod the flower. In *The Ghost Sonata* there was no angelic child to bring poor mortals peace, no goddess to pity their woe. The betrayed dead man and the drowned milkmaid walked instead; the façade of the house was torn away and the awful figure in the cupboard, the ancient mummy of a woman with the ways of a parrot, finally disclosed the original crime of old Hummel, the Creditor (the antithesis of Lindkvist), on whose first sin the whole edifice of hypocrisy was raised. The mummy woman could stop time, wipe out the past and undo what was done. She made all further bribes or threats invalid and left the soul only one way out of its hell—the way of retribution.

Only then could love flower between the Student and the Young Girl whose hyacinths were the image of the Cosmos, of Buddha holding the earth-bulb in his hand and waiting for it to grow into a heaven. And still the clairvoyant Student, touching truth and beauty at last, must be thwarted. When he cried for music, the girl protested that labour had to come first, 'the labour of keeping the dirt of life at a distance,' and their tender idyll was violated by the vampire cook, fat with the nourishment she had sucked from her employers' food. Strindberg knew well the power of the enemy to steal the goodness out of food.

The Student must welcome Death as the liberator of his innocent love—'When you wake again may you be greeted by a sun that does not burn, in a home with no dust, by friends without stain, by a love without flaw. . . .' And left alone, he must pray to Buddha in the name of all humanity for patience, and be comforted by a revelation of the power of the Sun and the peace of the Isle of the Dead.

On the opening night of the Intimate Theatre, November 26th, 1907, the hundred and sixty-one seats were packed with critics and society. Strindberg wrote a prologue in blank verse, but he was not present—only his laurel-crowned bust in the foyer. The event was smart, the little theatre admired, but *The Pelican* was not well received, and on the next nights the seats were almost empty. Falck did not want to trouble Strindberg with this disaster, but he insisted on knowing every detail, and after his immediate despair in which he advised closing down, his optimism rose again and he and Falck planned a campaign. Strindberg had always doubted if *The Pelican* was the right choice for the opening, and now, in between trying out the other chamber plays, they decided to put on *Miss Julie*, which Falck had already presented successfully in Lund.

So *The Burned Site* and the monologue *The Stronger*, written many years before, had their *premières* together, *Storm* followed and then *The Ghost Sonata*, but still the public did not come. The critics considered Falck was wasting his time on the new works of an author who had proved himself mentally and morally degenerate. But Falck was a fighter who welcomed difficulties—he arranged tours to the provinces and to Copenhagen, and Strindberg's spirits were kept up by the loyalty and enthusiasm of the company, working so hard for so little. The problems of putting *The Ghost Sonata* on a small stage bound them even closer together, and whenever Strindberg appeared at a rehearsal, the players were charged with his power and deeply touched by his appreciation and kindness.

But all their work was described as decadent and angrily Strindberg wrote in his *Open Letter to the Intimate Theatre*:

A blind man does not readily judge colour, but if he should agree to be the critic of an art exhibition, he must be prepared to put up with a reminder that he is blind, even if at other times it's unkind to draw attention to physical defects. If a tipsy or deaf person comes to the theatre and sets about writing (and having printed) a review of the play after a single performance, then I as the accused have the right to challenge the evidence or the judgment: 'He's drunk. He's deaf. Throw him out!'

So they went on, alternating so that new plays and old had their first performances together, some at less loss than others, but their first taste of success was when in the spring-time they put on *Easter*. Anna Flygare had already had a personal triumph in *The Bond*; now she played Eleanora. She had not Harriet Bosse's mysterious beauty, but she captured the fey wistful girl, living painfully in two worlds at once, and Strindberg's heart was wrung with pity. His sister Elisabeth had died in her asylum three years before—he had

213

sent her photograph to Harriet Bosse—'I want you just to see the Easter girl'—but now she lived again in Anna Flygare. He wrote to thank the actress:

Every evening now I feel both how you rejoice at coming up into the light, and how you suffer my Eleanora's sufferings, on account of which I wrote the piece.

The writer of tragedies often forgets how the player, evening after evening, goes through hours of agony for him. I thought of it first when I saw you tortured in *The Bond*, and for the first time realised my responsibility.

Poor Eleanora-Flygare! I say every evening at 8, and then I play (badly) *Sieben Worte*. . . .

With Strindberg's permission Falck had tried to borrow money from Bonnier, who had published several of his recent books, but this and many other attempts failed, and in desperation, while *Easter* was in rehearsal, the young director approached the highest source of help, the 'Artist-Prince' Eugen, painter brother of King Gustav V, who came this year to the throne. As surprisingly as, forty years before, his uncle, King Karl XV, had given August Strindberg a stipend to continue his education, Prince Eugen now paid the rent of his theatre. *Easter* melted the hearts of the critics, the house was full and the sun shone.

But although so many of his wishes were fulfilled, Strindberg was melancholy; he had made new enemies, he was in debt, his flat was large and empty, his domestic arrangements unsatisfactory, and even when he had a good housekeeper he had taken to an ascetic way of living which did not agree with him. Nowadays he very often felt ill, and when Bernard Shaw arrived in Stockholm and suggested calling on him that same afternoon at two o'clock, Strindberg's condition of nerves and health dictated the immediate and sincere reply: 'At two o'clock I shall be unwell.' He did, however, meet Bernard Shaw during his visit, take him to a performance of *Miss Julie* at the Intimate Theatre and show him proundly round. Shaw met the company and congratulated all concerned with a bewitching smile, but Falck wondered anxiously what the famous foreigner really thought. If Shaw expected something startlingly original from his Swedish colleague, it must have been disconcerting to see a Naturalist piece of the 'eighties.

214

Gordon Craig also came to Stockholm, but Strindberg did not see him. He was still trying to break through the convention of theatre, to show the real event behind the fortuitous action, to see man's soul rather than his painted face, to feel the power of the planets and forget the footlights. But although he was aiming at a complete revolution, he was no longer, as in his Naturalist period, in accord with the *avant-garde* of the day. Maeterlinck had given him something, but now he had left Maeterlinck behind and was still searching, alone. He read *The Mask*, as also *The Studio*, *The Art Journal* and *Die Kunst des Theaters*, marked passages, made notes and sketches and sent them down to Falck. But he could not accept Gordon Craig's main thesis; he had spent his life trying to free language from convention, how could he now want the word subjugated to stage design?

In July he left his flat and all its tormenting memories of Harriet Bosse and moved to the other side of Stockholm. This arranged itself; he asked a member of the company to lend him a lute and it was brought to Karlavägen by Fanny Falkner, a very young actress whose mother turned out to have a floor to let in her maisonette in Drottninggatan. Strindberg moved in with a handbag; the house was round with a spiral staircase paved in blue stone; he christened it the Blue Tower, sent for his desk, his books and a very few personal possessions and sold up the rest of his effects. A few weeks later Harriet Bosse was married to the actor Gunnar Wingårdh.

Now Strindberg was well cared for. His hostess attended to his food and an elderly servant gave him her complete devotion. His rooms were small, light and safe from intruders, but young Fanny's company was his for the asking, as was that of her small sisters whom he loved to spoil. He borrowed *The Arabian Nights* from them and wrote a new fairy play *Abu Casem's Slippers*, with his own little daughter also in mind. Without doubt the move revived him, for all that he complained to Falck that he was fed on Eskimo or pig food. In his heart he knew that he was settled at last, and even when Stockholm irked him, he believed that the powers willed him to travel no more.

He came more directly now into the management of the

theatre, writing the company—'because I am no speaker'—
endless memoranda as to how each character should feel,
move, speak and even breathe, although he was careful always
to treat the players as artists, never as 'workmen or school-
boys.' Over and over again he impressed on them the need to
keep their parts new to themselves, so that they should give
live and not studied performances. In the summer when *The
Father* went into rehearsal for the autumn season with Falck
in the name part, Strindberg took over the functions of producer, sitting silent in the darkened auditorium, only his
magnetism and the glimmer of his white hair informing the
players of his presence. Then that evening or the next day
they would find sheaves of notes in his neat handwriting,
criticising, encouraging, and signed 'The Producer.' The Press
was at last enthusiastic, although Strindberg now called *The
Father* his worst play and was inclined to think *The Dance of
Death*, still unperformed, his best.

His desire to be a producer soon flagged, but he used his
authority to bring Fanny Falkner into the company. He
coached her himself at home and then cast her for Swanwhite,
although he had already offered the part to Anna Flygare.
Everyone was upset, but Strindberg had his way and then
withdrew to the Blue Tower to write three more historical
plays—*The Last Knight*, *The National Director* and *The Earl
of Bjälbo*, and a final romantic chamber play *The Black
Glove*. Now, like the Master in *Storm*, Strindberg was settling
his accounts both with life and with people, and had 'already
began to pack for the journey.'

CHAPTER SIXTEEN

1909–1912

I had said all I wished to say . . .

STRINDBERG'S SIXTIETH birthday—on January 22nd, 1909—came sweetly. In the morning, two of the company called to leave a bouquet, and the door was opened by Strindberg himself at his most elegant, with a gracefully knotted cravat, shining silver hair brushed up from his great forehead and a pale flush in his cheeks. He ushered them warmly into the tiny hall, and beyond it they saw a luncheon table, exquisitely decorated with flowers and pink lights and laid for two. Embarrassed, Anna Flygare and her companion tried to slip away, but Strindberg explained that he was expecting his little daughter, whom he had not seen for two years, and presently they witnessed her arrival. Anne-Marie, now nearly seven years old, flung herself into her father's arms, while the tears ran down his cheeks, but a moment later he bade her greet 'Pappa's friends.'

The papers paid him generous tribute, and as the day passed Strindberg's rooms filled with telegrams, flowers, laurel wreaths, addresses from students and congratulations from known and unknown admirers. The Intimate Theatre gave the second performance of *Crime and Crime*, well received the night before, the Dramatic had the *première* of *The Last Knight*; *Gustavus Vasa* and *Lucky Peter's Journey* were also on in Stockholm, while another section of Falck's company played *Swanwhite* at Uppsala with Fanny Falkner in the title rôle.

After the excitement of the day and the drinking of many toasts, Strindberg was exhausted and retired early to bed, but soon came the tramp of feet beneath his window, the strains of the *International* and rousing cheers. He went out on to the balcony and found the street packed with members of the Social-Democrat youth clubs. The next day he sent them a message:

My thanks for your greeting, spokesmen of the common people, among whom I can never cease to count myself, since I am the son of a maidservant.

By now Strindberg had grown very fond of his 'little protégée' Fanny Falkner, and helped her in every possible way, and when the inevitable gossip started, he was careful of her reputation. He took the opportunity of her being away on tour to write to her of this delicate matter and explain that she must no longer visit his room alone. A few weeks later he told her more:

Do I need to write this letter? Eight days ago I discovered for the first time that they were saying I planned a new marriage with a young girl.
I find it so incredible, so unthinkable that I, old and sick, should want to bind a young person to my heavy fate which by the laws of nature is nearly over. That your name has been involved is not my doing. When they took my last child from me I lost interest in life, and now only wanted, from a quite unselfish motive, to have someone to work for. That was all.
Don't answer this, but just show the same confidence in me as before; then the gossip will subside.

And later still:

I am not fit company for a young girl. Go away into the country and seek youth. Go with Director Falck to-day . . . tell me before you start if you need money. . . .
I want to be alone and am right in this, but you who are young must go out and mix with people. . . .

So, before long, Fru Falkner took Fanny and the little girls away, and Strindberg was left alone—'the old man in the tower.'

The Intimate Theatre went on tour to Norway—against Strindberg's advice, for he could not believe his plays would ever suit the land of Ibsen and Björnson—'the Nora-men.' Nevertheless Falck had full houses in Christiania. Once Strindberg had believed that his seed had fallen into Ibsen's brain-pan. Now the great Norwegian had been dead three years, but in the latter part of his life he had hung a portrait of Strindberg over his writing-table and declared that although the Swede was his enemy, he could not write a word without 'the bold eyes of the madman' staring down at him.

Now Björnson, whose robust physique had so oppressed him in youth, was failing too, and Strindberg watched the bulletins with interest. When he read of his visit to Paris, he declared that the only purpose in the journey must be to have a double funeral—and indeed he had three, for on the return journey to Norway, Björnson's coffin was honoured both in Paris and in Copenhagen. Many of his old friends and enemies, including Gustaf af Geijerstam, had died in these last years, and Strindberg knew that his own turn was soon coming; in spite of growing weakness he pushed on to get the work of his lifetime finished. As his farewell he must write one more drama of the pilgrimage and express the unending conflict in himself between the terrible heights of heaven and the dear though dirty roads of earth.

He called this play *The Great Highway* after the road leading north out of the town past the corner where he now lived. To the south lay Old Stockholm, the city between the bridges where he was born, the Klara Church in whose shadows he had spent his earliest years, the Royal Library where he had worked, the Dramatic Theatre which had been the shrine of his hopes. To the north was the house where he had lived as a schoolboy, where his mother had died and where he had met Siri von Essen. In her he had looked for his mother; in other women he had looked for her, in all women and their children he had sought his own childhood. Now this was over and the road stretched on to the New Church Cemetery where, by his own wish, he would soon be buried—'not among the rich in idlers' ground.'

Gifts of inspiration helped him on. A child brought hand-painted crockery to the door, and on a plate he found the exact set for a scene—a little house in the woods with a broad white gate leading to the sea. He heard it said that a dying man had 'coughed up his heart,' and the phrase struck and became a leading theme. A pattern of blank verse came to him for the first and last passages in which he stood on the brink of heaven, and between were satirical scenes of earth's

219

topsyturvy ways in colloquial dialogue. He had had to write three plays to bring *To Damascus* to an end, and his autobiographies ran into many volumes; now with the use of poetic imagery he traced the passage of his soul on earth in a single play. By the end of the year *The Great Highway* was ready for Bonnier to publish and Falck to produce, and Strindberg felt that he had made his bow with his finest poetry and his sharpest wit. This time the public should laugh and cry but it would not be shocked—he had given it the last best shock in *The Dance of Death* which the Intimate Theatre had effectively presented a few weeks before.

A few writers liked *The Great Highway*, but neither critics nor public were pleased. Having rated Strindberg all his life for his violence, they now expected and enjoyed it and felt cheated by this uncharacteristic piece, and it had only a single performance.

The Intimate Theatre, never financially sound in spite of a good many successes, was now going steadily downhill, and Falck decided to have a complete change and present a play by Maeterlinck. Strindberg was deeply hurt; his time was short and many of his works were still unperformed. Falck had his way and produced *The Uninvited Guest*, but Strindberg could not forgive him, nor did the theatre recover its fortunes. At the end of 1910, after three years devoted entirely to Strindberg's work, it sold up and Falck took the company into other managements.

For a long time now, Strindberg had declared that he was not interested in politics and never read a newspaper, although callers sometimes saw one of these despised publications hastily concealed. The Socialists had, however, claimed him as their writer, and he was once more in a Rousseau vein. As a young man, appalled by industrial conditions, he had vowed to devote his life to the working people from whom his mother sprang. He felt that he had not done enough, so now, to everyone's astonishment, considering his ill-health and supposed indifference, Strindberg began to appear again in the daily papers as a convinced Radical and Republican. His articles denouncing the Monarchy and the upper classes were at once collected and published by the Socialists in three volumes—*Talks to the Swedish Nation, The People's State* and

Religious Renaissance, and Strindberg found that, tired though he was, he still had enough vitality to make enemies. This was not his intention, but although he preached complete tolerance, never in his life had he succeeded in being tolerant to those on top. Now he called for universal freedom of religion in which no King, State or Prelate should dictate, but only God, and he testified that the Bible, interpreted in the Swedenborgian way, was the best guide to truth.

But if he made new enemies, he was good friends now with his children, or at least with his eldest daughters, for his son Hans, married and living in Finland with his mother, was a stranger to him, and so was Frida Uhl's child Kerstin. But Greta had married her cousin Hugo von Philp, and Strindberg's son-in-law had become his own devoted physician, while Greta was still on the stage and often acted in his plays. And now the elder girl Karin became engaged to Wladimir Smirnoff, the Russian lecturer at Helsingfors, and to Strindberg's deep joy in the summer of 1911 they came to Stockholm and were married from the Blue Tower. Strindberg clung to his love for his children—and for all children—as the one unbroken emotion of his life, and he continued to lavish gifts and letters on young Anne-Marie.

He paid a last tribute now to his other lifelong love—the word—in a series of pamphlets on the origin of world languages and of the Swedish tongue. Fresh coals of fire fell on his head; he roundly criticised Swedish literature, describing, for instance, the verse of the 'nineties as 'chauvinistic kling-klang poetry.' Now many writers struck back, declaring that Strindberg was nothing but an unsuccessful author mad with jealousy and disappointment.

Nevertheless Strindberg felt curiously at peace; he indulged in some interesting correspondence with other students of philology and wrote an essay on China and Japan—his old interest in sinology had returned while he was writing *The Great Highway*, and he had let the Jap, called Hiroshima after his birth-place, speak his own epitaph in the original. Now this farewell to Eastern culture was paid too. One by one in his ordered way Strindberg gathered up the threads of his life. Ideas for future work still floated in his mind, but without urgency; fever claimed his body and released his spirit. At the

221

end of 1911 he was laid low with pneumonia, and wrote to friends in Finland:

> . . . I first noticed it on the morning of Christmas Day, when I was so tired, so tired that I neither wanted to get up nor to drink my coffee. I had no pain, but experienced a great calm and an indifference to the outer world, and felt that I had at last found peace. Usually I get up punctually at seven, take a walk and hurry home, driven by an irresistible desire to work. Now this restlessness had left me; I felt my life-work was completed. I had said all I wanted to say, and my unprinted manuscripts were put away in boxes in perfect order.

The notice taken of his sixtieth birthday had surprised and touched Strindberg, but when now in January 1912, four weeks after the Christmas morning of his illness, his sixty-third birthday was reached, it was a public event. Thirteen years before, Strindberg had refused Hjalmar Branting's help, declaring that he was no politician; now, as Labour leader, Branting led the workers' celebrations for their champion's anniversary. Strindberg, unable to resist a fight for long, had rallied, but everyone knew it was likely to be his last birthday. A public collection was made; money poured in, gala performances of many of his plays were arranged, and the workers organised a torch procession to the Blue Tower. A few nights before, Strindberg wrote to the painter Richard Bergh:

> Please tell Branting if that's what's going to happen, I must greet them: and that I'll come on to the balcony, but they mustn't stay or make speeches or sing, or else I'll be forced to kill myself doing the courtesies. I really am still ill, although I persuade myself I'm well. Have not been out.
> So that the procession can recognise my balcony among all the others, I'll put my most beautiful electric lamp out there with its red eye towards the Tégner-copse.
> If I'm really ill I'll get them to telephone headquarters, but will light up the window as a sign that I appreciate and thank them: perhaps am standing in the window.

This time the Blue Tower was overwhelmed with gifts and trophies; telegrams poured in from all over Europe and from America. Not only the Scandinavian Press, but the French and German papers carried articles on or by Strindberg, and Edmund Gosse saw to it that the occasion was not quite ignored in England.

222

STRINDBERG IN THE YEAR OF HIS DEATH

At night all over Stockholm laurel-wreathed busts and portraits were lighted up; people performed music, read poems, declaimed speeches all composed in the Master's honour, while his own words rang out to the packed auditoriums of the theatres. And when the long torch procession wound through the snowy streets to the Blue Tower, Strindberg was standing on the balcony beside his electric lamp with the red eye, and the ten-year-old Anne-Marie was with him. Hats and handkerchiefs waved and a roar of cheers went up. 'Long live Strindberg!' 'Long live Freedom's Poet!' 'Long live the People's Writer!'

Then Anne-Marie began to scatter rose petals on the heads of the crowd, and seeing this, Strindberg seized handfuls of his birthday flowers and showered them down on the people.

There was little more to be done. Strindberg had cancer of the stomach and was a dying man, but still he went on, making sure that nothing was forgotten. On March 18th he wrote to Nathan Söderblom, now a professor in Uppsala, who had been the Swedish Pastor in Paris at the time of the Inferno.

Herr Professor,

I had much to say to you about a great many things, but sick and old I must put my house in order and settle my accounts.—About 1892(?) I was—not by my own doing—in Paris without means, and by roundabout ways received help from the Swedish Colony's Relief Fund to the extent of 200fr. I have tried to console myself with the thought that since then, during the better last ten years, I have given substantial relief to others. But it doesn't help: that must be met with this. So I am sending you, and, as I don't know the address in Paris, begging you to be so kind as to forward, the enclosed 1000 kronor to the Relief Fund for compatriots in need. As it is a repayment it cannot be counted as charity, certainly not!

One little word is missing from this short letter, that small word which is so hard to get out: Thank you! for the help then and for the trouble you are kindly taking now.

Yours
AUGUST STRINDBERG

223

Occupied though he was with putting his own house in order, even to the exact arrangements for his funeral, and racking as often were his pains, Strindberg was still closely bound to the sufferings of others. When, on the fifteenth of April, news came of the *Titanic* disaster, he was consumed with pity and clothed himself in black—even now he did not stay in bed, but found relief in walking about the flat. Only a week later came a still more poignant personal grief; a telegram told him of Siri von Essen's death. Now he wore mourning in a full sense of its fitness; everyone should know what he had always known and had so often tried to deny, that he had loved Siri von Essen better than anyone on earth.

On the nineteenth of April he wrote his farewell letter to Anne-Marie:

My dear little daughter,
Thank you for your red flowers. But you mustn't visit me. Here there are so many medicine bottles, doctors and sights that it isn't pleasant at all.
Be happy in your youth with the young, and don't grieve for the old man, for he only wants to go.

FATHER

The doses of morphia were steadily increased and the relatives gathered at the Blue Tower. One evening when Karin was with him, Strindberg took the Bible from the table beside his bed, pressed it to his breast and murmured 'Everything is atoned for.'

Early in the morning of Tuesday, May 14th, 1912, August Strindberg's life came to an end.

He had asked to be buried quietly at eight o'clock in the morning—he loved the morning and he hated crowds—but his people would not allow him to go on his last journey unattended. Up the long High Road from the Blue Tower to the New Church Cemetery they trudged, following the funeral cortège with its full-dress, banners, insignia and all the pomp of mourning. White-capped students were there in

224

their hundreds, artists, actors, writers, musicians, politicians and an unending stream of workers—of ordinary people.

Professor Söderblom took the service, and August Strindberg's grave among the poor was marked, as he had directed, with a cross of dark oak bearing the words AVE CRUX SPES UNICA.

POSTSCRIPT

IN A preface—to one of the early autobiographies—written shortly before he died, Strindberg declared: 'The personality of the author is just as much a stranger to me as to the reader —and just as unsympathetic.' He invites us to dislike him, and provokes us into trying to understand the nature which produced such masterpieces of light and darkness.

Terms change with the times; Strindberg's first biographers speak of 'paranoia simplex chronica' and 'melancholia dæmomaniaca,' whereas nowadays we think of him as introverted, schizophrenic and the victim of an Œdipus complex. In any case his destiny appears so modern that it is difficult to remember that he lived it and analysed it before Freud, Jung and D. H. Lawrence led the next generations into sexual and psychological exploration. No ready-made labels suffice. To classify August Strindberg would be to make of him one of the 'strong,' 'either-or' characters he refused to create and certainly never became. He must be left as a 'both-and,' at once hypersensitive and crude, sensual and puritanical, harsh and sentimental, swinging between the poles of scepticism and faith, romanticism and realism, satanism and angelology. But one thing is certain, that Strindberg was ahead of his time—or rather this would be certain if one were not immediately reminded of Gertrude Stein's view that 'no one is ahead of his time, it is only that the particular variety of creating his time is the one that his contemporaries who are also creating their own time refuse to accept'—words particularly apt in the case of August Strindberg.

In the 'eighties he was a leader of Naturalism, at the turn of the century a pioneer of Expressionism, and his last poetic plays were reproductions of dream states, and drawings from the subconscious, which a quarter of a century later would

226

have been called surrealist. Not a single one of Strindberg's plays is a period piece; neither subject, situation nor language is dated. He wrote of all times for all times, and was always struggling to break through into further knowledge and new ways of expression. Strindberg should therefore never be imprisoned between the dates of his birth and his death, but given every advantage of modern and experimental theatre. *A Dream Play* with its growing castle, its glazier and its angelic visitor brings to mind Cocteau's *Orphée*, while Strindberg's *Swanwhite* is comparable with Cocteau's treatment of *La Belle et la Bête*. Strindberg's tragedies have their modern counterpart in the work of Eugene O'Neill, who acknowledges Strindberg as one of his main influences; Strindberg's effort to portray the lives of ordinary people while shunning 'that stage where all that is bourgeois has ever reigned supreme,' has been carried forward by Thornton Wilder, while his clairvoyant vision puts him among those adventurers whom Mr. R. A. Parker in *First Papers of Surrealism* calls 'Explorers of the Pluriverse.' Here Strindberg's obvious counterpart is Salvador Dali; each of these artists has for favourite picture Böcklin's *Isle of the Dead*, each recognises the object which contains or turns into a second image, and challenges materialists with his belief that the 'hallucinatory' image may be reality. Both of them believe that their imaginative work and their death-wish spring from a desire to hide again in the paradise of the womb—both are timid, yet attract attention by eccentricity, both know that they are geniuses and each balances on the edge of madness. Salvador Dali's illustrations to *Macbeth* make one doubly eager to see his interpretation of Strindberg's visionary work.

One contemporary of August Strindberg's, however, one must name with him, although they never met, probably never even heard of one another. Arthur Rimbaud, another writer of all times and all places, was born in 1854, six years after Strindberg, and died in 1891, having been through the *enfer* into which Strindberg was then descending. Just once, when in 1877 Strindberg went to France for the first time, these two writers, so different yet with so much in common, may have been in Paris together, but by the time—in the 'eighties

227

—that the Swede returned, Rimbaud had left Paris and poetry for ever.

There are passages in Dr. Enid Starkie's recent study of Arthur Rimbaud which could equally well refer to August Strindberg, and Dr. Starkie provides the explanation:

> It is interesting, both for a study of Rimbaud and of the nine-teenth century in general, to realise the prevalence of occult theories which were, amongst writers, the same common coin that Freudian and Marxian theory is to-day amongst many who have never read a line from these two thinkers. Baudelaire was much interested in the writings of Lavater, Swedenborg and Joseph de maistre. . . .
> Thus it can be seen that Rimbaud could, from the reading of Baudelaire alone, have absorbed much occult thought. . . .

We know that Strindberg read Baudelaire, and that in his struggle to understand and endure human existence, the Swede, like Rimbaud, was caught up in Paris occultism, although much later in life. Each was influenced by Poe, each practised magic and alchemy, and both of them developed a sense of superiority (on a basis of inferiority induced by lack of affection in childhood), that lifted them sky-high and then crashed them down into hell—a hell on the edge of madness which they acknowledged as retribution for overwhelming pride.

The keynote of the two men was the same, a passionate idealism which could not come to terms with ordinary life. Rimbaud turned to homosexuality; Strindberg pursued his own femininity in one woman after another without its ever being resolved, and both of them demanded that love be rescued from materialism. These words of Rimbaud's from *Une Saison en Enfer* could as well be Strindberg's:

> Je n'aime pas les femmes: l'amour est à réinventer, on le sait. Elles ne peuvent plus que vouloir une position assurée. La position gagnée, cœur et beauté sont mis de côté; il ne reste que froid dédain, l'aliment du mariage aujourd'hui.

In science, philology and metaphysics, the two poets sought for goodness and for truth, then Rimbaud broke away to a life of action, and Strindberg remained to walk round and round the circle of his fate, his feet on the treadmill, his head in the stars.

And the stars are his. Sean O'Casey in a letter to Robert Loraine has paid the tribute of twentieth-century theatre to the ageless Swedish genius:

Strindberg, Strindberg, Strindberg, the greatest of them all! Barrie mumbling as he silvers his little model stars and gilds his little model suns, while Strindberg shakes flame from the living planets and the fixed stars.

Ibsen can sit serenely in his Doll's House, while Strindberg is battling with his heaven and his hell.

APPENDIX I

August Strindberg's 29 answers to George Bröckner, May 1897

1. What is the predominant trait in your character?
   This strange mixture of the deepest pessimism and utter reckless-ness.
2. What quality do you rate highest in a man?
   Lack of pettiness.
3. . . . in a woman?
   Motherliness.
4. What power would you most like to possess?
   Power to solve the riddle of the world and the meaning of life.
5. What fault would you be most unwilling to have?
   Pettiness.
6. What is your favourite occupation?
   Writing plays.
7. What would give you the greatest joy?
   To hate no one and to have no enemies.
8. What position would you most like to have held?
   That of a constantly performed dramatist.
9. What would you consider the greatest misfortune?
   To lack inner peace and a quiet conscience.
10. Where would you prefer to live?
    In the Stockholm skerries.
11. Your favourite colours?
    Pale yellow and amethyst violet.
12. Your favourite flower?
    Mountain violet.
13. Favourite creature?
    Butterfly.
14. What are your favourite books?
    The Bible. Chateaubriand's Génie du Christianisme. *Sweden-borg's* Arcana Celestia. *Victor Hugo's* Les Misérables. *Dickens'* Little Dorrit. *Andersen's* Fairy Tales. *Bernardin de St. Pierre's* Harmonies.

15. Your favourite pictures?
   Th. Rousseau: Paysages Intimes. *Böcklin:* Isle of the Dead.
16. Favourite music?
   Beethoven's Sonatas.
17. What English author do you place highest?
   Dickens.
18. English painter?
   Turner.
19. What historical figures do you place highest?
   Henri IV of France and Bernard de Clairvaux.
20. Women in history?
   Elisabeth of Thuringen and Margaret of Provence.
21. What character in history do you most despise?
   One has no right to despise anyone.
22. What characters in fiction appeal to you most?
   Balzac's Louis Lambert and the Bishop in Les Misérables.
23. Women in fiction?
   Margareta of Faust *and Balzac's Séraphita.*
24. What name do you like best.
   Margareta.
25. What fault in another do you most easily forgive?
   Extravagance.
26. What social reform would you most like to see accomplished
   in your lifetime?
   Disarmament.
27. Your favourite drink and food?
   Ale and fish dishes.
28. What season and what weather do you like best?
   Full summer and warm rain.
29. Your motto?
   Speravit infestis.

APPENDIX II

LIST OF STRINDBERG'S MAIN WORKS

(a—autobiographical novels; d—drama; m—miscellaneous, including essays, stories, poems, philosophy, science, etc.; c.p.— chamber plays.)

Swedish Title	English Title	Category	Date
Hermione	Hermione	d	1869
I Rom	In Rome	d	1870
Fritänkaren	The Freethinker	d	1870
Den fredlöse	The Outlaw	d	1871
Mäster Olof	Master Olof	d	1872-6
Från Fjärdingen och Svartbäcken	From Fjärdingen and Svartbäcken	m	1877
Röda rummet	The Red Room	m	1879
Gillets hemlighet	The Secret of the Guild	d	1880
Gamla Stockholm	Old Stockholm	m	1880
Herr Bengts hustru	Herr Bengt's Wife	d	1881-2
Lycko-Pers resa	Lucky Peter's Journey	d	1882
Svenska folket i helg och söcken	The Swedish People	m	1882
Svenska öden och äventyr	Swedish Destinies & Ventures	m	1882-92
Det nya riket	The New Kingdom	m	1882
Dikter på vers ock prosa	Poems in Verse and Prose	m	1883
Sömngångarnätter	Somnambulist Nights	m	1884
Utopier i verkligheten	Utopias of Reality	m	1884-5
Giftas I & II	Married (2 vols.)	m	1884-6
Tjänstekvinnans son	The Son of a Maidservant	a	1886
Jäsningstiden	Fermentation Time	a	1886
I röda rummet	In the Red Room	a	1886

233

AUGUST STRINDBERG

Swedish Title	English Title	Category	Date
Författaren	The Author	a	1886
Marodörer (Kamraterna)	The Marauders (Comrades)	d	1886
Fadren	The Father	d	1887
Hemsöborna	The People of Hemsö	a	1887
En dåres försvärstal	A Fool's Defence	a	1887
Fröken Julie	Miss Julie	d	1888
Fordringsägare	Creditors	d	1888
Tschandala	Tschandala	m	1888
Paria	Pariah (one act)	d	1889
Den Starkare	The Stronger (one act)	d	1889
Samum	Samum (one act)	d	1889
Himmelrikets nycklar	The Keys of Heaven	d	1891
Debet och kredit	Debit and Credit (one act)	d	1891-2
Moderskärlek	Mother Love (one act)	d	1891-2
Inför döden	Facing Death (one act)	d	1891-2
Första varningen	The First Warning (one act)	d	1891-2
Bandet	The Bond (one act)	d	1892
Leka med elden	Playing with Fire (one act)	d	1892
Sylva Sylvarum	Sylva Sylvarum	m	1895
Antibarbarus	Antibarbarus	m	1896
Jardin des Plantes	Jardin des Plantes	m	1896
Inferno	Inferno	a	1897
Legender	Legends	a	1897-8
Till Damascus I & II	To Damascus I & II	d	1898
Advent	Advent	d	1898
Brott och Brott	Crime and Crime	d	1899
Folkungasagan	The Saga of the Folkungs	d	1899
Gustav Vasa	Gustavus Vasa	d	1899
Erik XIV	Erik XIV	d	1899
Gustav Adolf	Gustavus Adolphus	d	1899
Midsommar	Midsummer	d	1900
Påsk	Easter	d	1900
Dödsdansen	The Dance of Death	d	1901
Engelbrecht	Engelbrecht	d	1901
Carl XII	Charles XII	d	1901

APPENDIX II

Swedish Title	English Title	Category	Date
Kronbruden	The Bridal Crown	d	1901
Svanevit	Swanwhite	d	1901
Ett Drömspel	A Dream Play	d	1901
Fagervik och Skamsund	Fairhaven and Foulstrand	a	1902
Kristina	Queen Christina	d	1903
Gustav III	Gustavus III	d	1903
Världshistoriens Mystik	Mysticism and World History	m	1903
Näktergalen i Wittenberg	The Nightingale of Wittenberg	d	1903
Ensam	Alone	a	1903
Till Damascus III	To Damascus III	d	1904
Götiska Rummen	The Gothic Rooms	m	1904
Svarta Fanor	Black Banners	m	1904
Historiska miniatyrer	Historical Miniatures	m	1905
Taklagsöl	The Roof-laying Festival	m	1905
Syndabocken	The Scapegoat	m	1906
En Blå Bok I-II-III	A Blue Book I-II-III	m	1907–8
Oväder	The Storm	c.p.	1907
Brända Tomten	The Burned Lot	c.p.	1907
Spöksonaten	The Ghost Sonata	c.p.	1907
Pelikanen	The Pelican	c.p.	1907
Memorandum till Intima teatern	Memorandum to the Intimate Theatre	m	1908
Abu Casems tofflor	Abu Casem's Slippers	d	1908
Siste riddaren	The Last Knight	d	1908
Bjälbo-Jarlen	The Earl of Bjälbo	d	1908
Riksföreståndaren	The Regent	d	1908
Svarta handsken	The Black Glove	c.p.	1909
Stora Landsvägen	The Great Highway	d	1909
Tal till svenska nationen	Address to the Swedish Nation	m	1910
Modersmålets anor	Origins of our Mother Tongue	m	1910
Världsspråkens rötter	Roots of World Languages	m	1910
Folkstaten	The People's State	m	1910
Religiös renässans	Religious Renaissance	m	1910

APPENDIX III

LIST OF WORKS CONSULTED

Skrifter av August Strindberg (*The Works of August Strindberg*). *Strindberg*, by Erik Hedén. (Tidens Förlag, 1926.)

Strindbergs Första Hustru (*Strindberg's First Wife*), by Karin Smirnoff. (Albert Bonniers Förlag, 1926.)

Strindberg och hans Första Hustru (*Strindberg and his First Wife*), by Harry Jacobsen. (Bonniers, 1946).

Strindbergs Systrar Berätta om Barndoms Hemmet och om Bror August (*Strindberg's Sisters tell of their childhood home and of their brother August*). (P. A. Norstedt och Söners Förlag, 1926.)

Strindbergs Brev 1858–1876 (*Strindberg's Letters*), The Strindberg Society. (Bonniers, 1948.)

Den Strindberg Jag Känt (*The Strindberg I Knew*), by Birger Mörner. (Bonniers, 1924.)

Strindbergs Dramer (*The Plays of Strindberg*), by Martin Lamm. (Bonniers, 1926.)

Från Fjärdingen till Blå Tornet (*From Fjärdingen to the Blue Tower*): A Selection of Strindberg's Letters, 1870–1912, edited by Torsten Eklund. The Strindberg Society. (Bonniers, 1946.)

August Strindberg, by Martin Lamm. (Bonniers: Part 1, 1940; Part 2, 1942.)

Strindbergsproblem (*The Problem of Strindberg*), by Walter A. Berendsohn. (Kooperativa Förbundets Bokförlag, 1946.)

Strindbergs Brev till Harriet Bosse (*Strindberg's Letters to Harriet Bosse*) with commentaries by Harriet Bosse. (Natur och Kultur, 1932.)

Harriet Bosse, by Olof Molander. (P. A. Norstedt och Söner, 1920.)

Fem År med Strindberg (*Five Years with Strindberg*), by August Falck. (Wahlström och Widstrand, 1935.)

Strindberg på Stockholmsscenen (*Strindberg on the Stockholm Stage*), by Yngve Hedvall. (Victor Pettersons Bokindustriaktiebolag, 1923.)

Strindberg, by L. Lind-af-Hageby. (Stanley Paul, 1913.)

The Playwright as Thinker, by Eric Bentley. (Cornwall Press, New York, 1946.)

Marriage with Genius, by Frida Strindberg (Frida Uhl), edited by Frederic Whyte. (Jonathan Cape, 1937.)

August Strindberg, by V. J. McGill. (Noel Douglas, 1930.)

Strindberg, by G. A. Campbell. (Duckworth, 1933.)

Johan August Strindberg, by R. H. Ward, from *The New Spirit*, edited by E. W. Martin. (Dennis Dobson Ltd., 1946.)

INDEX